A Man of Faith

For
Jean & Vern
With our love
& Prayers
always,
Jim & Samille

Oct, 95

A Man of Faith

—Father Patrick Peyton, C.S.C.,
his life, mission and message

By Jeanne Gosselin Arnold

Family Theater, Inc.

Hollywood, California 90046

Nihil Obstat

REV. JOHN ROOS, STL., JCD.
Censor Librorum

Imprimatur

†HOWARD J. HUBBARD
BISHOP OF ALBANY

Albany, New York, June 2, 1983

ISBN 0-9608836-0-6

Library of Congress Catalog Card Number: 82-82300

Printed in the United States of America

Text of this book is set in 11 point Garamond on a 13 point base.
Type was set using the Univac/Compugraphic phototypesetting system of
the State University of New York at Albany.

Printed by Crest Litho, Colonie, N.Y.

Designed by Charles D. Hathaway, Media Services Unltd. (MSU),
Westerlo, N.Y. 12193.
Original bead design copyright 1981 by Linda D. Beattie/MSU.

Scriptural quotations are from the *New American Bible*,
Copyright 1978, Catholic Publishers Inc.

Cover design by H. Austin Peterson/Charles D. Hathaway

Preface

This book tells the story of the life and work of the Rev. Patrick Peyton, C.S.C, whose slogan, "The family that prays together stays together," originated by him in 1947, is now officially recognized as a proverb. Father Peyton's forty years of promoting daily family Rosary and daily family prayer has made him famous as the Rosary priest throughout the world. The story spans his life from birth in 1909 and childhood in Ireland to this date, which finds him still as active as ever in spreading his message of world and family unity through Jesus and Mary and the Rosary. The book is not intended, however, as a comprehensive biography. That would take volumes. The story focuses, rather, on highlights of his life and selected events typical of this great, but humble, priest. Its intent is to portray both the man and his message. It contains Father Peyton's first published original meditations on the fifteen Mysteries of the Rosary, written by him especially for this book.

Material for this book was gathered in countless hours patiently given by Father Peyton himself, through correspondence and interviews with people who have known and worked with him, and from the archives of Family Rosary, Inc. (1947) and Family Theater, Inc. (1947), of which he is founder and director and which are now under the umbrella corporation of Crusade for Family Prayer, Inc. (1954), and from Father Peyton's autobiography, *All for Her* (Doubleday & Co., Inc., 1967, and Family Theater Productions, 1973).

The narrative style encompasses no deviation from fact. All dialogue and direct quotes are taken from contemporary reports. The only exception is the story of Father Peyton's encounter with the young priest of social action in Part 5, which is a composite of several similar incidents at different times and places, but is essentially authentic. I wish to thank all those reporters and photographers and associates of Father Peyton who recorded the events as they occurred.

The unique format of this book with pictures integrated into the text as part of the narrative was accomplished only through close cooperation between the design and production people and myself to make all elements fit together properly. The original art for the Rosary bead design was modeled after Father Peyton's own Rosary. Photos are from Family Rosary Crusade and Family Theater files. Photos accompanying the mysteries are from Father Peyton's Rosary films.

I thank all who assisted in the compilation of this book, too numerous to list, including many who supported it with their prayers. I want to mention a few for their special roles. The Rev. George S. DePrizio, C.S.C., not only got the project and me together, but also personally interviewed some people of Latin America and translated those tapes and some correspondence in Spanish for me. Sister Mary J. Buckley, RSM, gave insights and support and, with Father Peyton, read every word, not in neat manuscript, but on difficult-to-read computer printouts, to check for factual accuracy. Patricia Spanbauer was indispensable in helping to obtain material from the Albany files and in supplying and checking many details. Charles D. Hathaway, my editor for the book as well as its designer, gave innumerable hours to listening, advising, criticizing and refining the work during the time it took to write and produce it between August, 1979, and May, 1982.

To all those who helped me put down in the record of this book the teachings of that holy man, Father Patrick Peyton, go, in addition to my humble thanks, those most powerful ones of all: As Father Peyton would say, "The Blessed Mother will thank you for it, too."

Jeanne Gosselin Arnold
May 1, 1982

Part 1

In the beginning
The early years

In the name
of the Father
and of the Son
and of the Holy Spirit

Credo

The two men were waiting in the papal antechamber.

They had flown together to the Vatican from New York on the businessman's private plane. They awaited the summons for the audience with the Pope.

"The Holy Father wishes to see Father Peyton for a few minutes alone," a papal chamberlain announced.

The tall white-haired man in the black cassock rose and made his excuses to his companion. Then he was ushered into the inner chamber, where he at once slipped to his knees and kissed the hand of the white-robed pontiff.

He felt strong hands on his arms pressing him to rise and was soon standing looking into the eyes of the Holy Father, almost as tall as the towering priest himself.

This was Pope John Paul II, who was soon to explode upon the world scene in travels and outspoken talks before huge throngs.

Now Pope John Paul II was inviting Father Patrick Peyton to sit beside him. As they walked together toward the chairs, the Pope was calling his visitor "a man of faith."

Pope John Paul II spoke briefly, ending with an invitation to Father Peyton to discuss his work.

Here was Father Peyton's chance to speak up on behalf of his Family Rosary Crusade.

Father Peyton had traveled all over the world urging families to pray the Rosary together every day. That was the single goal of the Family Rosary Crusade which he had founded in his early years as a priest of the Holy Cross Fathers.

He began to talk, grasping every second given him by his Holy Father. His words poured out in a rich Irish brogue.

The origin of the idea, he told Pope John Paul II, went back many years to his childhood in Ireland.

He told of his earliest memories of himself, first as an infant listening to the prayers of his family, then as a toddler struggling to recite the Our Fathers and the Hail Marys of the Rosary.

His parents, he said, had grown up in the Irish tradition of daily family Rosary. The Rosary had kept the faith of their ancestors alive, too, in the dark days of Irish history when the Catholic Church was forced to go underground.

John and Mary Peyton had made their poor three-room cottage a family Rosary home for their nine children. "It was our school, our community," Father Peyton told Pope John Paul II.

Some years later, he continued, he had good reason to devote his life and his priesthood to the service of Mary the Mother of God.

Through the Family Rosary Crusade, he was paying his debt to Our Blessed Mother for the favors of health and priesthood she had obtained for him when both seemed doomed. At the same time, he was repaying his debt to his family for the gifts of love and devotion to God and to Mary they had given him.

Pope John Paul II listened attentively and without interruption. He and his Polish countrymen were noted for their devotion to Our Lady.

Pope John Paul II, like every other Catholic leader in the world and those of many other faiths, was familiar with the unique mission of Father Peyton, that was unlike that of any other priest in the world. He knew that this Father Patrick Peyton had encircled the globe with his Rosary beads and had preached before multitudes devotion to Mary through the daily family Rosary.

Some months before, while still archbishop of Cracow, Poland, he had written a letter to Father Peyton commending him and encouraging him in his mission.

In his outpouring of words, Father Peyton spoke mainly of the origin of, and his hopes for the future of, the Family Rosary Crusade. Of the crusades themselves, he said little—only that "The record is imposing, but is history."

The thirty-seven years of the Family Rosary Crusade up to then had been so filled with activity that he could not have begun to recount it. He had used the media of print, broadcast and film, along with the crusades, to transmit his message.

Many small, but revealing, incidents, like one at a rally in Bruges, Belgium, were typical of the effect Father Peyton had upon the men, women and children who flocked to him at the rallies.

His basic message, as he spoke it at that Belgium rally, was always the same.

"Our Blessed Mother Mary is alive. She is here," the voice from the high platform chimed in Irish tones through the loudspeakers to the sea of upturned faces filling the streets. The praying hands of the black-robed priest on the platform were draped with a string of black Rosary beads.

His voice caressed every word. "She will help you if you ask her. She cannot deny you. She will come and pray with you to her Son Jesus who is with God His Father in heaven. He cannot deny His Blessed Mother anything she asks."

Silence was the only sound as he spread his arms to them as a child does when it sees its mother coming. Upturned eyes waited. It is possible that some in the crowd saw their Madonna beside the tall priest. It is certain that others could not see past the mist in their eyes. In the crowd, men wiped the sleeves of their workshirts across their eyes. Wrinkled old women blessed themselves with the Sign of the Cross and fingered the beads of their Rosaries.

"I know. I lived it," he said. Then he told them about praying the Rosary with his family every day in his boyhood in Ireland.

His concluding words, "The family that prays together stays together," ended with a flourish of his arms, lingered in the momentary hush.

As he descended the makeshift stairs from the platform, the crowd surged toward him.

His head could still be seen above those crowding to touch his robes, to shake his hand.

His translator in Belgium, Sister Marie Eymard, particularly remembers one small girl perched high on her daddy's shoulder who put her little hand in Father Peyton's big hand.

The little girl then turned to her daddy, gave him a big kiss, and said, "I think he is just like Jesus."

Father Peyton did not hear the little girl's remark, as others had by then pushed between them. It was one of countless reactions to the Rosary priest retold by those who witnessed or experienced them at the hundreds of crusades he conducted.

Now, at age 70, seated beside Pope John Paul II, Father Peyton knew the time was near to pass into other hands the torch he had so long carried for the promotion of daily family Rosary. This Pope's interest gave the yeast to his rising hopes that he had found the person who would take up that symbolic torch.

His emphasis upon the origin of his life's work was a statement of the faith of his parents, and that of their ancestors. It was, in effect, a statement of those Christian beliefs that are expressed in the introductory prayer of the Rosary, one of the prayers he had said every day of his life—the *Apostles' Creed.*

I believe in God, the Father Almighty, Creator of heaven and earth; and in Jesus Christ, His only Son, Our Lord; who was conceived by the Holy Spirit, born of the Virgin Mary, suffered under Pontius Pilate, was crucified, died, and was buried. He descended into hell; the third day He arose again from the dead; He ascended into heaven, sits at the right hand of God, the Father Almighty; from thence He shall come to judge the living and the dead.

I believe in the Holy Spirit, the Holy Catholic Church, the communion of saints, the forgiveness of sins, the resurrection of the body, and life everlasting. Amen.

"My time here is not to be much longer, I do not wish the Crusade to die with me," Father Peyton said simply. As he spoke, the memory of his years of devotion to Mary and the Rosary swept over him. He repeated to the Pope the words he had spoken to so many multitudes during those years:

"I know. I lived it."

A family Rosary home

The boy sat atop a pile of rocks hammering them into pebbles. His red-gold hair and blue eyes looked new and bright in contrast to the worn clothing that pulled tight on the thin tall frame. He pictured himself as the biblical Job sitting amidst the ruins of his life.

Patrick Peyton felt that the world, in particular the schoolmaster, had persecuted him. Deep down, however, he knew that his own rebelliousness had helped to bring him to this condition.

Each blow of the hammer became his wilfulness and the pebbles his shattered dreams.

A friend on the way home from school stopped to talk. Listening to the chatter about school, Patrick regretted his own defiance which had abruptly ended his education and brought him to this condition.

No longer able to attend school, he remained at home. He did the chores on the small farm and helped fill the ruts in the road with pebbles. The road repair work had been taken over more and more by the three oldest Peyton boys from their ailing father. The contract their father had to maintain the country roads provided the family's main income. It brought very few shillings.

Patrick's regret opened a small crack in his defiance, but it did not shatter it. His family watched the angry and frustrated boy patiently. They never lost their trust that he would overcome his rebelliousness and fulfill the destiny to which they believed him born.

The Peyton home was a three-room thatched cottage in the village of Carracastle, a few miles from the town of Ballina in County Mayo. The little settlement nestled in a pocket near the foothills of the Ox Mountains in the west of Ireland. Atlantic winds dropped a cold veil upon the landscape. On occasional summer days, the bright sun lifted the mist from the bright greens of the fields and mountainsides, and revealed the towering peaks. Sunday Mass took the family three miles away to a chapel in the foothills.

When the infant Patrick was born on January 9, 1909, there were already five children before him in that humble cabin.

The home bustled with work from early morning to after dusk. Even the littlest worked.

They cut turf in the bog and brought it home in the horse-drawn cart to burn away the chill in the cabin.

Their food was mostly the potatoes and cabbage they grew with sometimes a bit of fat meat for seasoning. There was never enough food. They were always hungry.

Patrick's earliest memory was seeing his family kneeling and praying every evening before bedtime. As a toddler, he learned the prayers and later learned their meanings.

Every night his father led the prayers of the Rosary. The rest of the family, numbering nine children with the three who came after Patrick, prayed the responses. Five decades, each with one

Our Father and ten *Hail Marys* counted on the beads of the Rosary, were prayed. John and Mary Peyton taught their children love for their Creator by this recitation.

Patrick learned the Bible stories of the lives of Jesus and Mary represented by each decade later during his school years. The fifteen decades of the full Rosary begin with the appearance of the Angel Gabriel to Mary telling her that she has been chosen to become the mother of the Son of God.

The stories, known as the *Mysteries of the Rosary*, continue through the crucifixion and resurrection of Christ and the assumption of Mary into heaven and her coronation.

Young Patrick learned that Christ dying on the cross had declared His mother the mother of all God's children and Himself their brother with the words, *"Woman, there is your son,"* and to His disciple, *"There is your mother."* (John 19: 26-27)

He learned that praying the Rosary was an invitation to Our Blessed Mother Mary to come into the home, to join the family in prayer to her Son Jesus. The family was saying to Our Blessed Mother "Our house is yours. Come in and bring Christ with you. You are welcome."

The child Patrick thought that Mary, hearing all those prayers, must say to her Son Jesus, "My Son, these Peytons besiege me every day. Give them all the beautiful love that will hold them together all over the world, wherever they may go, as much as they now have it in that little shack." The Son would say, "I hear them. They pray to me every night too. I know those Peytons. I'll pick one of them to do an extraordinary job."

The Peyton family was on daily speaking terms with Mary the Mother of God. Through her, they thanked God for their blessings and asked His help in guiding their family to its destiny.

A family photograph was taken when Patrick was twelve years old. John and Mary Gillard Peyton were seated in the center with son John standing between them and Annie Kate and Patrick standing on either side of them. The photographer placed

Michael, their aunt Annie Gillard (Mrs. Peter) Gilmartin, Tom and Nellie standing in a row behind them in such a way as to leave space to complete the family group with the inset facial photos of Mary, Beatrice, and Sarah, who were absent when the group photograph was taken.

The family hoped that Patrick would become a priest. But they did not know how a poor country lad could do this.

There was a difference in Patrick. The missionaries who came sometimes to the chapel nourished his religious fervor. Their words went to his heart like a magnet to hidden steel. He did not join the other teenagers at the weekly dances in the village but spent what spare time he had in the little church, especially after he became an altar boy.

He was happiest when serving Mass. He pictured himself as a grown man in the place of the parish priest. His spiritual horizons stretched far beyond the mountains that rimmed his physical world as the dream of priesthood grew in him.

Not everyone was as appreciative as his family of the difference in young Patrick Peyton. One day Tadhg O'Leary, the schoolmaster in the little village school, struck him in the face and called him a "lazy good-for-nothing." Patrick reacted to that rebuke with anger and walked out, never to return. He became a grade-school failure and a dropout at age fourteen.

As the family income declined along with John Peyton's health, the three oldest Peyton girls were sent to America. They worked as maids and sent part of their wages home.

The boy Patrick, by then tall and skinny, was torn with his frustration, but his defiance grew and he lashed out at those he loved most.

One day, he kicked his beloved father in the shin in rebellion against some good advice. There was nothing to be done after that monstrous deed but to run away from home. He had not gone far when his sister Sarah overtook him and brought him back home. His father never mentioned the incident.

At the family Rosary that evening, as his father began to lead the second prayer of the Rosary, the meaning of the *Our Father* became more real to him.

> *Our Father, who art in heaven, hallowed be Thy name;*
> *Thy kingdom come; Thy will be done on earth as it is in*
> *heaven.*

Patrick understood that his own patient father had forgiven him as he intoned with his family the response:

Give us this day our daily bread; and forgive us our trespasses as we forgive those who trespass against us; and lead us not into temptation, but deliver us from evil. Amen.

Patrick truly began to understand God the Father's love for all his children and forgiveness of their sins.

Although he continued to stumble when he wanted to soar, the evening prayer always brought Mary the Mother of Jesus into the home and she brought the peacefulness with her.

Patrick worked harder on the farm. At times, he found work with neighboring farmers.

One of these was a burly fellow whose family did not pray the Rosary together at the end of each day. During the week Patrick stayed at that home, his heart wept for the children. How could he, a mere boy, tell this grown man, that he was depriving his family? He prayed to Mary for advice.

On the last night, the man walked him part way home. They came to the point in the road where they would part, the farmer to return home and Patrick to go on alone.

They paused, two dark figures in the night. It was Patrick's last chance to speak up. The farmer might clout him on the ears, but it would not hurt much. He made a quick decision and began to blurt out the words.

He described daily Rosary in his own family. He told the farmer what his family was missing. They lived together; they worked together, played together; they worshipped together at Mass every Sunday. But they did not pray together. They did not invite the Blessed Mother Mary into their home and ask her to pray with them for help. They did not as a family thank God, through Mary, for the day's blessings.

Patrick did not get the box on the ears he feared. The man listened in growing astonishment, and then simply said, "Well, we'll see about it." Patrick heard later that this family was praying daily Rosary.

Patrick Peyton, at fifteen, had preached his first sermon.

It was basically the same sermon he was to preach the rest of his life.

11

With the words, which he could never recall exactly afterward, he had cast off a burden. He did not know that he had picked up another burden—one that would bring sacrifices and sorrows, as well as joys and triumphs.

Although he felt like a man that night, and did his work like a man, Patrick afterward occasionally reverted to boyhood.

Sandy Durkin, for whom he had gone to work in nearby Bonniconlon, caught him and a coworker one day, dancing with their brooms instead of sweeping the dancehall as they were hired to do. His companion accepted the rebuke, but Patrick, once again, replied angrily and walked away.

But childhood had to end. Patrick grew restless as he worked on the farm. He saw no path open for himself.

The oldest son Michael would inherit the farm. There was no work for Patrick in Carracastle, and work in Bonniconlon was barred to him because Sandy Durkin owned most of the businesses. Patrick decided he must go to America. His father consented, providing that his older brother Thomas would go with him. Tom agreed. Their three sisters in America agreed to help.

Shortly before the two young men were to leave, Patrick's father took him into another room. There, pointing to a picture of the Sacred Heart of Jesus, he said, delicately, "Get down on your knees."

His father stood beside him as he knelt before the picture. The father prayed for the safety of this strong-willed son. They prayed together. The father warned his son of the responsibility of being on his own.

"Be faithful to Our Lord in America," John Peyton counseled his son. It was the last advice Patrick was ever to receive from his father. He said of it later:

"My father, that blessed man, did not say to me 'Go to America and become wealthy.' No, he gave me the best advice a father could ever give to a son. It was the last advice my blessed father ever gave to me, for he died six years later, and I never saw him again."

Voices of destiny

"Scranton, The Electric City."

The big electric sign flashed its colored beams upon the buildings, the streets of Scranton, Pennsylvania, United States of America.

The light flickered across the upturned face of the young man, catching the red-gold glints in his hair.

He wore new garments instead of the worn farm clothing, but it was Patrick Peyton. He liked to stand looking up at the sign, which symbolized his new world. It seemed that he had been catapulted into a magician's world he had never imagined back in the Ox Mountains of Ireland.

He and Tom had waved goodbye to the tall figure standing behind the half-door of the thatched cottage until they could no longer see him.

The trip had begun by bicycle from home to the railroad station. Mary Peyton had gone with Michael in the horse-drawn cart to give her two sons up to the world. "It's glad I am to be sending you to America," she had said; and Patrick had realized that her sorrow at losing her sons was outweighed by her concern for their futures.

The journey by train, steamship, then ferry to Hoboken and a train again to Scranton, ending May 23, took just ten days. His sister Nellie and her employers, a prominent family, had met the young men at the station. They took them to the home of their sister Beatrice and her husband Michael Gallagher, where their other sister, Mary, was also staying. There they were to live until they got jobs and were on their own.

The big electric sign had drawn him that evening to ease his conscience after the scene with his sisters earlier. Nellie had told Monsignor Paul Kelly that her brother Patrick wanted to become a priest. She had made an appointment for Patrick to meet the pastor of St. Peter's Cathedral after a service that first Sunday in America.

As Nellie and Mary turned toward the rectory, Patrick bolted in the opposite direction.

13

"What's the matter with you?" Nellie called after him. He turned and saw the look of pain that passed swiftly over her face as she realized all that her brother's refusal to keep the appointment meant.

As he gazed up at the sign, the lights seemed to whirl and fade, and he was seeing again the picture of the Sacred Heart of Jesus in the dark bedroom back home. He saw himself kneeling before the picture, and his father standing over him, like a twentieth century patriarch of the Old Testament.

"Be faithful to Our Lord in America," his father's voice came back to him. It seemed to echo from the sides of the buildings around him.

Then he remembered Tadhg O'Leary and Sandy Durkin and his vision of returning a wealthy man to show them the errors of their judgment of him.

He thought he would get a job as a bus driver and go all the way to Los Angeles to see the other wonders of this big country.

He turned from the sign and strolled down the street to the Casey block where the young Irish immigrants gathered. He did not know that destiny followed at his heels, and that the big electric sign and the thought of Los Angeles were a part of that destiny.

In those booming pre-depression days of 1928, it seemed that everyone had work except Patrick. Michael Gallagher had helped Tom to get a job with him in the coal mines only a few days after their arrival. He had refused to help Patrick, saying he would not survive a year in the mines. The 19-year-old immigrant with the thick Irish brogue was turned down everywhere. He was too young, too frail, or too inexperienced.

In mid-June, Monsignor Kelly told Nellie Peyton to bring her brother who wanted to be a priest to see him about a job as sexton of the cathedral. Desperate for a job, Patrick this time went to see Monsignor Kelly and got the job.

He was to begin on July 1.

While waiting, he got temporary work on a construction job. Then a co-worker told him two men were to be laid off. One was a family man and the other a drifter who had settled down to steady work. Patrick asked the boss to let him go instead, saying he had another job lined up.

"You're a fool," the boss told him. "You can stay here and make good money."

14

Patrick shook his head. "No," he decided, "it would not be right for me to take a job away from a family man."

He gave up the job that was to start him on the way to becoming wealthy.

Later, as he worked at his new job as sexton, which he soon learned was janitor, a friend told him the construction boss had been so impressed by Patrick's concern for those two workers that he had juggled the work to keep them both on.

Young Patrick Peyton had again taught a grown man the meaning of the love of God and fellow man, this time by example, as he had done by words as a boy back on that country road in Ireland.

He never felt alone in the empty church. He greeted his Lord God at the altar. He stopped to talk to Mary the Mother of Jesus whenever he passed her statue.

He knelt before the statue praying his Rosary. After the *Apostle's Creed* and the *Lord's Prayer* and as he started the first of the three *Hail Marys* that precede the decades, he voiced caressingly the familiar words:

Hail Mary, full of grace! the Lord is with thee; blessed art thou among women, and blessed is the fruit of thy womb, Jesus.

Holy Mary, Mother of God, pray for us sinners, now and at the hour of our death. Amen.

He began to feel again the peacefulness of those evening prayers with his family and the joy of serving Mass in the chapel on the mountainside.

He was like a person lost in a cave who, while seeing the light far ahead, had still sought an exit in the nearby tunnels of

15

darkness. One day his dream flooded over him. The sacrifice of worldly pleasures and the hardship he had struggled to avoid became the goal to be reached.

Leaving the paint and the brush where he had been painting behind the main altar, he dashed to the rectory.

"I want to be a priest," he burst out to Monsignor Kelly.

Patrick had accepted his destiny. He was headed toward the light and he knew that, no matter how hard the way, there would be no turning back.

It was the last day of enrollment at the Christian Brothers school and Monsignor Kelly, not the least surprised, sent him to enroll. He said to Patrick when he returned, "Now bring your brother out of the coal mines. Too many are being killed. He can take over as sexton."

Patrick entered high school at an age when most already have graduated. But the taunts of his classmates against this immigrant giant did not bother him. Tom came out of the coal mines and became the new sexton.

As the brothers walked home together from the cathedral one evening, Tom said, "It must be wonderful to be a priest."

A few days later, Patrick visited Monsignor Kelly again. "My brother wants to be a priest too," he told him. The monsignor agreed to pay Tom's tuition also and told Patrick to have him enroll in the same school, even though he would have to make up the month of studies he had missed.

Patrick rushed to the home of Nellie's employer where he, Mary and Tom were invited for dinner in the kitchen. Bursting into the room, he shouted to Tom, "You have until Monday morning to decide whether you want to be a priest."

Tom decided to follow Patrick's lead and enrolled. The two brothers shared the job of sexton.

That year, four Holy Cross priests from Notre Dame, Indiana, came to give a mission at the cathedral. Their visit revived Patrick's boyhood dream of becoming a missionary and he decided he wanted to join their order.

The following September of 1929, therefore, Patrick, with Tom again following, went to Indiana to finish high school and enter the seminary at the University of Notre Dame staffed by the Holy Cross Fathers. Both brothers worked at odd jobs at the university to help pay their tuition. Patrick enjoyed the wooded paths and lakes on the campus grounds. He liked to stop at the grotto of Our Lady to say his Rosary. The family-like atmosphere of the order suited him.

The Holy Cross order's two principal works in the United States were teaching in universities and high schools and staffing parishes. At that time priests were also sent to the foreign missions in Bengal. The seminarians were allowed to choose between work in the United States or in the Bengal mission.

Tom chose the United States and Patrick chose the mission. To prepare for their assignments, they were sent to complete their theological studies in Washington, D.C., Tom at Holy Cross College and Patrick at the special mission school called the Bengalese.

They were well on their way to ordination and priesthood. Patrick devoted every waking moment to work and his studies.

Years later, Father Thomas Peyton recalled, "I had to study hard for everything I learned, but Pat had a phenomenal memory. He could hear a lecture and repeat it the next day almost word for word. Or he could read something once in a book and remember it."

In spite of this, added Father Tom, "Pat pushed himself too hard."

Though no one realized it as he came and went to classes, overwork was beginning to take its toll of the young seminarian.

A dream in peril

Patrick Peyton knelt before the statue of Our Lady. He tensed his body against its drooping weariness as he made the Sign of the Cross. He began the prayer of the pendant part of his Rosary beads.

His fatigue lifted like a clearing fog as his fingers reached for the bead of the second *Hail Mary* and he silently prayed:

Hail Mary, full of grace! the Lord is with thee; blessed art thou among women, and blessed is the fruit of thy womb, Jesus.
Holy Mary, Mother of God, pray for us sinners, now and at the hour of our death. Amen.

When he had finished his Rosary, he lingered, thanking her and asking her to pray with him to her Son Jesus to make him a good priest. The effort to rise from his knees brought the tiredness back to his body. His footsteps dragged along the path and it seemed that he was plodding through a driving blizzard. He had completed ten years of study with the Holy Cross Fathers since he entered their seminary on the campus of Notre Dame in Indiana. This fall semester of 1939 had barely begun and he should not be this early so tired.

He ignored the fits of coughing which brought occasional specks of blood, and the flushed cheeks spotting the pallor of his face.

When he began to hemorrhage, however, he had to tell his superior, who sent him to a doctor. After a brief examination and a recounting by Patrick of his symptoms, which somehow that day seemed less serious, the doctor told him, "You do not have to worry. Your lungs are sound and strong."

With that reassurance, Patrick pushed even harder against the exhaustion that weighted his body down.

One February night he awoke and reached for his handkerchief. Suddenly he realized there was blood, and he was hemorrhaging more than ever. He staggered out seeking help. The doctor called to attend him did not expect him to live through the night, as he said later. Tom was called from Holy Cross College. Patrick was taken by ambulance to a hospital.

The hammer came crashing down again on his dreams. But this time it was not his own wilfulness shattering his dreams like those long ago pebbles, but a disease every Irishman knew meant lingering months until certain death. He had tuberculosis.

After three months in the hospital bed, and no improvement in his condition, he was transferred to the infirmary at Notre Dame. The doctors and his superior agreed that he might benefit from the Indiana air and the treatment of specialists at a nearby tuberculosis sanitorium.

He went periodically to the sanitorium for examinations. He prayed constantly. Winter passed into the budding of spring, then the bloom of summer.

Patrick did not respond to the only TB treatment then known to physicians—complete bed rest, good food and fresh air. As a last resort, the doctors could try to arrest the disease by collapsing the infected lung, but fluid in the lung prohibited this drastic step. His condition worsened and there was little hope that he would ever resume his studies for the priesthood.

One day in early August, he looked up from his bed to see his sister Nellie standing in the doorway. Her statuesque figure, tall and large-boned like all the Peytons, and her attractive face, were like sunshine entering that small room.

Nellie, who was working as a housekeeper at St. Paul's Rectory in Scranton, had been given time off to go to Indiana to be with Patrick.

Nellie's prayers and firm faith revived Patrick's hope. The two talked about their mother, who had suffered a severe stroke.

One bleak October day, Patrick's trio of doctors gave him their verdict. He could put himself in their hands for a series of opera-

19

tions that would allow the lung to rest, but would leave him deformed for the rest of his life.

"Or," his Protestant and Jewish doctors challenged him, "you can pray."

When he got back from the doctors he told his superior the verdict. Then he returned to his room and lay in his bed with tears overflowing the wells in his eyes.

He had a decision to make, one that would mean life or death for him, and also for his faith.

He asked himself the same question Father Cornelius Hagerty asked him later that night: Was his faith a sham or a reality?

"You have the faith," the eminent professor Father Cornelius assured him.

"But you're not using it," he added. "You brought it from Ireland. Your mother gave it to you just as her mother gave it to her."

The words are not exact, but the gist of Father Cornelius's observations as they talked was this:

"Our Lady will be as good as you think she is. If you think she will be a hundred percenter, she will be for you a hundred percenter. No one of us ever does as much as he is capable of doing. We always fall short.

"Even Our Lord and Our Lady do not do as much as they could do, but the reason is that we think that they are not able. We limit them by the extent of our faith."

Father Cornelius summed up his thinking in three statements: "Mary is omnipotent in the power of her prayer. Mary is omnipotent in the power of her intercession with her Son. Mary can do anything that God can do."

He explained that "The difference is not in what God can do and what Mary can do. The difference is in the way they do it. God wills something and it happens. Mary prays to Him for something and He does it. He will never say 'no' to her."

Father Cornelius's words gave Patrick a new sense of the reality of Mary, of her nearness and sensitivity to our needs so that he could pray:

"Blessed Mother Mary, I believe you are alive, that you are real, that you are a woman, that you have eyes, a face, a smile, a memory, an intelligence, a heart. You have a mother and father of your own. You have a Son, who is truly God, who loves you, who will deny you nothing you ask."

That sense of Mary's reality never left him. He could ever afterwards invoke her presence for others, whether speaking to millions or to a single individual.

"I realized how strong my position would be with Mary,"he afterward declared. "She could not say to me 'Who are you?' I had paid tribute to her all my life. Those 53 'Hail Marys' I said every night of my life were like an insurance a man pays on a house. Now the house was burning down and he would claim his insurance.

"That night," he has since said many times, "I put my life in prayer. I put my life in the hands of God and Our Blessed Mother."

He prayed kneeling on his bed, palms outstretched against the wall on either side of a picture of Mary. He asked her to give him his life, to intercede with her Son Jesus for his life.

"If you ask Him," he told her, "He cannot refuse, He cannot deny you anything." So intense were his prayers, the then President of Notre Dame, the late Cardinal John F. O'Hara, revealed later, that there were imprints from his hands on the wall.

He did not pray alone.

Praying with him and for him were his colleagues, his brothers, sisters, and his mother in Ireland.

"He can do more for souls than I can," Mary Peyton was saying back in Ireland to her sister Annie as her son lay sick and probably dying far away in America.

Patrick's mother had been a widow now for five years. John Peyton had died in 1934 at the age of 67.

"I was never a good soldier; now I have to be one,"she told her sister. Nellie had written only that Patrick had to take a rest from his studies because he had been working too hard. But Mary Peyton knew her son. He would not be taking a rest unless he was seriously ill.

She prayed to God to take upon herself those sufferings that were consuming the life of her son. She asked God to take her life in place of his.

All of this she told her sister. Others knew it too. They believed the stroke she suffered was God's answer. She died on December 3.

Patrick knew nothing of this as he prayed and slept and visited the doctors for weekly checkups and grew ever weaker. Later he was to say of his mother's offering, "It was more than the natural

21

love of a mother for her son. It was more like that beautiful woman's supernatural love for all mankind. She offered her life in exchange for mine, not just for me, but for all people everywhere. She gave her life because, as she said and believed, I could do more for souls than she could.''

Another member of the family was offering her life for Patrick, too, but it was not until later that he learned of this.

Across a bridge of prayer

A long night of inner exploration after the talk with Father Hagerty uncovered the way to a spiritual world. "Prayer is the bridge to another world,'' Patrick discovered.

As Patrick prayed with ever-increasing intensity, the power of his prayers became stronger.

Like the pounds hefted by a weightlifter's growing muscles, the burden of his illness became lighter.

On the eve of All Saints Day, less than a week after Father Hagerty's visit, the fog suddenly lifted from his soul. After one final vast effort he was crossing the bridge easily. It seemed that Mary came and took him by the hand to lead him to the other side, into a spiritual world brighter than the blaze of autumn outside.

It was like one of those occasional days of his boyhood in Ireland when the fog lifted from a world he could not see and showed it to be real.

The new power of his prayer developed and strengthened that bridge so that he could ever afterward invoke Mary's help to lead others with natural ease into that world of spirituality.

Patrick knew that he was getting well. But his doctors at the clinic refused to give him the semi-annual checkup with x-rays and laboratory tests before its scheduled date. So he went around

A Man of Faith

Special
Offer
Inside!

By Jeanne Gosselin Arnold

Dear Friend of Our Lady,

From your friendship and support I know you wish to help me reach families everywhere, especially troubled ones, with the comforting message of the power of prayer—particularly the rosary.

A way for you to further this goal is through the distribution of A MAN OF FAITH, a true story of how powerful is Mary's intercession with her Divine Son when we turn to her.

By purchasing copies as a gift for relatives or friends, you will be a catalyst in spreading far beyond its present boundaries the truth of the message: THE FAMILY THAT PRAYS TOGETHER, STAYS TOGETHER.

May God love and bless you always.

Patrick Peyton, c.s.c.

Dear Father Peyton,

I do believe in your work of spreading the message of family prayer, especially the rosary, and want to help you.

☐ Please send me _____ copy(ies) of A MAN OF FAITH at $8.95.

☐ I would like to take advantage of your SPECIAL OFFER OF 10 BOOKS FOR $65.

☐ I am not ordering books but I want to aid the Family Rosary Crusade by my gift of $ _____.

SEND CHECK OR MONEY ORDER TO:

The Family Rosary, Inc.
Executive Park Drive
Albany, N.Y. 12203

Name   _____
Address   _____
            _____
            Amount Enclosed $_____

MY PLEDGE AND PRAYER—Mary, I ask your intercession with your Divine Son for myself, my family, my country, my world. I shall do this through the Rosary that I will
pray daily with all or some of my family or alone if
necessary, because I so firmly believe in the words of your
son:

"*Again I tell you, if two of you join your voices on earth
to pray for anything whatever, it shall be granted you by my
Father in heaven. Where two or three are gathered in my
name, there am I in their midst.*"

(Matthew 18: 19-20)

them and, with some assistance, secured an examination at St. Joseph's Hospital in South Bend.

Confirmation of his improvement came quickly. The doctor sent word in two days that he could get up and go to Mass the next day, the Feast of the Immaculate Conception. From that time on, he equated every step of his recovery and every accomplishment of his life with a feast day in the lives of Jesus and Mary.

The Mass that day had special meaning for him, and he was jubilant.

He did not know that his mother was being buried in Ireland that very day. His family had felt his distress at such news would worsen his condition, so had not told him that she had died.

The doctors who had pronounced him incurable were forced to admit the disease was "arrested," but would not term it "cured." They released him to return to his studies, but with many admonitions and restrictions.

Tom was at the station to meet him when he stepped off the train in Washington, D.C., after an all-night ride from Indiana. It was Monday, February 5, 1940, exactly a year since he had been carried by ambulance to the hospital.

Upon his arrival with Tom at Holy Cross College he was ordered immediately to bed. But he would not be returning to the Bengalese. His superiors felt that he would never be strong enough to become a missionary.

Patrick, still under doctor's orders, received most of his instruction and did most of his studying in bed. Occasionally Patrick was allowed to leave his room for special instruction or special events. Tom was assigned as guardian of his activities. The two brothers were together once again, but Tom was a year ahead of Patrick in his studies.

Father George De Prizio was one of many frequent visitors. The young priest would become Father Peyton's superior two decades later and remain his friend and adviser for the rest of his life. He always came bearing a cup of tea.

One day he took Father Peyton to a classroom to coach him in oratory.

"As I listened," Father De Prizio related, "I observed that this man had his own natural style of speech. I realized that the training in oratory should not be such that this would be lost." He added, "I am firmly convinced that Father Pat would have been the

23

founder of his own order of priests had it not been for the way his work took him all over the world with the Rosary.''

Winter melted into spring that brought the buds of May and the processions of little girls in their white dresses, enacting the crowning of Mary as Queen of Heaven.

In that month of the Glorious Mystery of the Coronation of Mary, the Peytons suffered a great loss, more deeply sorrowful because it was also a gift.

"Nellie, you are going to die,'' the priest told their sister as she lay in the Scranton hospital.

"Yes, I know,'' Nellie Peyton replied calmly.

Monsignor William Farrell, then chancellor of the Scranton diocese, administered the sacrament of the Anointing of the Sick and gave her the Holy Eucharist. Then he asked her:

"Have you a message for your brothers?''

"I have,'' she replied. "Tell them that, if it be God's Holy Will that they become priests, I pray that they will be true priests like Jesus Christ.''

Nellie Peyton had entered the hospital for surgery. But the day she was put on the recovery list, she suffered a heart attack. Tom and Patrick were summoned, but she died before they could reach her.

Nellie Peyton departed from them forever. But she gave them her life in losing it.

Patrick was given a piece of paper found in her room. She had written on it:

I, Nellie Peyton, offer Thee, Dear Lord, all my thoughts, words and actions of this day, and every day, and even life itself, for my two brothers, Thomas Francis Peyton and Patrick Joseph Peyton, that if it be Thy Holy Will that they become priests, that never in their priestly lives will they commit a mortal sin.

"Even life itself,'' Patrick mused over those words and repeated them all the rest of his life whenever he was called upon to explain his debt.

He was indebted to his parents for their gift of faith. He was indebted to his whole family for the love they had given him and the losses they had suffered for him, especially to his mother and his sister Nellie, who had given their lives for his.

24

Now he also owed all the good that Nellie would have done for others had God not accepted her offer by taking her early.

He owed another tremendous debt to the Blessed Mother Mary, who had saved his life.

He would devote his life to repaying those debts, he told himself as he and Tom sadly returned to Washington and their studies.

Tom was going to become a priest before the brother who had led him all the way from Ireland and toward priesthood. Patrick prayed to be ordained along with Tom. He told no one, but put his trust in Mary, the Blessed Mother, to find the way.

Some mortal must have divined Patrick's prayers. This is not unlikely, because Patrick prayed and studied constantly. In any case, the human apparently became God's instrument in answering them. In a few months a cablegram came from the Vatican. It read:

SPECIAL DISPENSATIONS ARE GRANTED FOR THE IMMEDIATE ORDINATION TO THE PRIESTHOOD OF SEMINARIAN PATRICK PEYTON.

Patrick Joseph Peyton and Thomas Francis Peyton were ordained priests on June 15, 1941, in the Church of the Sacred Heart at Notre Dame.

The farm boy with the religious heritage of an Irish home, the altar boy who had dreamed of becoming a priest, the school dropout whose dream had been shattered, the lad who had dared to preach to a grownup, the young man who had resisted his own dream, he whose faith death had challenged, who had cried out to his Blessed Mother and had been saved by her, was ordained now to walk in the footsteps of Jesus Christ. He would henceforth preach Christ's Word and administer His Sacraments.

As the yoke of Christ was placed upon him, he felt the power given him lifting up the weight of that yoke.

That day, Father Patrick Peyton pledged every one of his priestly actions to Mary, the Mother of God. Some who misunderstood would say later that he was keeping a promise to her for having saved his life, but that is not true.

"I never bargained with her," he later explained. "I never said to her that I would do this if she would do that. She helped me out of her own love in answer to my prayers, and I wanted to thank her by dedicating my life, my every action, every merit of my priesthood to her."

The brothers celebrated their first Masses in Scranton among family and friends. Then Father Tom Peyton was assigned to a parish and Father Patrick Peyton went back to finish his studies.

The question now was how to fulfill his pledge to Mary.

Holy Cross Fathers are allowed some choice in their type of work, subject to the approval of the superiors.

Any idea of Father Peyton's would have to be considered practical, workable and attainable by Father Thomas A. Steiner, provincial superior of Notre Dame Province. Father Steiner, in turn, was responsible to Bishop Albert Cousineau, the superior general of the Congregatio Sanctae Crucis (Holy Cross).

Father Steiner was not noted for imagination or love of innovation.

Father Peyton prayed, trusting Mary to tell him what she wanted him to do.

His inspiration came on the last Sunday of January, in his room, where he was alone for a prescribed day of retreat and meditation.

In those early days of 1942 there was no end in sight for the destructive forces of World War II. Japanese had attacked Pearl Harbor on December 7, 1941, and Hitler's Nazi troops were still swarming out of Germany. America was at war on two fronts.

Father Peyton envisioned millions of people praying together to bring an end to the war. Then he imagined winning and maintaining peace forever through worldwide practice of the daily family Rosary as it was prayed in his youth by his family in Ireland.

"I knew I had found my lifework," he said later. "I would get every family in the United States—in the whole world—to pray the Rosary daily. It would repay my debt to Our Blessed Mother and bring peace to the world by bringing peace to the family on its knees before God every single day."

He also knew that Father Steiner would consider the idea completely unrealistic for one priest, especially one in delicate health, to accomplish.

Now he knew what Mary wanted him to do, but not how to do it. He prayed his Rosary. One evening, as he prayed, he came to the last of the first three *Hail Marys* that represent to him faith, hope and love. He mused as he prayed that third bead of love:

> *Hail Mary, full of grace! the Lord is with thee; blessed art thou among women, and blessed is the fruit of thy womb, Jesus.*
> *Holy Mary, Mother of God, pray for us sinners, now and at the hour of our death. Amen.*

"The one thing I want to do with my life is to devote every minute of it to restoring the family Rosary in America," he confided to Father Christopher O'Toole, his immediate superior at Holy Cross, as they sat on the porch one June evening. By then, Father Peyton was allowed more frequent and longer periods out of bed. The campus was almost deserted, as the seminarians had left for vacation.

Father O'Toole authorized him to write a letter explaining his idea to Bishop Edwin O'Hara of Kansas City, who had spoken some time before at Holy Cross and who Father Peyton believed would be receptive.

He wrote, scratching out and putting in and rewriting many times, and got a young seminarian to type it for him.

Many, many years later, that helper described the occasion in a letter.

> University of Notre Dame
> Notre Dame, Indiana 46556
> October 17, 1977

My first contact with Father Pat Peyton's Rosary Campaign was to type a letter for him to Bishop O'Hara of Kansas City requesting help to get the Campaign started. This was during the time that Father Pat was staying in bed most of the day recovering from tuberculosis in our seminary at Holy Cross College in Washington, D.C. I used to stop by his room to tutor him in Theology, covering the classes missed because of his illness. After the tutoring, he would always talk to me about his idea of the Rosary Campaign and that led to the letter which led to the beginning of the Campaign. Much has happened in all of the years that followed, but we're all proud of what Father Pat has been able to accomplish.

(Rev.) Theodore M. Hesburgh, C.S.C.
President

Bishop O'Hara's response was enthusiastic and encouraging. Father O'Toole authorized Father Peyton to continue exploring and planning through other religious leaders and heads of the large national Catholic organizations.

Father Peyton found more support as he continued to write letters and went about Washington, where several of the organizations had their national headquarters.

By mid-August he had all the Catholic chaplains in the military under the jurisdiction of Bishop John F. O'Hara praying the Rosary before their troops and requesting the servicemen to ask their families to pray the Rosary for their safety.

Father Patrick Peyton was on his way.

Then came his first assignment. He was to go to Albany, New York, as chaplain to the Holy Cross Brothers who taught at a Catholic high school there. It was an easy assignment that would not tax his health.

Father Peyton felt that his chosen work had been derailed, or at least sidetracked.

He began praying the Rosary. He concluded the introductory prayers of the pendant part of the beads:

> Glory be to the Father, and to the Son, and to the Holy Spirit.
> As it was in the beginning, is now, and ever shall be, world without end. Amen.

Then he realized that pendant part of the beads represented a runway to the main event—like the runway for an airplane to take off to the skies. He did not feel so unhappy about going to Albany.

Part 2

First decade—the forties
Going to the top

Commitment to a mission

So Father Peyton went to Albany. He packed up his belongings and took a train from Washington, the capital of the country, to Albany, the capital of New York State.

When he arrived, and before even going to his room, he asked for a place to pray. He was directed to the little chapel in his new home.

Alone in the chapel, he slipped into a chair at the rear. Almost automatically, his Rosary beads were in his hands. He began his prayer with the graceful movement and words of the Sign of the Cross. He gave thanks for his safe arrival and for all the other benefits that God had bestowed upon him, through Mary's intercession.

Suddenly, as he prayed, alone in the chapel, he knew that he could not do it. He was but a single priest, and frail in health, with an impossible dream. He saw himself through the eyes of more practical men.

How could he hope ever to reach ten million American families? And, if he could reach them, how could he hope to convince them that they should pray together as families? How could he sell them on the idea of daily family Rosary?

Here he was, at this place, at this time, fenced in by other limitations added to his own inability. He had been sent to this upstate diocese, away from the big city centers of activity. His work was restricted to being performed in the diocese. The tremendous task he was committed to perform was far beyond his poor human capacity.

He rose from his chair and strode down the aisle to the altar. Grasping the tabernacle, the ark containing the consecrated Host, he spoke to God. He, Father Patrick Peyton, was inadequate for this mission. He could not do it. But God could. He pleaded with Jesus to do it as a gift to His Mother Mary. He asked that ten million American families and Catholic families throughout the world become Rosary homes.

The answer came as a clear voice in his mind: He was to spread the message to the ends of the earth that families should pray

30

united as families, and that they should pray the Rosary, the most fruitful of family prayers; he was to harness the airwaves as a pulpit, with the best artists to help him; he was to ask the bishops to gather their flocks to hear the message. It was like that day of inspiration the previous January, only more far-reaching.

His task was to be even more gigantic than he had first perceived, but he had now been shown the way to do it. His doubts and fears were gone. He accepted the task in the words of the familiar *Our Father* as he prayed:

Our Father, who art in heaven, hallowed be Thy name; Thy kingdom come; Thy will be done on earth as it is in heaven.

Give us this day our daily bread; and forgive us our trespasses as we forgive those who trespass against us; and lead us not into temptation, but deliver us from evil. Amen.

He had been chosen for a special role as an apostle of Mary the Mother of God, and he accepted, humbly and without hesitation, whatever it might entail, wherever it might lead him.

He was following the example of Mary, the humble maid of Nazareth who had been chosen by God for the highest role of all womankind. She had accepted God's will, without doubt or hesitation. With her acceptance had begun those events of almost two thousand years ago that had brought salvation to mankind and changed the history of the world.

The First Joyful Mystery
The Annunciation

Zachary was the priest chosen on a certain day to offer the incense before the Holy of Holies in the temple at Jerusalem. He felt unworthy because he and his wife Elizabeth were childless. They were bereft of the children who would have been a sign of grace in the eyes of God.

As Zachary was burning the incense, Gabriel, an angel of the Lord, appeared before him and told him that Elizabeth his wife would conceive and bear a son, and that he was to name the child John. John would be the one who would come before to prepare the way for the Lord.

Zachary did not believe the angel, because he and his wife were old. For his disbelief, he was struck dumb. When he came out of the temple, he could not speak to the other priests to tell what had happened. But he made signs to them, and they perceived that he had seen a vision.

In the sixth month, the angel Gabriel was sent from God to a town of Galilee named Nazareth,
to a virgin betrothed to a man named Joseph, of the house of David. The virgin's name was Mary.
Upon arriving, the angel said to her: "Rejoice, O highly favored daughter! The Lord is with you. Blessed are you among women."
She was deeply troubled by his words, and wondered what his greeting meant.
The angel went on to say to her: "Do not fear, Mary. You have found favor with God.

You shall conceive and bear a son and give him the name
Jesus.
Great will be his dignity and he will be called Son of the
Most High. The Lord God will give him the throne of David
his father. He will rule over the house of Jacob forever
and his reign will be without end.''
Mary said to the angel, "How can this be since I do not
know man?''
The angel answered her: "The Holy Spirit will come upon
you and the power of the Most High will overshadow you;
hence, the holy offspring to be born will be called Son of
God.
Know that Elizabeth your kinswoman has conceived a son in
her old age; she who was thought to be sterile is now in her
sixth month,
for nothing is impossible with God.''
Mary said: "I am the servant of the Lord. Let it be done to
me as you say.'' With that the angel left her.

(Luke 1: 26-38)

Father Peyton's meditation
on The Annunciation

God takes the initiative to redeem and save us. He chooses Mary
to speak for us all. God seeks and asks for her cooperation. Mary
gives her response. She chooses to be chosen and the Word of God
becomes Man and dwells among us.

Mary is our example as day by day, God invites each of us to
choose to be chosen. He takes the initiative and we but give the
response. When our response is joyous, generous and total like
Mary's, God has then the full freedom to do great things for us, in
us, with us, and through us.

Answered prayers

Sister Magdalena's long black habit with its stiff white bib rustled as she crossed the classroom to open the door to the knocking outside.

She raised her face, framed in all its youthful freshness and beauty by the white band low on the forehead and the folds of the headdress close to her cheeks.

"Have you got a girl that can type a letter?" the tall priest greeted her. From behind her came the clatter of typewriters from girls in deep-blue jumpers and white blouses seated at long tables.

"I want to get ten million families to pray the Rosary every day," Father Peyton explained.

"Why not!" Sister Magdalena's reply was a statement, not a question. She was not a bit surprised at the priest's introduction. "I just looked up and saw that tall Irish priest with the red hair and the blue eyes and it seemed perfectly natural," she described that first meeting years later.

Not one girl, but many, answered Father Peyton's request for a typist. And they wrote not one letter, but many, stenciled

thousands of copies and addressed thousands of envelopes.

His chosen work had gained the approval of his provincial superior. He had finally been forced to seek that permission when he left the jurisdiction of Father O'Toole, his immediate superior

34

at Holy Cross. While perhaps not approved enthusiastically, at least it had not been disapproved.

When Father Peyton, supported by letters of endorsement from two bishops, had approached him, Father Steiner had said he had no objections as long as the bishop of the Albany diocese approved. Bishop Edmund F. Gibbons, leader of the Albany diocese, gave that approval.

Father Peyton wanted to write to every bishop in the country asking their support for his idea of daily family Rosary. But he had neither money, office nor typewriter. A few days after his arrival, one of the Holy Cross Brothers led him to Sister Magdalena's classroom door at Vincentian Institute, where the Brothers taught the boys and the Sisters of Mercy taught the girls.

That first meeting between the priest and the nun fermented new values into many lives, including their own.

For Father Peyton, it answered the question of how he could pursue his chosen work in Albany. Many of the secretarial students became involved in Father Peyton's campaign, and some found their own professional careers in his work.

As one secretarial class after another took up Father Peyton's work during the next few years, other groups of educators often invited Sister Magdalena to come and explain her successful system of teaching. "The girls were learning on something real, something they were interested in, that was important to them. That was the secret of their success and of my system," she explained later.

The contagion of helping Father Peyton spread. Wherever he or his helpers went, they infected others with their enthusiasm. Sister Mary Adrian described the library at the Sisters of Mercy motherhouse as a beehive of activity, sometimes until midnight. Any spare moments between tasks were spent by the novices addressing envelopes and stuffing letters into them.

Father Peyton's frail health and financial poverty were shown in her words years later: "Father had to make many visits to the Mother House. He may have walked over, but we always saw that he had a ride back. We were always happy to serve him lunch or to see that he never left without at least a glass of milk. We were concerned about his keeping well."

The response of the bishops to Father Peyton's initial mailing was more than encouraging. Some sent him copies of church newsletters and diocesan newspapers with stories and editorials about his campaign for the Rosary. One editorial prompted him to request an appointment to call and personally thank Bishop Thomas Molloy of Brooklyn.

Father Peyton was not used to face-to-face encounters with bishops. He was frightened. But Bishop Molloy's words softened the impact of his austere presence. Father Peyton returned to Albany with a promise of $5,000 to launch his crusade for daily family Rosary.

Father Peyton celebrated Mass for the twelve Holy Cross Brothers under his spiritual care in the chapel in their residence. But it was Our Lady's grotto at Vincentian Institute that beckoned him to his private prayer. He could pass unnoticed through a side entrance of the school building and down a short hall to the darkness of the grotto. He could be alone there to pray with undisturbed intensity. He went there frequently during the week as he worked and on Sunday evenings after the Brothers had all retired to their own occupations.

Early one February morning, he slipped from the brightness of sun on new snow into the darkness of this shrine. He groped his way to the granite slab stretching across the front of the grotto's arch of stone and knelt there. He could hear the whispering of the fountain that ran like a little stream down the rocks near the niche where he knew Our Lady's statue stood.

The figure of Our Lady gathered light as he gazed into the darkness under the arch of stone. She stood, with the Rosary beads draped over praying hands, looking down at him from the raised niche in the rocks as artists had depicted her looking down at the young Bernadette at Lourdes. This grotto had been built as a replica of the shrine of Our Lady of Lourdes.

Mary's figure seemed to cast a halo of light all around her and he began to see the sparks dancing in the little stream near her feet. Then a shattered rainbow of color became visible to his eyes. It slanted from the stained-glass picture of the Nativity scene upon the rocks of the grotto and the small altar under its arch. Stained-glass windows along one side of the rows of seats facing the grotto provided the only light in the chapel. They sprinkled their colors upon the black robes of the priest kneeling erect on the hard stone slab.

No sound but the trickle of the fountain broke through the dimness to Father Peyton at his prayers. Silently he prayed his *Hail Mary* and a *Memorare* reminding Mary of her promise to mankind and her influence with her Son Jesus. Then he began his plea for help.

Twelve thousand and six hundred letters were all ready to be mailed to all the pastors of the country, ready, except for the stamps. Encouraged by the responses of the bishops to his first mailing, Father Peyton had had a letter drafted and duplicated, telling about the benefits of daily family Rosary and explaining his ideas for fostering it. The Sisters of Mercy and the girls at Vincentian had worked hard for months preparing the letters and addressing the envelopes.

Father Peyton had no money for stamps. He needed three hundred and sixty dollars for the three-cent postage for first-class mailing. He asked his heavenly mother to pray with him to find the money somehow and he thanked her for the help he was confident she would give.

As he slipped again out into the street, the bright sun on the snow dazzled his eyes. A figure approaching him from down the street appeared a dark silhouette. As the silhouette drew nearer he saw that it was one of the Brothers. Handing him an envelope, the Brother said, "Here is a little donation collected by the boys in my class."

As Father Peyton continued on, around the corner to the main entrance of the school, others hailed him and rushed to hand him more money, sometimes in envelopes, sometimes in fistfuls of coins they dug from pockets and pocketbooks. He found other bills and coins on the table in the hallway that he called his office. In the school cafeteria, where he went for lunch, there was money under his plate. Nuns and students came to give him their donations, large and small. When he went to his room that night, he found more money on his dresser and under his pillow.

The same sort of thing was repeated as the days passed and the mailing date grew closer. By February 11, he had the money for the stamps.

After he and his helpers had stamped all the envelopes, they put them in mail sacks and lugged them into the grotto. There they remained all night at the feet of Our Lady. The letters were mailed the next morning on the scheduled date.

The mail continued to go out in sacks. The replies started to pour in. Before long, the table in the hallway at Vincentian became an impossible mailroom.

During those months, Father Peyton also went from parish to

parish preaching triduums. These were a series of services on three consecutive days and provided the pulpit for his pleas for daily family Rosary. The collections provided the staple of support for his work. This was the only money he would accept for his activities as a priest. He never would, and never has, accepted stipends for his Masses, for these had been committed to Mary.

Families were praying the Rosary daily. The helpers took the idea to their homes. The Brothers and Sisters taught the children in their classes to promote it with their parents. Parishioners took it home from the triduums.

Heroic offering

The sophomores at Albany's College of Saint Rose were having an election. It was the second semester, the spring of 1943, and they were choosing class officers for their coming junior year.

Before the ballots were half counted, Mary Grace Reutemann was the lead for class president. In the final count, she won an overwhelming majority.

Mary Grace was a vivacious, joyful young woman, friendly and helpful to her classmates, and a good student—an obvious leader.

A few months earlier, Father Peyton had been introduced to the young students by their chaplain, Father Francis F. Woods, a priest of the Albany diocese who had helped him from the beginning. Father Woods's main job was secretary to the diocesan marriage tribunal.

At Father Woods's invitation, Father Peyton had spoken before a group of the college students about his idea for daily family Rosary and had asked their help. They gave it generously.

Mary Grace Reutemann, generally in the forefront of any student activity, was one of Father Peyton's most enthusiastic volunteers.

With summer came the end of the school year. The student volunteers dispersed to their own homes and summer activities. Mary Grace Reutemann, wishing to contribute to the war effort, took a job for the summer in a plant manufacturing war materials. A few weeks later the Holy Cross Brothers departed for their vacations.

Father Peyton, his duties in Albany temporarily halted, was assigned as chaplain to a group of Holy Cross seminarians vacationing at Deer Park, Maryland, for the summer.

A few weeks after Mary Grace began work in the war plant in the nearby Village of Watervliet, a strange sickness attacked her lungs, sapping the strength of the robust young college girl.

Her grief-stricken family watched helplessly as her condition grew rapidly worse.

Father Peyton was busy preparing to leave Albany when Father Woods asked him to go with him to the hospital to pray for Mary Grace. With characteristic concern for every individual soul, Father Peyton dropped everything to go to her bedside and offer his prayers.

Father Peyton took with him to Deer Park the hundreds of letters he had received in response to his first mail campaign explaining his idea of daily family Rosary. He enlisted a group of seminarians there to help him analyze and correlate the reactions in order to write an evaluation report.

The natural beauty of the vacation camp site invited meditations on the Creator. Rustic structures stood in the open green space between the line of woodland behind and the shoreline of Deep Creek Lake around the promontory of land thrusting into the long lake. Father Peyton liked to stroll along the banks of the lake, praying the Rosary.

Seminarian Albert J. Heinzer, talking and praying with him as they strolled together there, felt the presence of the Blessed Mother. Eight years before, he had for a brief time been a classmate of Patrick Peyton's at Notre Dame. Financial problems had forced a four-year interruption in his studies, but he had returned and graduated in 1941. He was to enter his second year of theological studies at Holy Cross College after the summer at Deer Park.

As he prayed with Father Peyton by the lake, he felt that Our Lady was with them. "I felt that the appearance of Mary there along the shore would not be abnormal," he said later.

In the midst of Father Peyton's work at Deer Park, something happened that gave impetus and urgency to his crusade for daily family Rosary.

The rest of the events are told by Sister Emily Joseph Daly, of the Sisters of Saint Joseph and the College of Saint Rose:

> What transpired in that hospital room as some simple words were uttered in barely audible tones was, on Father Peyton's own testimony and on the witness given by events, of incalculable significance. For as Mary Grace recognized the important part that sacrifice plays in winning grace for souls, she heroically offered her life for the success of Father Peyton's mission for Mary. With a gentle firmness which created the impression Our Lady was beside her, she directed her family to unite each day in saying the family Rosary—a request which was faithfully heeded for all the years the family remained together. And as word spread of the unexpected illness which had come upon Mary Grace, of her insistence upon the significance of the family Rosary and of the intimate role she was playing in Father Peyton's crusade, family friends and ac- quaintances felt impelled to initiate in home after home the group recitation of the Rosary.
>
> July 19, 1943, marked the date on which Father Peyton's Rosary Crusade felt the impetus of a mighty force. Grace from heaven moved hearts to respond to the simple plea that families should pray the Rosary together, and the instrument of that grace was Mary Grace whose soul on that day returned to her Creator.

The flowers that would have heralded her inauguration as junior class president and other joyful fulfillments of a life were now heaped upon Mary Grace Reutemann's grave. For the family and friends who loved her, her absence was her presence everywhere. Her silenced voice was a record in their heads turned on by the sound of the wind, a song, a word.

The more that people took portions of her faith, the more it grew and her name spread, and her dying words became a chorus.

Her sacrifice created a pattern followed by many others throughout the years who offered their sufferings. To Father Peyton these heroic pledges became a shield that warded off negative forces.

Mary Grace's sacrifice, and the loss felt by her dear ones, became Father Peyton's pain. His suffering was also his strength. It was not easy to do God's work. It was not easy to get families to pray. Outside pressures crowded out daily family worship. And evil forces were always at work to destroy or disrupt families.

Father Peyton had powerful weapons to combat those evil forces. He had the help of Jesus and Mary. He had the added support of those who had made the supreme sacrifice. He returned to Albany after the vacation period, knowing he must use every means to get families to unite every day in praying the Rosary. With him he brought a fifteen page report on the responses to the idea of daily family Rosary. He began his second year as chaplain to the Holy Cross Brothers.

The small table that served as his office was once again set up in the hallway of Vincentian Institute outside Sister Magdalena's classroom.

Father Woods was becoming more involved in Father Peyton's work. His own experience with troubled marriages had made him wonder whether Father Peyton's way of saving families was not better than his own. But the final push had come from the death of Mary Grace Reutemann. He had been deeply affected by her sacrifice and could not forget it. If a young college girl's faith could be so strong, could his own be any less? He, too, was deeply devoted to Our Lady. He gave every moment he could spare from his other duties to helping Father Peyton.

Father Peyton discussed with Father Woods his need for a pamphlet on why families should pray the Rosary. Father Woods saw the value of such writings for his own work as secretary of the matrimonial court. In this work, he counseled husbands and wives whose marriages were breaking up. He had seen all kinds of problems that could destroy families. Since Father Peyton's arrival, he had been suggesting to the couples he counseled that they try the daily family Rosary, and he had seen it work. Many marriages had been saved. Father Woods volunteered to write the pamphlets. They later grew to a series, including a booklet called *The Story of the Family Rosary*, and they were distributed in the hundreds of thousands nationwide.

That fall, Father Woods also got Father Peyton a spot on ''The Voice of the College of Saint Rose,'' a weekly radio broadcast over local Station WABY. The idea of the two priests was to have a prominent family pray the Rosary on the program.

The response to that broadcast was so great that it completely dissolved the initial doubts of students who produced it. Afterward, they gave time to Father Peyton regularly. This led to the station giving him a time slot of his own for weekly family Rosary recitation. That program lasted for two years.

It demonstrated family Rosary by having a family itself, never a priest, reciting the prayers of the Rosary. Listeners heard a well-known man of their own community, perhaps even a neighbor, praying over the air, *"Hail Mary, full of grace, the Lord is with thee; blessed art thou among women, and blessed is the fruit of thy womb, Jesus."*

Then they heard the chorus of that man's wife and children in the responses: *"Holy Mary, Mother of God, pray for us sinners, now and at the hour of our death. Amen."* Thus they learned that a family by itself could pray the Rosary.

People in their homes tuned in and prayed along.

Father Peyton was again assigned to Deer Park for the summer of 1944. Father Woods went with him to work on the pamphlet.

Father Peyton took along with him his ideas, the first install-ment of Bishop Molloy's promised $5,000, and a lot of paper. He asked the seminarians to help write the pamphlet.

It was there that he encountered the first strong skepticism toward the whole idea of family prayer.

One of the seminarians, Paul Bailey, who favored private prayer, challenged Father Peyton's belief. Father Peyton im-mediately recognized that this objection might be a recurring obstacle. He set about the task of formulating for others the ex-pression of what he had taken for granted.

As Father Peyton reasoned out his case for family prayer he drew upon his own lifelong experiences, his religious training, and Scripture.

Jesus had said, *"Where two or three are gathered in my name, there am I in their midst."* (Matthew 18: 20.) Family prayer made the home a little church and brought Jesus into the home. When a family prays together, it recognizes its dependence upon God. It begs God to make that family everything it could be.

The family is the basic unit of the larger community. It is already united in a bond of mutual love. When such a unit raises its voice in prayer, the power of the prayer increases as the family becomes one with Jesus Christ.

Praying together as a group brings unity and peace to the fami-ly. Daily family prayer resolves whatever conflicts have arisen among the members of the family during the day. The bond of mutual love is strengthened in the love of God.

The Rosary is the ideal family prayer. It is prayed "In the name of the Father and of the Son and of the Holy Spirit." The children hear their father say, "I believe in God" as he begins the *Apostles' Creed*. The family honors God and asks his help when they pray the *Our Father*, the perfect prayer given to man by Jesus Christ Himself. All those *Hail Marys* cannot help but attract the attention of the Blessed Mother. She hears again the very words of the Angel Gabriel when he appeared to tell her she was chosen, and she remembers, like any young mother, the birth of her Infant Son Jesus. The father and the mother and the children cannot help but want to be like that holy family as the family prays its Rosary. The soul of the Rosary is the Mysteries. As we pray each decade, we reflect upon these Mysteries in the lives of Jesus and Mary. We cannot completely comprehend them, but we are reminded that with God, nothing is impossible.

Families were being threatened, from both within and without. Husbands and fathers were absent from the home, far away in horrible battle. Mothers were absent from the home, working in the war plants. The lives of children were disrupted. They needed, more than ever, the unity of family prayer. Without prayer, families would dissolve. Only prayer could save families. Only God can save families.

Through the Rosary, families can appeal to Mary the Mother of God to pray with them for help from her Son Jesus in saving their family and all families. The family must be saved if the world is to be saved. The Rosary has saved the world in the past. It will help save the world now by saving families.

Father Peyton would sorely need these statements as he met others' unbelief or indifference in his efforts to get families to pray the Rosary daily.

At that time, the doubting seminarian was completely won over by Father Peyton's faith. Work began on the pamphlet, *The Story of Family Rosary*, which was completed that summer. Father Peyton's mailings from the seminarians' camp became so massive that eventually the government decided Deer Park needed a better post office and upgraded the one there.

Father Woods and Father Peyton returned to Albany at the end of the summer.

Eileen Soraghan was one of the first of Sister Magdalena's typing students to enlist in the Peyton campaign for Our Blessed Mother Mary. He missed her capable leadership after she

43

graduated from Vincentian Institute in the spring of 1944 and went to work for an insurance company.

She had been working only a short time when she got a phone call at home. "Eileen, Father Pat needs you," Sister Magdalena told her on the phone. Soon afterward, Father Pat called her and said, "Dear Eileen, Our Blessed Mother needs you. I can't pay you the fine salary you are getting now, but Our Lady will thank you if you come to work for me." Father Peyton had been offered an office in the nearby Dominican Convent. The task of moving and sorting and filing had left his accumulated material a jumbled mess.

In October, 1944, Eileen exchanged the material security of her job for another kind of security with Father Peyton. She became his first paid secretary at an indeterminate salary.

One day that fall Father Woods asked her to type a confidential letter to his bishop. In it he asked the bishop to relieve him of his important duties in order to work full-time with Father Peyton.

Bishop Gibbons assigned Father Woods to the Church of Saint Madeleine Sophie in nearby Schenectady. It was a mission church that would not require much of his time. It would give him some security, which Bishop Gibbons knew he would not find with Father Peyton.

Eileen found security for her family when she and Edward Gerwin, at their marriage later, took a pledge to make their home a family Rosary home. Many years later, Eileen Soraghan Gerwin of Williamsport, Pennsylvania, told the story of that first letter of resignation she typed for Father Woods. She said:

> Father Woods was an Albany diocesan priest, ordained in Rome, and a Doctor of Sacred Theology. In the 1940s it seemed certain that he was destined to become the next bishop of Albany.
>
> Shortly after the office was opened in the Dominican Convent in the autumn of 1944, Father Woods asked me to take a letter that was to go to the bishop.
>
> In his letter, Father asked the bishop to release him from his diocesan duties, the tribunal, etc., so that he might devote all his efforts and energy to helping Father Pat win families for Mary's Rosary... In one short letter, Father Woods relinquished all possibility of temporal honor or ecclesiastical power. Father Pat, through his giving of his whole life for Mary had completely won Father Woods over to her cause. The loss to the Albany diocese

was truly the world's gain, for he worked side by side with Father Pat for many years and must now be interceding in heaven for the success of Father Pat's efforts.

Father Peyton got added exposure in the public media through newspaper articles. The radio broadcasts continued. The massive mailings all over the world continued.

This beginning in Albany was the seed that would grow into a worldwide harvest of family Rosaries and prayer. The seed contained all the elements that would bloom and bear fruit. In it were Father Peyton's willingness to ask and his unerring choice of the top and the best people to ask, either for skills or financial support. In it also were his manner of appeal that made it a privilege to give, not to him, but to Mary the Mother of God, and his confidence that his appeal could not be denied.

He turned to professional communications specialists. George Nelson was head of his own advertising and public relations firm in Schenectady. Although a Protestant, he was a vocal promoter of the daily family Rosary and Father Peyton. He helped with publicity through the print and broadcast media.

But the actual work was still limited to the Albany diocese, and the triduums took up much of Father Peyton's time.

As he prayed constantly for Our Blessed Mother's guidance and help, his success in Albany began to be a frustration to him. He needed a larger pulpit. There were much greater heights to soar. He needed a longer and wider runway. George Nelson was to become the co-pilot of Father Peyton's next far-reaching project.

Father Peyton set his course for the nationwide airways of network radio.

The whole country would hear the recitation of the Rosary, and millions would pray along.

"Why not!" Sister Magdalena's unquestioning response to his appeal for help came back to him. She had said "Yes." Many others had said "Yes" to Father Peyton. Millions of others in the years to come were to say "Yes." Through the corridors of two thousand years, their "Yeses" echoed Mary's "I am the servant of the Lord..."

Not merely by their assent, but also by their action, because they could not ignore the needs of families, they followed where Father Peyton's footsteps led them.

He followed in the footsteps of those who filled twenty centuries of Christianity with action.

Most especially, he followed Mary who cannot ignore the needs of others, just as she could not ignore Elizabeth's need, when she learned of it those two thousand years ago.

The Second Joyful Mystery
The Visitation

Mary, on learning from the Angel Gabriel that her aged kinswoman Elizabeth was in her sixth month with child, journeyed through the dangerous hill country to the home of Zachary and Elizabeth in Judea. She knew that Elizabeth would need help and went to her aid.

When Elizabeth heard Mary's greeting, the baby leapt in her womb. Elizabeth was filled with the Holy Spirit

and cried out in a loud voice: "Blest are you among women and blest is the fruit of your womb.

But who am I that the mother of my Lord should come to me?

The moment your greeting sounded in my ears, the baby leapt in my womb for joy.

Blest is she who trusted that the Lord's words to her would be fulfilled."

Then Mary said: "My being proclaims the greatness of the Lord,

my spirit finds joy in God my savior,

For he has looked upon his servant in her lowliness; all ages to come shall call me blessed.

God who is mighty has done great things for me, holy is his name;..."

(Luke 1: 41-49)

Mary stayed with Elizabeth and helped with the household chores.

Joseph, her betrothed, who was of the House of David, meanwhile was troubled. But an angel appeared to him in a dream and said:

"Joseph, son of David, have no fear about taking Mary as your wife. It is by the Holy Spirit that she has conceived this child."

(Matthew 1: 20)

When Elizabeth's time came, she bore a son. On the eighth day afterward, when the neighbors gathered for the circumcision ceremony, they all said the child should be called Zachary after his father. But Zachary wrote on a pad that his son's name was John. As soon as he had done this, his voice was restored and he could speak again.

Then, with the voice of a prophet, he spoke of the coming fulfillment of God's ancient promise of salvation for His people.

Still with the voice of the prophet, he said to his son:

"And you, O child, shall be called prophet of the Most High;

47

For you shall go before the Lord
to prepare straight paths for him,
Giving his people a knowledge of salvation
in freedom from their sins,
All this is the work of the kindness of our
God;
he, the Dayspring, shall visit us in his mercy
To shine on those who sit in darkness and
in the shadow of death,
to guide our feet into the way of peace.''

(Luke 1: 76-79)

The son of Zachary and Elizabeth grew and became known as John the Baptist, who prepared the people for the coming of Jesus.

Father Peyton's meditation
on The Visitation

To love God alone is to love Him not at all.

The measure of our love for God is the love we have for our neighbor.

Mary loves God and so she loves her neighbor. Her cousin Elizabeth, elderly, pregnant and with a husband who is unable to speak to her, is in desperate need. Mary hurries through a long hazardous journey of some sixty miles to help Elizabeth. Mary enters their home and their problems are solved. Zachary and Elizabeth are blessed with blessings beyond their believing.

Families today are in grave need of help. Mary is as responsive today to any cry for help as she was to the needs of Zachary and Elizabeth. Countless families the world over invite Mary to their homes through the Family Rosary. She comes. They sense her presence. They solve their problems because where Mary is present there is Christ, her Divine Son.

The winning of Elsie Dick

"You can't get it," Elsie Dick told the tall priest in front of her desk. With great difficulty Father Peyton had obtained an interview with the director of religious programs in the New York studio of the Mutual Broadcasting Company. "You have no organization or group to back you. If I gave it to you, there would be a storm. I can't give it to individuals," she told him brusquely.

He had asked her for a free half hour of network time to recite the Rosary. He had been told by George Nelson that his goal was unreachable, that it was bad radio. Others had told him he was reaching for the stars. George had, nevertheless, introduced him to Edgar Kobak, the president of Mutual, who had resisted but had finally referred him to Elsie Dick. She like the others had pooh-poohed his idea.

Father Peyton did not believe them. Hundreds of people had told him their families prayed the Rosary in their living rooms as they listened to his weekly radio program. Many had told him their families had begun praying the Rosary together daily. The fact that the population of Albany was seventy-five per cent Catholic at the time did not bother him. After all, the majority of the country's population was Christian—believers in Christ and beholden to Mary who gave birth to God incarnate. The Rosary would be a powerful prayer for all Christians.

This was the first time Father Peyton had ever asked anyone in the world of big business for anything. He had felt out of place when he had entered this environment of glittering glass, plush carpets and fashionable men and women hurrying to and fro.

His request had been bluntly and ungraciously refused. Realizing he could not penetrate this cold world of materialism, he rose to leave. With his hand on the doorknob ready to open the door, he turned back toward Elsie Dick, straightening the shoulders that had drooped dejectedly. For the first time since his defiant teen years, he spoke in anger.

Emotion thickened his brogue as he retorted, "It's extraordinary how preoccupied we are with other people's problems, so long as it doesn't cost us anything. It's a pleasure to hear you speak theoretically about the problems of the family, the decay and disintegration of family life, so long as nobody asks you to raise your hand to help save it. And that's what you are now refusing, because I'm not coming in here to glorify your network by having some great orator talk, but I'm suggesting some husband and wife, some father and mother, to pray and ask other families to join in prayer, and you won't have it.''

Elsie Dick regarded him calmly. Unlike most people, she did not counter his anger with anger of her own. She said, ''Well why didn't you say that in the first place? I will have it. I have no choice when you put it that way. I can't say no.''

That network executive, a young Jewish woman, had said ''Yes'' to Father Peyton.

She made it clear that the entire responsibility for the production was Father Peyton's, and that it had better be good. She was putting her job on the line. On the train back to Albany, he agonized over how to carry out the tremendous responsibility he had demanded. The program was only a few weeks hence. With some juggling of commitments, Elsie had been able to give him the date he wanted—May 13, Mother's Day.

The broadcast was to be in honor of the greatest mother the world had ever known, Mary the Mother of Jesus.

''Hail Mary, full of grace, the Lord is with thee; blessed art thou among women, and blessed is the fruit of thy womb, Jesus.'' He prayed to the rhythm of the wheels of the train rumbling along the railroad tracks. And it seemed that the wheels of the train were voices in holy procession giving the response: ''Holy Mary, Mother of God, pray for us sinners, now and at the hour of our death.''

No sooner had he reached the second Hail Mary of the decade than peacefulness engulfed him. Mary wanted the broadcast. She had obtained the time for it against all odds. She would show the way to its fulfillment.

A gift for the greatest mother

Father Peyton picked up the telephone and dialed "O". To the operator he said, "I would like to speak to Mr. Bing Crosby in Hollywood, California."

Eileen Soraghan's mouth dropped open. She was standing by the desk at which Father Pat was sitting. A few other people were stuffing letters into envelopes at other desks in the donated office space in the basement of the College of Saint Rose.

Eileen had helped organize Father Peyton's first real office in donated space at the Dominican Convent. Later she supervised the move into the larger quarters donated by the Sisters of Saint Joseph in their college basement.

Eileen knew that Father Peyton had never met the famous crooner-actor.

The telephone operator soon came back on the line. "Mr. Crosby is on the lot right now and will call you as soon as he comes in if you will leave your number," she told Father Pat.

"God bless you," he replied and gave her the number. He hung up the phone to wait.

Bing Crosby was on the set filming *The Bells of St. Mary's* when an aide told him, "Some priest from the East Coast" was calling. Less than an hour later, he returned Father Peyton's call.

Father Peyton picked up the phone on the first ring.

"This is Bing Crosby," crooned the voice across the the continent.

"Thanks be to God," exclaimed Father Peyton. "I'm a priest in Albany. Will you do something for the Blessed Virgin Mary?"

He plunged into the reason for his call. Would Mr. Crosby speak—free—on a radio broadcast featuring a famous family reciting the Rosary? It would help Father Peyton get ten million families to pray the Rosary every day if he could have Mr. Crosby on the program.

Bing Crosby said "Yes" on that April 23, the first Monday after Easter. "You have me," were his words to Father Peyton.

"Thanks be to God," Father Peyton exclaimed again. "Now I will say a little prayer for you." And over long distance telephone, he prayed a quick *Hail Mary* and asked her to help Mr. Crosby and himself in their endeavor and to watch over and help Bing Crosby in all his ventures.

"Our Blessed Mother will thank you," Father Peyton promised as he and Bing Crosby ended their conversation. Father Peyton always prayed for the success of any project being arranged by telephone, long distance or not. To him, the prayer was the most important part of the conversation.

"I was awed," Eileen Soraghan Gerwin whispered as she described that phone call to the film star.

In response to all the gloomy prophecies of failure, Father Peyton was determined to make the Mother's Day program interesting. George Nelson helped him put it together. George also sent out hundreds of letters to local station managers urging them to use the network program.

They decided they must have someone to recite the Rosary who would attract attention.

They got the Sullivans of Waterloo, Iowa. Mr. and Mrs. Thomas F. Sullivan had lost all five of their sons in one naval battle when they went down with the cruiser *Juneau* in the Pacific.

Their loss had shocked the country. It had led to President Roosevelt's order that the last of a number of sons would not be taken for the war.

A movie had been made of the Sullivans' lives and loss. Theater managers in some areas would not even show it because they felt it was too heart-breaking.

As the time for the broadcast drew near Father Peyton visited the studio. He shuddered at the drabness of the stage set. Even though it would not be seen by the radio audience, he wanted it to look like what it was—people at prayer with listeners tuned in all over the country.

He saw a statue of a madonna and child in a religious store window. He borrowed it and brought it to the studio. Dozens of roses were placed around the statue. Later, he bought the statue and its mate, "Our Lady of Providence." They occupy spaces in the organization's Albany and Hollywood offices.

The rehearsal the night before the broadcast was terrible. Elsie Dick wondered how to word her resignation. Everyone left the studio sure that the program would flop.

It was a disturbed Father Peyton who left the studio at eleven o'clock that night and took his first bite of food, a sandwich in a little Broadway restaurant. During the long walk with Father Woods to the French Hospital where they were to spend the night, all of Father Peyton's soul poured forth in a silent prayer for help. Finally, in a timid voice, like that of a beaten man, he said, "Let's say the Rosary; but tonight we'll say it differently than we have ever said it before. You know, it might be embarrassing to Our Lady if we asked her now to make her own program a success. After all, this program is a gift to her; so, we'll offer this Rosary...to God, the Father, that He may not permit His daughter, Mary, to be humiliated tomorrow...to God, the Son, that He will help us to make perfect our special gift to Mary, His mother...to God, the Holy Spirit, that He inspire us to present a program worthy of Mary, His spouse...to St. Joseph, that he may watch over our program as he ever guarded on earth those things which were concerned with the honor and glory of Mary, his beloved wife..."

Father Peyton said that Rosary with all the fervor of his soul, and Father Woods soon was convinced that six persons were combining efforts to make a futile cause successful for the Lady they loved. Four of those were in Heaven, and the other two walked the darkened streets of New York.

It was very early the next morning of May 13.

In the little chapel of the French Hospital the two priests offered their masses to "The Four," and, kneeling before the Tabernacle, they recited together fifteen decades of the Rosary. Then, spiritually fortified, they set out for the radio theater.

First network program

May 7, 1945, the Monday before the program, brought news of Allied victory in Europe.

President Harry Truman declared that first Sunday after V-E Day a day of national celebration.

All across the country the churches filled with those giving thanks to God. People danced in the streets, and strangers greeted one another with smiles and happy words. Radios were kept on everywhere for the latest news bulletins.

The horrors that were just beginning to surface of the Nazi concentration camps rocked civilization. The other conflict raged on in the Pacific. The drums of war still played their ominous thunder under the victory chants. But for a day, Americans gave their thanks and dared to hope.

It was also Mother's Day. Mothers smiled at the gifts from little hands and clasped their children, praying for a world at peace for them. Other mothers sorrowed for the absence of their sons and husbands, or wept for their loss in battle.

It was into this national mood of joy and sorrow that Father Peyton unfolded the story told by the Rosary.

Archbishop Francis Spellman spoke. Choirs sang the hymns. Bing Crosby spoke on a hookup from Hollywood.

The Sullivans, with their daughter Genevieve, prayed the five Joyful Mysteries of the Rosary. As their voices rose and fell with their own loss and suffering and faith in God, not once did their ''script'' seem repetitious or monotonous.

The Sullivans captured the hearts of the nation with their prayers.

The promise of deliverance told by the mysteries of the Rosary had a personal and timely meaning for the nation of listeners.

The story of the greatest mother the world has ever known—the Mother of God—honored all mothers on their special day. The birth of Mary's Son Jesus, recalled as the prayers of The Nativity came into their living rooms, reminded the mothers of the births of their own children.

The Third Joyful Mystery
The Nativity

Caesar Augustus issued a decree in those days ordering all to return to their own cities to be counted. Joseph, with his espoused wife Mary, who was with child, went from Nazareth in Galilee into Judea to the city of Bethlehem, which was the city of David. He went there because he was of the house and line of David. Many others were there, and

Joseph was turned away from the inn when he sought a room for himself and Mary.

While they were there the days of her confinement were completed.
She gave birth to her first-born son and wrapped him in swaddling clothes and laid him in a manger, because there was no room for them in the place where travelers lodged.

(Luke 2: 6-7)

Shepherds were watching their sheep that night when an angel of the Lord appeared to them.

The angel said to them: "You have nothing to fear! I come to proclaim good news to you—tidings of great joy to be shared by the whole people.

This day in David's city a savior has been born to you, the Messiah and Lord.
Let this be a sign to you: in a manger you will find an infant wrapped in swaddling clothes."
Suddenly, there was with the angel a multitude of the heavenly host, praising God and saying,
"Glory to God in high heaven,
peace on earth to those on whom his favor rests."

(Luke 2: 10-14)

The shepherds left their flocks and went into the city of Bethlehem to see this Christ Child which the angel had announced to them. And they found Joseph and Mary and the Babe lying in a manger. Later the wise men came from the east, following a new star that rose in the east and led them to Bethlehem. And when they saw the child, they fell to their knees and worshipped Him, and presented Him with gifts of gold and frankincense and myrrh.

Father Peyton's meditation
on The Nativity

God is now with His people. He has come among us. He is visible in the Infant Jesus—helpless and totally surrendered to the care, love and protection of His Mother, the young girl Mary.

God made no mistake in His choice of her for so unbelievable a responsibility. His heaven is now her arms that enfold Him, her heart that loves Him, her eyes that watch for His every need.

The shepherds and the Wise men—the poor and rich—both find their God when they find Mary. Like the shepherds and Wise men, all of us will find Jesus Christ, the Eternal Word of God, when and where we find Mary.

Most reviewers pronounced Father Peyton's Rosary broadcast the best of the victory celebration programs.

Father Peyton had reached the goal others had told him was

impossible. The triumphant return to Albany eventually subsided into the normal hectic pace of everyday activity.

It was only natural for Father Peyton to reach for even more difficult goals. The dream of a weekly network program with families praying the Rosary over nationwide broadcasts began to grow in him.

Traveling about like the peddlers of pioneer days, Father Peyton was selling daily Family Rosary from parish to parish in the Albany diocese. He began to get invitations to parishes in other dioceses and other states as word spread and response grew to the mass mailings of letters and pamphlets.

Father Peyton faced a dilemma. He had his provincial's permission to work only in the Albany diocese. The dilemma was quickly resolved when the Bishop of Louisville, Kentucky, refused to let him speak to a group of nuns who had invited him unless he had written permission from his superior.

He telephoned Father Steiner, and, instead of the reprimand he expected, got an unexpected and broad authorization to go anywhere he was invited, provided he had permission of the bishops where he went.

Father Steiner told him, "I want every possible effort made to move Our Lady to bring this terrible war to an end."

To Eileen Soraghan Father Peyton had to leave more and more of the direction of the bulging office.

Individuals in some of the places he visited began to carry the torches lit by his ideas. A fund-raising luncheon for his work in Pittsburgh, Pennsylvania, resulted in the first club organized for an annual benefit. As friend talked to friend, similar clubs were formed in Rochester and Syracuse. A club was organized in Cleveland, Ohio. Invitations began to pour in to conduct parish programs in the Midwest.

Father Peyton was traveling most of the time by then. He knew he must, for the first time, ask his provincial superior for help. Father Steiner laconically assigned the post of assisting him to Father Jerome Lawyer, who had just been rescued from a Japanese prisoner-of-war camp in the Philippines. It was supposed to be a rest assignment.

Father Lawyer's posting in Albany as chaplain to the Holy Cross Brothers gave Father Peyton more freedom to travel and pursue his dream of a weekly radio network program. It did not give Father Lawyer much rest.

Father Peyton was summoned back to Pittsburgh many times. There his special torch-bearers were trying to find the way for him to reach his new goal.

"You must go to Hollywood, where the stars are," one of them, Fritz Wilson, finally concluded after much discussion.

Reaching Los Angeles would in itself be almost impossible to accomplish at that time. Little transportation of any kind was available to civilians.

The war in Europe over, U.S. troops were being shipped home across the Atlantic, then to the west coast, and across the Pacific for battle against Japan.

Father Peyton got his ticket for the trip with the help of others who spread the word that he needed it. Not one, but two, train tickets to Los Angeles were given up to him by a nun who had obtained them after long waiting.

Father Peyton had grasped one star when he had reached for Bing. It was only natural for him to then reach for a whole galaxy.

Harnessing the mass media

Col. Thomas H.A. Lewis was tired.

The war was coming to an end, and his work for the Armed Forces was done. He had taken leave from his civilian job as a top advertising and promotion executive for the movie industry in the early part of the war to set up and direct the vast network of the Armed Forces Radio Services. All he wanted now was to get away from his desk.

He had done his share of public service and deserved a rest, he mused on that day Father Patrick Peyton invaded his office and his life.

Tom Lewis, also a movie, radio, and television producer and script-writer, has on request written his story of that encounter and some of its consequences. Colonel Lewis's own description:

The invasion of Father Peyton

I first met Father Patrick Peyton very near the end of World War II, at the Los Angeles headquarters of the Armed Forces Radio Service, of which I was the commandant.

A college friend of mine in New York had written me insisting I see Father, telling me little about him except that he would be unlike anyone I had ever met before.

He was "right on" about that.

Such an operation as the Armed Forces Radio Service was very difficult to penetrate during wartime. There were several check-points before one reached the commandant's office: the barrier beside the reception desk; the staff sergeant's office; the adjutant's office; the executive officer's office; and my secretary's office and waiting room.

Father Peyton cleared all points without breaking stride, giving each person he passed a hale, hearty, "God bless ya!" in his rich Irish brogue, and confirming the blessing with his glistening Irish face.

Father sweated a lot in those days. He had a dream. He longed to share with the world his devotion to Mary, the Mother of Jesus, and he burned with zeal to make his dream come true.

"May God, and Our Lady bless ya!" he roared at me, pulling out a long well-worn Rosary and kneeling on the floor in front of my desk. "Kneel down now and let's say a little prayer before we say anything about my business," he said. We knelt—I facing the fervent, perspiring face of Father Peyton across the top of my desk.

And that's the way Sergeant Pettitto saw us as he burst into the room a moment later. I motioned the sergeant back toward the door where now stood my secretary and three or four other persons Father Peyton had bypassed on his way in.

Father was the fastest man with a Rosary I have ever met, faster than Wyatt Earp with a gun. And when he whipped it out, you were in for more than the prayers on the beads. You got a litany, a *Memorare*, and a few trimmin's as well.

One night in New York in a drenching downpour, after we drove up to the entrance of the Waldorf Astoria Hotel in Peter Grace's limousine, a line of cars stacked up behind us and a door-man under a huge umbrella was waiting at the curb for us, but Father Pat calmly finished up his trimmin's.

It could get embarrassing.

As a matter of fact, it did.

It was no small matter to get, free-of-charge, a half-hour in evening prime time on a major radio network. The war was over and I was back at my job with Young and Rubicam. I asked for volunteers among my staff there, to get the program started, notably Al Scalpone, he of "The Family that Prays Together Stays Together" fame.

Several times when I was on the verge of making a deal and had called Father for a consultation, I discovered he was away giving a "triduum." A triduum is a three-day period of prayer.

When I finally reached him I said, "Father, do you want a local pulpit from which to direct a series of three days of prayer?—or—do you want a national pulpit?"

"Why Tom, that's why I came out here..."

"Well, then Father—let's forget the 'triduum', or whatever, and stay in town until I get a deal—will you?"

"I will," said he, with that contagious brogue.

I made another study of the network's positions in prime time. There was a soft half hour on Mutual struggling for audience against two strong shows on NBC and CBS.

We tied up a number of top stars, like Roz Russell and Bing Crosby, and writers like True Boardman. I offered this package to the Mutual Network, and the Family Theater became a reality.

In time, of course, Father Peyton exchanged his national pulpit for an international one. He was giving on-the-spot massive Rosary Crusades by then.

I remember the first Crusade he embarked upon—in Spain.

He was frightened.

He had a right to be.

He could not speak a word of Spanish.

I brought him down to see Father Aloysius Ellacuria, a holy man, a man whom I was most fortunate to have as a spiritual adviser, and the first 'Charismatic' I have ever known. (That was before Pope John and I and precious few other Catholics knew what a 'Charismatic' was!)

Father Peyton and Father Aloysius did not eat much lunch but they prayed a lot.

Father Aloysius was a Basque from Northern Spain. As Father Pat and I were leaving, Father Aloysius called me back.

"Tell him not to worry" he said, "It does not matter if he does not speak Spanish—he speaks from in here." He touched his breast. "The people will understand him—but remind him that God can give him *any* language *instantly*. Jesus has done this before with His disciples. Tell him not to worry—but to pray that he becomes what God has planned for him—that he becomes the *Modern* St. John, whom Jesus committed to protect his Mother in this uncaring world!"

And I think that's what Father Peyton's apostolate has been—don't you?

Colonel Lewis's story spans several periods in the chronology of Father Peyton's activities. It was not until after months of discouraging pleas to network executives that he returned to again seek out Colonel Lewis in his civilian job, and it would be eight years before he would go to Spain.

Father Peyton remembers his pleas to Colonel Lewis at that first meeting.

"I have come to Hollywood to harness the mass media for the glory of Our Lady," said he to the colonel.

"The war is just about over and the world is entering an era of readjustment. Families have been disrupted and dismembered. Now they must be reunited, and the ties that bind the family together must be restored and strengthened. Unless we do this, winning the war will mean losing the peace. Our Christian civilization for which we fought will decline and atheistic materialism will take its place. And this is where Hollywood comes in. It can be used positively. I want its facilities and its stars to project this message, to tell the world that family unity is the key to world peace, and that family prayer is the key to family unity."

In the end, Father Peyton asked the colonel, "Can I ask you, dear Tom, to introduce me to your wife? That would be close to heaven." Loretta Young, the famous movie star, was Tom's wife.

When Father Peyton had arrived in Los Angeles, it was not as the bus driver he had aspired to become that long ago night under the electric sign in Scranton, but as a priest with an important mission.

He had watched America through the coach windows as the train snaked from the east across the continent. Father Peyton occasionally dozed, only to be startled awake by bursts of laughter, song or conflict. Soldiers trod or staggered along the narrow aisle, to join or leave the perpetual poker game. Litter filled the cars. Whiskey fumes and cigarette smoke filled the air. Even as he grew more hungry and exhausted, Father Peyton felt grateful for his ticket to the stars. Occasional stops revived him as he stretched his legs and gulped down a stale sandwich. At one stop he dashed to a nearby church to say a Mass of thanksgiving. The long journey by night and by day had taken him through cities, past lakes, along great rivers, across the wide plains and through the rugged Rocky Mountains to the shore of the Pacific Ocean.

He stepped off the train at Los Angeles, a rare black-robed figure among the throngs of khaki-clad soldiers surging out.

The vastness of the country had filled him with a sense of the enormity of his mission. He had a mandate to bring the message of Mary the Mother of God to the country's diverse peoples. He was reaching for the brightest stars of Hollywood to help him deliver that message.

He entered a taxi and told the driver to take him to the nearest Catholic church. The driver apparently heard enough of his speech to decide to take him past the Spanish mission church to the Cathedral of St. Vibiana, where there were other Irish priests.

Monsignor John J. Cawley, vicar general of the cathedral, a native of Ireland, welcomed him into the rectory. The archbishop of Los Angeles, Archbishop John J. Cantwell, himself a devotee of the family Rosary, remembered the letter he had received from Father Peyton a few years earlier and gave his support to Father Peyton's activities in his archdiocese. He arranged Father Peyton's introduction to Monsignor John J. Devlin, the chancery's contact with the film industry.

Monsignor Cawley introduced him to Monsignor Patrick Concannon, a native of County Galway, who invited Father Peyton to speak at the Church of the Good Shepherd in Beverly Hills, where he was pastor.

A lot of movie stars would be among the congregation on that Sunday, August 5, 1945, the feast of Our Lady of the Snows.

Galaxy of stars

The congregation facing Father Peyton in the Church of the Good Shepherd in Beverly Hills was studded with stars, handsome actors and beautiful actresses of Hollywood's golden age.

The ladies were glamorous, their dresses and hats created by the top designers of the period.

The religious faithful of that Hollywood world of make-believe watched and listened intently to the tall priest with the red-gold hair as he asked them to give their talents for the glory of God and the salvation of the world. A sudden smile banished the solemnity of his expression and lit his face with its Irish charm.

Father Peyton's long angular face suited his large heavy-boned frame. His features had a prominence generally associated with sculpture in granite, except for a softening curve here and there and the pallor left by tuberculosis that could be more suitable to marble. His eyes, under the ledge of brow, were as blue as the Madonna's mantle of the statue behind him.

"You can save the world if you will only help me save families through prayer," Father Peyton continued.

"What a blessed thing it would be if we could pray the Rosary over nationwide radio and bring Our Blessed Mother into every home in America," he said. He mentioned briefly his idea for a network radio program. "We can do it," he exclaimed. Whenever Father Peyton talked to anyone about a project, it immediately became "we" doing it and "our" project.

He knew exactly what he wanted them to do to help him, but he did not tell them then. He was following advice given him by Loretta Young.

He had met that great lady of the screen the night before, when Tom Lewis took him to their home. Loretta's recently born son, Peter, was in a crib beside her chair as they talked.

"Sell them on the idea of family Rosary, but don't give them any details of how you want them to help," she told him. "Have Monsignor Concannon in the front of the church as they leave; to invite them to come back to the sacristy to meet you personally. Then clinch the sale."

Among the stars who accepted the monsignor's invitation after the Mass and met

Father Peyton were Irene Dunne, Charles Boyer, Maureen O'Sullivan, Ethel Barrymore, and three others. They all agreed to participate in his radio programs.

The very next day, the power was released that sent waves of shock around the world. The news of the atom bomb screamed from the front pages of every newspaper in the world and into every radio in every home in the world in every language, riding the telephone lines and air waves like voices from the Tower of Babel. The mushroom cloud rising over Hiroshima told the world's people that they would never again be safe from the terrible new weapon that had been built in such secrecy by the United States.

Only God could save mankind from destroying itself. A priest of God was at that very time going among the stars of Hollywood asking them to help save mankind. With beads in hand and prayers on his lips, he was telling them that the Rosary was the way to Mary the Mother of God and that she would add her powerful prayers to theirs to implore God's salvation of mankind. He was preaching that family unity is the way to world peace and that daily family Rosary is the way to family unity. He was asking the most visible entertainers of America to lend their talents and their fame to get this message into every American home. They could not refuse him.

He contacted them first for an appointment by phoning their unlisted numbers gotten for him by Monsignor Concannon.

He was at the home of Maureen O'Hara when the bulletin came over the radio that the war was at an end. The news of Japan's surrender on August 15 crossed the international dateline to reach the western world on August 14. Maureen O'Hara pledged her help.

Father Peyton rode the trolley back to the cathedral in downtown Los Angeles, amidst fireworks and hordes of people shouting in the streets.

The fighting was over. Planes and ships were bringing the survivors back home. Families would be reunited. Disembarking on the shores of America were large numbers of war brides. New families would mushroom. There would be many problems. America, a have-not nation for five years, was entering a period of post-war readjustment.

All kinds of wounds of war would have to be healed, not only in America, but over all the globe. The healing would leave its scars but hope blossomed that the disease of war had been cured.

It was in this national mood that Father Peyton came among the stars of Hollywood preaching that "There can be no peace without prayer." He offered to those stars a cause.

Irene Dunne, one of the first to volunteer, recalled her response to Father Peyton thus:

> I really believe I am one of the first persons to know about Father Peyton's Rosary Crusade. I can see him standing in my hallway taking his leave after we had been talking over his plans. In his very confident yet humble way he said, "Mary will see this whole thing through. You can be sure of that." He spoke of Mary with such (what is the word) assurance maybe—familiarity, perhaps. He seemed so near to her I honestly felt her presence.
>
> Irene Dunne

Ruth Hussey and her husband Robert Longnecker promised their help. They were to play a very important part later in production of the radio programs.

It did not hurt Father Peyton's cause that one of his most ardent admirers was Luella Parsons, Hearst Hollywood gossip columnist, friend and dragoon whose favor was sought by everyone connected with the movie industry. Although not a Catholic, she promoted his project among the stars. She was reported as having said at a party, "I would carry a sandwich board anytime for Father Peyton."

Jimmy Durante heard about what was going on and wanted to know why he had not been invited to help. The beak-nosed comedian and his talents were welcomed joyfully.

Jimmy joined a group of stars Father Peyton was recruiting one Sunday at the Church of the Good Shepherd. The priest was surrounded by a cast of stars for his real-life drama. In the group were June Haver, Irene Dunne, Jeanne Crain, and Maureen O'Hara.

Father Peyton, as usual, began his recruiting effort with a *Hail Mary* to invoke the Blessed Mother's presence and support.

After Father Peyton's *"Hail Mary, full of grace, the Lord is with thee; blessed art thou among women, and blessed is the fruit of thy womb Jesus"*, the voices of the others joined in the response. Jimmy's voice was a rasping disharmony to the dulcet tones of the actresses.

"I'll always remember," said June Haver, "how touching it was to hear Jimmy Durante in his gravelly voice saying, 'Holy Mary, MUDDER of God, pray for us sinners, now and at the hour of our death.'" Then with a dramatic pause after the others said their "Amens" came Jimmy's "Amen" emphatically solo and with the accent on both syllables.

Father Peyton flew back to the East Coast, hopes bulging like the briefcase with all the pledges of the stars locked up in it. He looked around him on that first plane ride of his life and saw that he had reached a summit.

"The stars were on my side," he said later of that period.

There was Ethel Barrymore, June Haver,
Pat O'Brien, Lizabeth Scott, Jimmy Durante, Ann Blythe, Betty Lynn,

Bobby Driscoll, Rosemary
De Camp, Jeanne Cagney,

Bing Crosby,
Gene Kelly, Mrs. (Betsy Blair) Kelly,

and many, many others.

The ever-increasing activities, along with the frequent absence of Father Peyton, and also of Father Woods, drew Father Lawyer more and more into the operations of the Albany office. Eileen Soraghan worked long hours managing the office and the work of the many volunteers. With more triduums, more publications, more letters to write, phone calls to receive and to make, more and more details, it became necessary to hire a couple of office helpers. One helper hired in the fall of 1945 was Patricia Spanbauer. Only a few months out of high school, the young woman brought to Father Peyton's small staff the steno skills learned in Sister Magdalena's class and the experience she had gained as one of Father Peyton's most valuable volunteers.

When Father Peyton went to New York and offered his package of stars to the network executives, they looked down on it. He soon discovered that his summit was merely a high plateau.

Even if his stars had been a choir of angels, their voices would not be heard over national radio in prayer, especially the Rosary, except within the accepted format. Father Peyton would have to offer a package complete with a weekly half-hour of quality entertainment to sugar-coat the commercial, even if the product he wanted to sell was prayer.

Months went by, filled with efforts to sell the practical professionals of network radio on the idea of broadcasting the Rosary. He approached them through friends, and through friends of friends, many of them fellow Notre Dame alumni. He called upon other persons who might help whenever the frequent triduums he meanwhile conducted took him to or near New York. But the answer continued to be "No". The Rosary was still "bad radio." He prayed fervently and constantly for Mary's help, breaking many chains of beads in his intensity.

Finally a progression of people with influence one upon another got him an appointment with Ed Kobak, president of the Mutual Broadcasting network. Kobak had dodged Father Peyton for a year because, as he told one of Father Peyton's contacts, "I'm afraid that man will sell me the Empire State Building."

Kobak surrendered, but conditionally, to Father Peyton's persuasiveness. A half-hour weekly free time would be given to Father Peyton for a program of top-quality entertainment. Any religious commercial would have to be non-sectarian. All production costs would have to be borne by Father Peyton.

Kobak's associates, who drafted the rules, told him he needed a man like Tom Lewis with his expertise in broadcast production and public relations to help him. That meant a trip back to Hollywood.

No Rosary, he thought. Above all, no Rosary, the network had told him. Father Peyton knew that the role he had accepted regardless of its hardships and its sacrifices would not be an easy one.

A cherished vision died. His fantasy of millions of families sitting around or kneeling in their living rooms praying the Rosary along with their radios died like a mirage before his eyes.

There was still family prayer. He could sell that as nonsectarian. But that posed a double-pronged dilemma. Would it be acceptable to Mary? Would it be acceptable to the Catholic Church? Ecumenism was still just a word in the dictionary known only to a cultured elite. A practical streak in Father Peyton told him that strategy was needed even for the most lofty goals.

He took his dilemma to his provincial superior. Father Steiner sent him out to seek and bring back the opinions of three nationally famous priests.

Bishop Michael Reedy of Columbus, Ohio, who had been associated with "The Catholic Hour" radio broadcast, neither approved nor rejected a program for family prayer.

Monsignor Fulton J. Sheen, the famous radio priest, told him to go ahead.

But it was Archbishop Spellman's spokesman and secretary, Monsignor Francis X. Shea, whose words solved Father Peyton's personal problem and eased his anguish. Monsignor Shea, who said he was speaking for the archbishop, said, "If Our Lady can't get a full loaf, she will take half; and if she is not even offered a half, she will take the crumbs."

His Blessed Mother would accept the small gift from her son. But it was a severe blow to Father Peyton to offer only crumbs to her whom he wished to honor with his whole life.

Return to a childhood home

He knelt before the graves of his parents, gazing at the headstone engraved with both their names. He wore his cassock for this first visit since he had left them eighteen years before. They could not welcome him home with joy. His father could no longer speak his blessed words of advice; nor his mother, her loving words of encouragement. They were silent now. But he could tell his father that he had kept his promise. He could thank his mother for having given her life in exchange for his.

The son pledged to John and Mary Peyton, there upon the sod over their bodies, repayment of the debt he owed them for the gifts they had given him. With memories and love foaming within him, he reaffirmed his pledge to devote his life to the Blessed Mother Mary in thanksgiving for her help in guiding them all to their destiny. There was no one there to see the pain in his face as he lifted it in silent supplication toward the sky.

His big hands moved gently along the beads of his Rosary. Each prayer on each bead brought back the scenes of his childhood. He heard his father's voice: *"I believe in God"*—his father's legacy to his children. He heard the prayer of his mother. He saw the children growing up as they knelt and heard a choir of changing voices reaching a crescendo of *Hail Marys*. He could almost smell the warmth of the turf burning on the hearth and feel the moisture of the heavy morning mists upon his face.

The creases of pain smoothed on his face as he silently prayed. His thoughts drifted with the breeze of the gentle summer day over the gravestones of many cherished ones who had peopled the long ago years of his past.

Father Peyton left the Kileen Cemetery, the graveyard of the ancient little church that had once stood there, and walked to the chapel, some five minutes away. He went into the chapel to pray and looked back through the years at the boy Patrick as an altar boy serving the Mass there and dreaming of himself in the place of the priest.

Several times during that return home, he walked the three miles, as he had done with his family as a child, from the farm to that little chapel at Attymass and visited his departed parents in their final resting place.

The farm at Carracastle was thriving. With the acquisition of farm machinery and the advent of better fertilizers and improved seed, his brother Michael had been able to acquire more land and build a new house. Michael and his younger sister Kitty were the only family members still living on the farm. Both were unmarried. Father Peyton introduced Kitty, by pre-arrangement, to Michael Maloney, the brother of Sisters Cecelia and Theophilus, who were on the ship to Ireland. Kitty later married this man. Not long afterward, Michael brought a bride to the farm.

There was little rest for Father Peyton on his vacation. With him had come his brother Father Tom and his sister Mary and Father Woods. He and Father Woods spent their vacation recruiting priests, nuns and lay people of Ireland to support their broadcasting program in America. They gained much continuing support, both spiritual and financial, from these contacts.

Father Peyton accepted an invitation to preach at the shrine of Our Lady at Knock in his native County Mayo. In this and talks in other parts of the country, he urged his Irish countrymen to hold fast their heritage of daily family Rosary and asked their prayers for his success in spreading the practice in America.

Father Peyton had come to Ireland at the insistence of friends who said he had been working too hard and needed the vacation that neither he nor his brother Father Tom had ever taken. He was thirty-seven years old and well established in his chosen role as the apostle of Mary.

In his decision to go back home to Ireland, Father Peyton wanted a time to look back before looking further ahead.

On the voyage across the Atlantic, the Peyton party had met Basil Harris, president of the United States Lines, and his wife Mary. The Harrises and their friends had promised a donation of four thousand dollars to Father Peyton's radio productions. They were also later to help him meet J. Peter Grace Jr., another wealthy shipping magnate and businessman, who was to become a lifelong friend and benefactor.

A whole year had passed since he had first reached for the galaxy of stars in Hollywood. A feeling of urgency began to nudge at Father Peyton. He felt that the Blessed Mother Mary had accepted his small gift, even though he could not offer her the Rosary on network radio. Perhaps that would come later.

Father Peyton cut short his vacation. After only six weeks, he and Father Woods booked passage on a ship sailing on September 8, the Blessed Mother's birthday, and they sailed back across the Atlantic.

Birth of Family Theater

Father Peyton's return to Hollywood was far different from his first visit a year before. Friends greeted him warmly. A place to stay awaited him at the convent of the Immaculate Heart of Mary. The sisters, headed by Mother Eucharia Harney and later Mother Regina McPartlin, for twenty years were to provide him, and sometimes staff members, with a home in Hollywood.

He was no longer penniless. He had pledges of twenty thousand dollars, money that would come soon. Eight thousand dollars each had been promised to him by the Redemptorist Fathers at Esopus, New York, and the Servite Fathers of the famous Shrine of Our Sorrowful Mother at Chicago. Father Peyton interpreted these contributions as signs that the "crumbs" he offered were acceptable to Mary. This stilled some of his misgivings and encouraged him to return to Hollywood.

It was a new Hollywood. The war over, love stories of the movies could once again have happy endings.

It was a whole new country, in fact. Civilians, no longer deprived by the massive needs of the military, were free to travel. They could once again buy automobiles and sewing needles. Industry had retooled for a vast variety of consumer goods.

The men and women of the armed forces were home, except for the occupation forces—and the 407,316 who would never come home. More than six hundred and fifty thousand were wounded in the war. Many were trying to readjust to their disabled lives, at home or in VA hospitals. Huge numbers of veterans, many with new war brides, could not find places to live.

A massive housing shortage had greeted their return. And families kept on expanding, with the biggest baby boom ever conceived in the country's history.

These were some of the needs of families that kept Father Peyton on his knees begging for divine help whenever he was not going from person to person begging for money and other help.

He renewed his friendships with the stars, on the sets, in their offices, visiting their homes in Beverly Hills, or striding along Sunset Boulevard. With his tall figure, handsome face and engaging smile, he could have been one of them, cast in the role of a priest. But, as he moved amidst the glitter and glamour, he was not a part of it. His life was a very different one.

He rode the Los Angeles streetcars to churches where he was invited to give triduums. These kept alive his personal mission and produced enough money for the taxis to Beverly Hills. Finally, a poor black lady who lived in Watts, Virginia Majors, gave him an old car, the only one she had. The car looked like a poor relative, if indeed, any relative at all, to the luxury cars it parked amongst.

His office was the nearest telephone booth, or occasionally, an empty desk in a friend's office.

The stars reaffirmed their promises to appear on the radio shows. Many other people helped him. But there were a few who, with no intention of helping but not wanting to refuse him outright, wasted his precious hours by listening and giving non-committal answers.

He had free stars and free radio time. He still needed many other talents—writers, directors, technical crews. He still needed a lot of money to pay union wages to supporting casts and other costs of production. The estimated one to two thousand dollars per weekly half-hour show added up to fifty to one hundred thousand dollars a year.

Despite his efforts, Father Peyton was not having much success in getting his show on the road.

One evening, as he visited Loretta Young in her home, he told her of his failure. Her husband, Tom Lewis, was upstairs working. He was by then back in civilian life and heading west coast operations for Young and Rubicam. While Loretta had continued to support Father Peyton, Tom had remained aloof since his initial help the year before.

"I've got an idea," the actress said suddenly to the distressed priest. "I'm going to get Tom to come down and talk. They pay him fifty or sixty thousand dollars a year to do the kind of thing you're talking about. Let's draft him."

Tom came downstairs. Loretta explained their dilemma and told him Father Peyton needed his help. Father Peyton told him about his progress to date—about the free radio time and pledges from the stars. But now he desperately needed someone who could put it all together.

"I am not asking you to do it for me, dear Tom, but for Our Blessed Mother," he said. "If you do it, you will be doing a favor for her, She will thank you for it."

Tom could not refuse. Caught in the cross fire of his wife's entreaties and Father Peyton's persuasiveness, he surrendered. He said "Yes" to Father Peyton.

"I'll get you on the air," he said. "I'll get my whole team working and we'll put the package together. After that, you're on your own."

The next day, Tom called Ed Kobak at Mutual in New York. He said, "I've watched this operation all the time without committing myself to it. Now I'm committed." Tom garnered the professional expertise of his associates at Young and Rubicam. He knew they could not long carry the extra workload as spare-time volunteers, so, at the very beginning, he hired Bob Longenecker, actress Ruth Hussey's husband, as full-time producer.

The group of professionals followed the formula proven successful to sell soap and other products on radio to "sell" family prayer—entertainment with short, simple commercials. They insisted on presenting dramatic plots with realistic characters. The scripts were written around family situations, moral but not religious. Al Scalpone wrote the commercials.

"The family that prays together stays together."

That was the slogan chosen by Al Scalpone to end every weekly show. It caught the fancy of Americans and soon became a household saying. Father Peyton was identified by his slogan. People who had never heard of him were familiar with the slogan. It has continued to be repeated, and ofttimes parodied. Many do not even know its origin. Some think it is from the Bible, or Shakespeare, or some other classic writer.

A second slogan, "A world at prayer is a world at peace," became almost equally famous.

The slogans later became a part of the language of many other countries as the shows were beamed abroad.

On February 13, 1947, millions of Americans heard the first Family Theater of the Air production, "Flight from Home," starring Loretta Young and Don Ameche. Jimmy Stewart, a non-Catholic, was narrator.

The reaction was swift. Catholics who had expected a program based on the Rosary were so bitterly critical that even Father Woods advised quitting. But Father Peyton decided to continue offering Mary the crumbs, in the hope that someday he could give her the full loaf of the Rosary on national radio.

His decision was upheld. The public reaction that came in a few days turned the seeming disaster into a triumph.

Later, as the plays continued, a letter came which was a complete surprise to Father Peyton. It was from Pope Pius XII. It congratulated him on the programs. Father Peyton read the letter as a message from his Blessed Mother sent through the Vicar of her Son Jesus and telling him that his gift, no matter how small, had pleased her.

That letter, dated January 14, 1948, said in part:

> The radio apostolate, to which you have been giving the full measure of your priestly devotion during the past seven years, in furtherance of the pastoral mission of Our indefatigable brethren in the Hierarchy of the United States, has been, as you are well aware, a constant object of Our paternal interest and solicitude.
>
> In the admirable selection of *Family Theater* recordings you are presenting to Us in affectionate filial homage, as in the nation-wide repute and spiritual fecundity of the Family Rosary devotion to which they bear eloquent witness, it gives Us no little joy to discern a faithful and dramatic echo of Our own repeated pleadings, with pastors and with mothers, fathers and the newly wed, to make sure that the new homes they are courageously building for their children and for the Family of Nations are modelled on the prayer, labor and sacrifice of the Holy Home of Nazareth.

That first letter fom a pope gave Father Peyton added authority for the continuation of his work.

Critics acclaimed the weekly shows the best religious programs on the air. Many top awards and citations went to the programs and to several other specials produced for radio, and later for television. Family Theater of the Air and Father Peyton gained national and international recognition as the leading producers of religious programs on radio.

The search for money to continue led Father Peyton, through Mary Harris, to J. Peter Grace. Shortly after the debut of Family Theater, Father Peyton, carrying a victrola and a record of one of the shows, invaded the New York office of that shipping magnate and international industrialist.

He played the record and came away with a contribution of four thousand dollars. He also gained the promise of another four thousand dollars from a charitable foundation operated by Peter's brother, Michael Grace.

Father Peyton traveled around the country begging money from wealthy men, religious organizations and other individuals. The hard seats of buses and trains were his bed, and the quick lunches at grimy bus stations were his bread. His garments were only what he could carry in a suitcase. Every donation and every word of encouragement pushed him to greater efforts. The need for money was a continuing problem. Many times there was not enough for the next show. When his own efforts failed, he turned the entire problem over to Our Blessed Mother, knowing that, if she wanted the programs, she would help find a way to pay for them. He was never disappointed.

On trips between the east and west coasts, Father Peyton occasionally stopped over in South Bend, Indiana, to visit his friend, Father Heinzer. The seminarian of the Deer Park days for whom Father Peyton had invoked the presence of Our Lady was serving his first assignment as a priest after his ordination in 1945. He was the assistant pastor of St. Joseph's Parish in South Bend.

On one occasion, as Father Peyton was telling Father Heinzer something he wanted to do, Father Heinzer felt compelled to give him the eight dollars that made up his own meager monthly personal allowance.

The continuing high ratings persuaded Ed Kobak to agree to Father Peyton's proposal for a Christmas show—based on the Rosary. The show would have to be a super-special, his Christmas gift to Mary and to the nation.

The hour-long program, "The Joyful Hour," was broadcast over Mutual live from Hollywood and New York with a star-studded cast on December 20, 1947.

Tony La Frano narrated the story, which took the nation of listeners through the five Joyful Mysteries of the Rosary, on a pilgrimage to Bethlehem and the first Christmas, and through Jesus's childhood.

Familiar voices ringing through the songs and prayers included Bing Crosby and Perry Como singing familiar Christmas hymns. Other Christmas carols were sung by the Ken Darby Glee Club and St. Vibiana's Cathedral Choir.

Ethel Barrymore introduced each decade with selections from the New Testament that told of The Annunciation, The Visitation, The Nativity, and The Presentation and The Finding of the Child Jesus in the Temple. Other famous voices joined in retelling these dramatic events.

The Irish voice of Father Peyton introduced the Rosary with its first prayer, the *Apostles' Creed*. The prayers of the Rosary came, against a background of music, like a cantata, swiftly, on cue and in the voices, solo and in chorus, of MacDonald Carey, Jeanne Crain, Dennis Day, Pedro de Cordoba, Dick Haymes, Joan Leslie, Christopher Lynch, Roddy McDowall, Ricardo Montalban, Maureen O'Hara and Maureen O'Sullivan.

The impeccable voice of Ethel Barrymore relating the story of the presentation of the Infant Jesus by his parents to the Lord was joined by the voices of other stars playing out the drama and giving the first foreshadow of sorrow.

The Fourth Joyful Mystery
The Presentation

And, according to the law of Moses, when the days of Mary's purification were ended, they took the child Jesus to Jerusalem, to present Him to the Lord.

There, at the temple, waited an old man called Simeon, who was devout and filled with the Holy Spirit. Simeon had been promised by the Holy Spirit that he would not see death before he had seen the Christ Child. He knew that the promised Savior was to be born in the city of David, for it had been so prophesied. Simeon had waited for a very long time at the temple and had watched for such a babe.

When Joseph and Mary appeared with their Son Jesus, Simeon rushed to them and blessed God and said to them:

"Now, Master, you can dismiss your servant in peace; you have fulfilled your word.
For my eyes have witnessed your saving deed

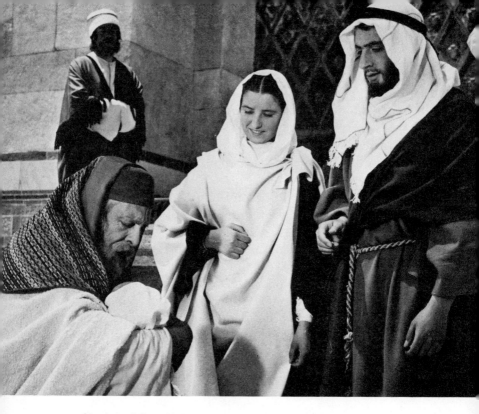

displayed for all the peoples to see:
A revealing light to the Gentiles, the glory of your people Israel."
The child's father and mother were marveling at what was being said about him.
Simeon blessed them and said to Mary his mother: "This child is destined to be the downfall and the rise of many in Israel, a sign that will be opposed
and you yourself shall be pierced with a sword—so that the thoughts of many hearts may be laid bare."

(Luke 2: 29-35)

Anna, a prophetess and widow of great age who remained always at the temple to serve God with fasting and praying, came to them as Simeon was speaking his prophecy to Mary. She, likewise, gave thanks to the Lord and after Joseph and Mary had done everything according to the law of the Lord, they left Jerusalem and took their Child back to their home in Galilee, in the city of Nazareth.

Father Peyton's meditation
on The Presentation

No one of us is an island—we cannot make it alone. We are meant to live in community—in family, in society, in the church. Even hereafter we shall find our bliss in the family that is God—the Most Holy Trinity.

In this mystery Mary takes her child to church. The church—in her time the temple—is the place where the faithful Jew finds support, togetherness and the rites and rituals that foster his faith and fellowship with fellow believers. Mary accepts the Temple, its laws and regulations, its rites and rituals. In a word, she accepts the *institutional church* of her time. Her presence in the temple, her fellowship with its members, her obedience to its laws, her acceptance of its authority, open up the floodgates of heaven for her child, for herself, for Joseph, for Simeon and Anna.

The old man, Simeon, cries out his *Nunc Dimittis*. Anna gave *thanks to God and talked about the child to all who looked forward to the deliverance of Jerusalem.* Mary heard words that forewarned her of a future of great sorrow and suffering. They returned home and the *child grew in size and strength, filled with wisdom, and the grace of God was upon Him.*

What does all this mean for you and me? The Church is where we find those who believe in the Risen Christ. In the Church, we support one another; grow in fellowship; profess the same faith; partake of the same sacraments; eat at the same table and follow the same rites and rituals. There, one with our fellow believers, we become a *sign*—a *sacrament*—for all men and women to come to know and experience that in this assembly—the Church—Christ is present because the Church is His Mystical Body.

Father Peyton finally had the Rosary on a nationwide network. He gave Our Blessed Mother the full loaf he had so long yearned to give her. His anguish over offering her the crumbs vanished.

In his concluding words on the program, Father Peyton told the nation that "Its purpose is to cry out to the very heavens and the earth that Our God is alive, that He is lovable, that he is personal, that He is omnipotent, that He is your greatest friend and benefactor, that it is He and He alone Who gave you, father and mother who are listening to me, your little child. He and He alone gave to your child the eyes to see you, the voice to call you 'Father,' 'Mother,' the heart to love you, the little feet to run to you and the hands to clasp you. This is the God this 'Joyful Hour' proclaims, a God so wonderful Who measures His love for you in these and a thousand other ways. This is the God of your home and of your family.''

The program was repeated annually and several times revised. The last one had Gregory Peck as narrator, and added the voices of Anne Jamison, Lannie Ross and Jo Stafford in song, and Anne Blythe, Ruth Hussey, Marina Koshetz, Pat O'Brien, Robert Ryan and Jimmy Durante with his "Mudder of God" and strong "A-Men" accented on both syllables.

During the first year, Family Theater of the Air radio shows were broadcast live from Station KHJ, in the new Mutual-Don Lee building, the network's Los Angeles headquarters.

Father Peyton had been given a small office by the Immaculate Heart Sisters in their convent in Los Angeles. Among his many activities was a time-consuming search for a suitable permanent office. Since he could not afford rent, this would have to be donated. He made his need known wherever he went.

When the gift came, it was one he could not refuse, although it would mean adding the cost of maintenance to all the other expenses.

Mrs. Jacoba Buchenau, who became a lifelong friend, gave him a house. It was a frame building at 7201 Sunset Boulevard in Hollywood. Family Theater moved there in 1948. The house became its administration center.

The radio shows continued for twelve years. Every one featured famous actors and actresses, donating their time and talent. The shows were later syndicated by Family Theater and broadcast for another ten years under the name "Marian Theater."

Another super-special, "The Triumphant Hour" was produced and aired for Easter. Two others were done for Mother's Day and Thanksgiving. Most of these radio programs were so successful that they afterward became annual broadcasts.

All of the specials, except the Thanksgiving program, featured the Rosary.

When television came Father Peyton was ready to tackle that too. He was already committed to modern mass communication to sell family prayer. He had the organization and the format. All that was needed was to adapt these to the new medium. But he would somehow have to raise the enormous sums of money the new method would require.

As Family Theater led the field in the production of religious drama for radio, it became the leader in television. Praise from the nation's critics, both in and outside the entertainment industry, as well as awards poured in for the various television programs produced by Family Theater.

Father Peyton got his Rosary on his very first television program. It was "The Triumphant Hour," the story of the passion, death and resurrection of Jesus. The cast included Pat O'Brien, Maureen O'Sullivan, Jane Wyatt, Don Ameche, Roddy McDowell, Morton Downey, Pedro de Cordoba, Jack Haley, and the Bob Hope family. The Dionne quintuplets and their mother prayed the Rosary with Father Peyton.

That first special was shown, at separate times, on all networks during the Easter 1951 season.

Productions that followed were, "The Joyful Hour," "Hill Number One," "That I May See," "The Search," "Prince of Peace," and many many more.

"When my minister sees this film on television, he will want equal time," Buddy Ebsen, TV's "Barnaby Jones," quipped to Father Peyton after a filmed interview on his faith.

Family Theater produced a number of such interviews with 15 prominent stars for the "Prince of Peace" series. These were 30-minute shows begun in 1964 and shown widely on television. It was the project that brought Hollywood film editor John C. Fuller back into Father Peyton's fold as a volunteer.

The Family Theater of the Air charted Father Peyton's course into a new dimension of his work. He asked for and was granted a booth at a Marian Congress in Ottawa, Canada, to demonstrate and explain the dramas. That Congress in the fall of 1947 brought together the leading Marian thinkers of the world. Father Woods and Father Lawyer went to Ottawa to help Father Peyton set up the booth.

As a result of the display, Father Peyton received his first invitation outside the United States. He was asked by Father John T. Maloney to preach a triduum at his parish, St. Mary's in London, Ontario. Father Maloney had a deep devotion to Mary and a deep faith in her willingness and power to help.

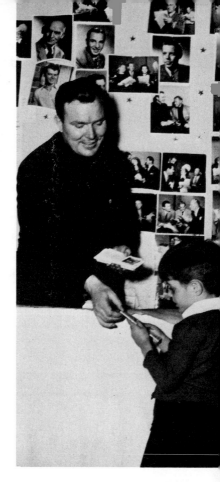

First diocesan-wide Crusade

"If only there was some way to organize a whole diocese at one time," Father Peyton appealed to Father Maloney.

"Perhaps we can," replied the pastor of St. Mary's Church as they talked in his rectory. Father Peyton had come to Canada early to make final plans for the triduum he was to begin in a few days at St. Mary's. The two priests had arranged the last details and gone on to a discussion of Father Peyton's growing dream of a world-wide crusade for daily family Rosary.

By that time, Family Theater of the Air had been broadcasting its weekly shows for nine months. The tremendous response had proved the value of reaching a mass audience. Father Peyton had begun to ponder ways of reaching a mass audience at one time in his personal ministry. He had been lamenting to the Canadian priest about the slowness of reaching people parish by parish.

Father Maloney needed no convincing about the willingness and power of Mary to help. Together, the two priests prayed on their Rosary beads the decade of The Annunciation. They asked Mary to help them in carrying out Father Peyton's chosen task.

Father Maloney said, "When Mary hears the call of those who love her, she answers but never stops at herself. She leads all those who love her to the feet of her Son Jesus."

Like many before and after him, Father Maloney took up as his own Father Peyton's hope of promoting daily family Rosary throughout the world. He felt that the goal could be reached only through the cooperation of the religious leaders. If they could convince the bishops of the world, then the bishops would instruct the pastors. The leadership of the pastors was vital.

He said, "If the flock is in the desert, it is because the pastor led it there. If it is in rich green pasture, that is where the pastor led it."

Father Maloney then described a very successful building campaign recently completed in the diocese by a professional fundraising firm. He thought the system could be adapted to getting pledges of daily family recitation of the Rosary. Father Peyton had already discovered, in the success of Family Theater of the Air, that the methods used by the professionals in selling soap and other products worked as well to sell prayer.

They decided to approach Bishop John T. Kidd of the London diocese through influential priests. They therefore invited a group of high-ranking dignitaries of the diocese to attend the final service of the triduum and to meet Father Peyton afterward at the rectory.

At that meeting, Father Peyton told the gathered priests of his and Father Maloney's idea of a diocesan-wide campaign for daily family Rosary. They were convinced enough that they chose three among them to visit the old bishop the next day.

Father Peyton could not wait that day to hear the bishop's verdict. He had to leave early to meet a commitment in Buffalo. But he was told by telephone that evening that Bishop Kidd had encouraged the idea, and promised his support.

Father Peyton punctuated his many engagements in the northeastern United States with frequent return trips to Canada. Bishop Kidd assigned Father Maloney as his personal liaison. Auxiliary Bishop John C. Cody was named diocesan director of the Crusade. The provincial at Notre Dame assigned Father Ray Finan to work with Father Peyton.

During the next three months, the Crusade team developed the organization and recruited more than seven thousand lay volunteers. They also planned a publicity campaign to insure maximum attendance. The main feature of this was a weekly Crusade news publication, *The Time for Family Prayer*, founded and edited by Arthur Carty, a dedicated supporter.

As each issue of this newspaper came off the press, Father Maloney and Father Peyton saw the tangible results of their

original idea to expand the Family Rosary Crusade into a diocesan event.

That first diocesan-wide Crusade was conducted from February through May, 1948.

The organization worked out at that first diocesan Crusade for Family Prayer in London became the model, with some later adjustments, for the hundreds of crusades that were to follow throughout the world.

The first step was always to obtain the support, or at least the permission, of the bishop of the diocese.

The pastor of each parish then selected two leading laymen of the parish. These laymen became a central committee directing all activities of the Crusade.

The two laymen then selected a district chairman for every one hundred homes in their parish. These district chairmen in turn each selected five team captains, making a team captain for every twenty families.

The team captains each recruited three other volunteers, thus creating a team of four men for every twenty homes, or one man out of every five families of the diocese.

Each team of four men formed pairs and each pair visited ten homes with the two pairs covering the twenty homes assigned to the team. Thus every Catholic family of the diocese was visited by a neighbor they knew. Later, in other countries, the system was expanded to include families of other faiths.

A card was printed, pledging the family to recite the Rosary together every day. Every member of the family who was able was asked to sign the card.

Father Peyton and his aides had decided to enlist only men for these visitations, in order to bring them more actively into the religious life of the family.

Volunteer ambassadors of Our Lady from every social and economic level visited the families and obtained signed pledge cards for daily family Rosary. They told the families they would be doing a favor for Our Blessed Mother by praying the Rosary. Many who had neglected their religion were brought back into the Church.

Father Maloney arranged talks in every parish of the diocese for Father Peyton. He addressed three parishes a day over a thirty-day period.

The new archbishop of Regina, Michael C. O'Neill, promised Our Lady he would have one of those crusades described to him by his friend Father Maloney. He himself needed her help in overcoming the depression that still would not leave him three years after the horrors of war he had witnessed as a chaplain in the Canadian Army.

He called together all the bishops of his archdiocese from the Province of Saskatchewan to hear Father Peyton explain the idea of diocesan crusades. All the bishops agreed.

That meeting opened up new horizons for what had become Father Peyton's Family Rosary Crusade. He was invited to conduct crusades in several dioceses of the province.

That meant that Father Peyton would have to keep a Family Rosary Crusade team in Canada. Patricia Spanbauer, who had been summoned to help with the London campaign, was desperately needed back in Albany, where the staff had been depleted. Another priest was needed there, also, to help Father Lawyer, who had been struggling to keep things going.

Father Peyton remembered the deep devotion to Mary shown by his friend Father Heinzer, both as a seminarian at Deer Park and as an assistant pastor at South Bend. He knew Father Heinzer would willingly join him, and so asked his provincial for him. Father Heinzer joined that June. He was specifically assigned to take over Father Woods's pastorate at St. Madeleine Sophie. His coming to Albany relieved Father Woods and Father Finan to continue in Canada.

The two, with Father Maloney still helping, went ahead to do the preparatory work in the various dioceses.

During this preparatory phase in the dioceses of Saskatchewan, a feature was added that became the most spectacular event of later crusades, attracting crowds of thousands and even millions.

This was the Crusade rally. It brought people to hear Father Peyton speak at one central location instead of at each parish.

This saved Father Peyton both his voice and his time. In addition, it made his dream of a vaster audience for his personal ministry an even greater reality than he had hoped for.

The first rally was at the Benedictine Abbey of Our Lady of Mount Carmel in Milville, Saskatchewan, on October 11. It was a comparatively small gathering. The second rally on October 17 in Regina drew a crowd of twenty-five thousand people. Altogether, five rallies were staged in the dioceses of Saskatchewan during those closing months of 1948.

News of the Family Rosary Crusade spread, and invitations began to pour in from bishops all over the North American continent. For the next two years Father Peyton shuttled between the United States and Canada.

The Crusade teams swept west and crisscrossed between the western and central provinces of Canada, then up into the Yukon and Alaska, and to the Arctic Circle and beyond.

Among those with the teams were Archbishop O'Neill and Bishop Philip Popock of Saskatoon who volunteered their services for rallies throughout this vast region.

Father Peyton and his Crusade teams covered this vast region in all kinds of weather and in conveyances as varied as airplane and dogsled, sometimes even on snowshoes. The rally sites were chosen according to density of population and availability of transportation. Attendance at the rallies ranged from tens of thousands in the cities to as low as five hundred in some wilderness missions. An estimated sixty thousand at Edmondton and seventy thousand at Vancouver came to hear Father Peyton speak.

In the fall of 1949, Father Peyton was invited to conduct his first diocesan-wide crusade in the United States—in Scranton, his first home in America. News reports estimated that rally crowd at fifty thousand people. Crusades in other cities of Pennsylvania that year gathered a total of another fifty thousand people at the rallies.

Father Peyton's private prayer and group prayer of workers beseeched Mary's help and intercession before every Crusade and thanked her after each.

In Scranton a new dimension of prayer was added. The sacrifice exemplified by Mary Grace Reutemann was formalized as an official part of the Crusade, and a man was appointed to head the "Heroic Pledge" committee. In this, workers went into every institution in the diocese where people were ill or dying and asked the terminally ill patients to dedicate their sufferings to the success of the campaign.

The year 1950 took the crusades east in Canada and west in the United States to the North Central state of Indiana, thence southeast to Kentucky. Father Peyton delivered his message for Mary in ten eastern Canadian cities and in seven cities of the United States. Again Patricia Spanbauer found herself summoned from Albany to help with all kinds of work in the big cities.

With the expansion and growth of the crusades, more help was needed. Father John Murphy and Father Joseph Quinn were assigned by the Holy Cross provincial, Father James Connerton, C.S.C., to the Family Rosary Crusade.

Crusade teams went ahead to set up the organization and oversee the work of the volunteers. By the time Father Peyton arrived a few days before the rally—or in some cases, just in time for it—volunteers were ready to visit every Catholic family.

In the United States, Father Peyton's spreading fame through the weekly radio broadcasts gave the crusades an added advantage. Extra publicity was gained by huge outdoor billboards along busy highways proclaiming the crusade slogan, "The Family That Prays Together Stays Together." These billboards were donated by the Outdoor Advertising Association of America.

Father Peyton kept on preaching the salvation of families through prayer. He would tell his audiences, "In a home where the Rosary is prayed devoutly each day, families are reminded constantly of what Jesus and Mary suffered for their sakes. Their gratitude is renewed daily. They give thanks in the daily actions of their own lives. In such a home, there cannot be an unfaithful husband or wife or a parent or child without love and kindness.

In those days of the great American move to the suburbs, and two cars in many a garage, Father Peyton told families that, "Affluence is a balloon that will burst. Spirituality is far superior to the material."

Rally crowds ranged from five thousand in Montreal to the tens of thousands in other cities.

Fifty thousand people gathered for the rally at Indianapolis. The 1951 Washington, D.C., rally drew 70,000.

Part 3

Second decade—the fifties
Circling the globe

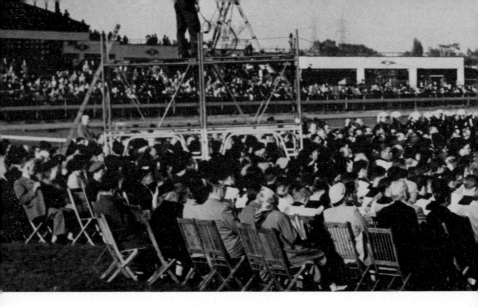

There were 75,000 people in attendance at Providence in 1951.

The donkey and the driver

The more people he reached the more Father Peyton yearned to reach as many families as he could as soon as he could. He could not go fast enough nor far enough. He saw that families were wounded. They were the victims of outside forces that exerted tremendous pressures upon them. They were plagued with new fears and new doubts.

The world quaked with the fear of atomic devastation. The United States had been unsuccessful in guarding its secret of nuclear fission. The allegiances of some countries had been realigned. New nations were born. The nation of Israel was

90

declared on May 14, 1948. On October 1, 1949, the proclamation
of the Peoples Republic of China had drawn a bamboo curtain
around her vast borders. And the fear of Russian aggression grew
as an iron curtain clanged down around Eastern Europe.

One of the booby traps left by an uneasy peace exploded on
June 25, 1950, when North Korea, armed by Russia, invaded
South Korea. Families were again disrupted, their young men
sent into battle. Although the ceasefire was declared in July,
1951, it was not until two years later that the armistice was
signed.

The stage was set for the decade of the 1950s to be a period of
decolonization and of emerging Third World countries, of cries
for freedom, justice, equality by nations, races and individuals.

Father Peyton saw these world troubles as only the tip of an
iceberg. He believed that the invisible underlying force, far more
devastating than what could be seen, was a crisis of faith. Individual faith had been shaken by world events.

Parents wanted security and a world at peace for their children.
People were asking for answers.

Father Peyton had the answer, and he felt a great urgency to
shout it out to the whole world at once. It had been given very
precisely by Our Lady of Fatima in 1917.

In six appearances before three children tending the flocks in
the parish of Fatima, Portugal, Our Lady had said there would be
no peace without prayer.

91

Father Peyton was passing on her answer with his slogan, "A world at prayer is a world at peace."

He was telling them to talk to God, to express their gratitude to Him, to honor Him, saying *"Our Father, who art in heaven, hallowed be Thy name; Thy kingdom come; Thy will be done on earth as it is in heaven."*

He was telling them they would find their answers in God if they would only ask Him, *"Give us this day our daily bread; and forgive us our trespasses as we forgive those who trespass against us; and lead us not into temptation, but deliver us from evil. Amen."*

He was showing them the way to God through the Rosary. He was urging them to arm their children for the battle against atheism with the prayers of the family Rosary.

The decade of the fifties was to take Father Peyton and his Crusade team from continent to continent, all over the globe. He would make himself homeless to answer the call of every bishop who asked him to bring the message of the Rosary through the Family Rosary Crusade.

He subjected himself completely to Mary. He went where she willed, did what she wished.

He frequently repeated a parable of two donkeys who met at evening and bragged about their long day's haul of turf from the bog, with no mention of the driver who had guided them. "I am the donkey, and Mary is the driver," he said. Without her, he would not know which way to turn and could accomplish nothing.

Under Mary's guidance, he sought to grow in wisdom in order to better fulfill the role God had assigned to him. He followed the example of Jesus, Who subjected Himself to His Mother as is told in the last Joyful Mystery of the Rosary—The Finding in the Temple. As Father Peyton reflected on the Mysteries of the Rosary, he thought how much they reflected the pattern of every man's life as one of joy, sorrow and finally triumph of the spirit.

The Fifth Joyful Mystery
The Finding in the Temple

His parents used to go every year to Jerusalem for the feast of the Passover, and when he was twelve they went up for the celebration as was their custom. As they were return-

ing at the end of the feast, the child Jesus remained behind
unknown to his parents. Thinking he was in the party, they
continued their journey for a day, looking for him among
their relatives and acquaintances.

Not finding him, they returned to Jerusalem in search of
him. On the third day they came upon him in the temple
sitting in the midst of the teachers, listening to them and
asking them questions. All who heard him were amazed at
his intelligence and his answers.

When his parents saw him they were astonished, and his
mother said to him: "Son, why have you done this to us?
You see that your father and I have been searching for you
in sorrow." He said to them: "Why did you search for me?
Did you not know I had to be in my Father's house?" But
they did not grasp what he said to them.

He went down with them then, and came to Nazareth,
and was obedient to them. His mother meanwhile kept all
these things in memory. Jesus, for his part, progressed
steadily in wisdom and age and grace before God and men.

(Luke 2: 41-52)

93

In the wake of the Crusade, reports of reaction deluged the workers. They were told in person to the teams and in thousands of letters that poured into the Albany office. A woman reported that the Rosary brought her family together all at the same time for the first time in years. A father stopped his nightly visits to the neighborhood bar and got acquainted with his children.

Husbands and wives began talking to one another, and children began to respect their parents. A teenager drew back from the trouble he was headed for. The wife on the verge of divorce learned a deeper love for her children. The husband pondering desertion grew closer to his family. A young couple on the way to Las Vegas for a divorce saw one of the billboards and turned back home to give their marriage another try.

Similar stories were told by hundreds of grateful individuals, some with tears in their eyes as they related the salvation of one or another member of the family.

During those two years ending the first decade of his work and beginning the second, Father Peyton's apostolate for Mary was gaining momentum in two directions—through the diocesan crusades and through the Family Theater of the Air. He was, at the same time, jigsawing across the United States in his continual search for money and talent to keep the programs going and to initiate new projects.

Manna from heaven

A shabby old car pulled up in front of Sacred Heart Church in New Orleans, Louisiana.

A raggedly dressed old man and woman were in the car. The woman heaved herself out and hobbled toward the priest and the nun nearby.

The woman handed a package to the nun, demanding, "Give this to Father Patrick Peyton."

She emphasized the "Patrick."

The two watched as she limped back to the car and the car drove away.

The nun sniffed at the small package tied with dirty string as she held it by one corner. "It's for your brother," she said, handing it to the priest.

Father Thomas Peyton took the unsightly thing, wrapped in greasy brown paper. He thought it was a cheese sandwich made at least two weeks ago. His first inclination was to toss it into the trash can. But he went into the rectory and, feeling a duty to examine its contents, opened it.

He stared at two sheaves of bills, each secured with a rubber band. He counted the money twice. It was eight thousand dollars.

That was exactly the amount Father Patrick Peyton had said he still needed to produce a television show for the coming Mother's Day. In fact, Father Pat was at that moment out seeking backing for the production. Father Pat was staying at his brother's parish while planning for a Family Rosary Crusade in New Orleans.

Father Patrick returned a few minutes later. Father Tom handed him the package, describing its arrival.

"Thanks be to God," said Father Pat. It was a prayer rather than an exclamation. He showed no surprise at receiving the money, but told his brother, "Our Blessed Mother wants that television show."

Father Tom Peyton, reporting the incident years later, said, "I felt uncomfortable all the rest of that day, with the thought that something supernatural had happened." He never found out who the shabbily dressed couple were. He had never seen them in his parish before and never saw them again.

That television show, "The World's Greatest Mother," was aired over the Mutual Broadcasting System on Mother's Day 1952 as a tribute to Mary and all mothers everywhere. The show received the same critical and public acclaim as had its predecessors.

Even with free television time and free stars, the productions were costly—sometimes as high as several thousand dollars. That was a lot of money for a wandering priest who also had to raise money for diocesan crusades and who depended solely upon donations.

Just as he had gone to the top for talent, he went to the top for money. He sought out the wealthiest men he could find to ask for aid. "I would rather ask those who could afford it than the poor people who were struggling for a living," he said. He called these men of wealth and industry the "giants" of the Family Rosary Crusade. His friend, Peter Grace, became one of his regular backers.

Overseas to England

Bishop Angel Herrera Oria looked around at the tapestry of people that seemed to be drawn like curving drapes around the oval turf of Wembley Stadium. He had been about to leave London to return home to Málaga when he read in the London newspapers about this rally. He had obtained his ticket with great difficulty, through the help of a friend. Huge throngs massed outside, unable to gain entrance, had slowed his progress into the stadium, and he was glad finally to be seated just as the ceremonies were about to begin.

The buzz of voices was blown away by the strains of the British national anthem bouncing from the loudspeakers. The montage of faces in the bleachers turned toward a small mass of movement on the far rim of the grounds below.

The long procession trod along the rim of the oval. A circle of priests formed in the center of turf around a raised platform. Dignitaries took their places along the side. They stood motionless as the words of the *Ave María* wafted over the hushed crowd in the pure notes of a solo singer.

Presiding over all was Cardinal Archbishop of Westminster Bernard Cardinal Griffin. Fourteen other bishops in their magnificent robes made a colorful picture. Silhouetted clearly amidst this splendor was the figure of a tall black-robed priest. Across the oval, facing them and dominating the whole scene, was a beautiful statue of Our Lady of Fatima.

Fifteen hundred young people formed a living Rosary.

Upon the green began the reenactment of scenes from the Bible.

As they were acted the prayers of the Rosary were recited. The responses prayed by the entire assemblage pounded like ocean waves of sound upon the air. The short introductory speeches were received with bursts of applause by the ninety thousand spectators. The black-robed priest finally ascended the platform and began speaking into the microphone in soft Irish tones.

Bishop Herrera was struck by a most profound religious impression. He had never before heard of this Father Patrick Peyton but, according to the newspapers he had read, this American priest who was speaking in an Irish voice so simply and so beautifully about Our Blessed Mother was very famous in America. The Spanish bishop thought that it was the most magnificent Marian spectacle he had ever witnessed.

He wanted Málaga to have such a spectacle, for the benefits of both faith and of devotion to the Blessed Mother. After the rally, he sought out Father Peyton in the place where he was staying and found him at Cardinal Griffin's residence.

Bishop Herrera invited Father Peyton to bring his Family Rosary Crusade to Málaga. Father Peyton was at first hesitant, fearing the barrier of language. He did not know Spanish, but so eloquent and so convincing was the bishop's appeal that the two quickly agreed.

Father Peyton would come the following year to the bishop's diocese on the sunny southern coast of Spain. Never had Bishop Herrera imagined that it would be London that would afford to Málaga such a benefit of faith and devotion to Our Blessed Mother.

The rally in London had climaxed a series of crusades and 40 rallies in England, Father Peyton's first experience abroad. The first invitation had come in 1951 from Lancaster, England.

Father Woods had gone ahead to set up the organization which would test the system abroad. Father Peyton had remained in

America to fulfill the commitments for the many crusades and rallies scheduled there.

During 1951 and 1952 Father Peyton had flown across the Atlantic several times for rallies in England.

The intensive promotion carried on by the Crusade teams brought a great deal of publicity in England as elsewhere. Even in this land of the Anglican Church, the secular press found the doings and personality of this Roman Catholic priest newsworthy.

Picture Post Magazine, the English equivalent of *Life*, sent a photographer and writer to do a story on the Crusade in the diocese of Hexham-Newcastle in 1951.

Father John Murphy, C.S.C., who was then also traveling with the team, told the story of that coverage as an example of English reaction to Father Peyton. He related: "The two men accompanied us everywhere we went for a couple of days. They questioned Father Peyton constantly and took pictures of him in his room at Ushaw College, in homes, in schools and at meetings and rallies. Slim the photographer was not a Catholic, but he was evidently impressed by Father Pat. When Slim and his partner had the material they wanted and were taking their leave, Slim said: 'I've covered a lot of hot shot American gospellers on many assignments, but this assignment really has me puzzled because Father Peyton is for real.'"

Slim's reaction to Father Peyton was typical of the reactions of people of all faiths and at every level of society across the world.

Those crusades had led to the grand finale in London, with the rally of July 27, 1952. Pat Spanbauer had once again been brought from the Albany office to help Fathers Woods and Murphy with the many details.

Pope Pius XII contributed to the success of the London rally with a July 14 letter of support to Cardinal Griffin in which he wrote in part:

> And what form of collective prayer could be more simple and yet more efficacious than the *Family Rosary*, in which parents and children join together in supplicating the *Eternal Father*, through the intercession of their most *loving Mother, meditating meanwhile on the sacred mysteries of our faith?* There is no surer means of calling down God's blessings upon the *family* and especially of preserving peace and happiness *in the home* than the daily recitation of the *Rosary*. And apart from its supplicatory power, the

Family Rosary can have far-reaching effects, for if the habit of this pious practice is inculcated into children at a young and impressionable age, they too will be faithful to the Rosary in after life and their faith will thereby be nourished and strengthened...

Because the Bishop of Málaga was there, that rally became the launching pad that took Father Peyton and his Family Rosary Crusade eventually to Latin America, where the great needs of the people would propel him into the greatest part of his missionary years. But there were to be many other stops on the way.

Crusade in Spain

Father Mark G. McGrath waited in the residence of Bishop Herrera. He was waiting for Father Peyton to finish writing the speech that he would translate into Spanish for the Málaga rally.

Father Peyton came from his writing room, greeted Father McGrath and passed into the chapel. Some time later he went back to the writing room.

Father McGrath waited. Father Peyton again went to the chapel, nodding as he passed back and forth. This happened several more times during the writing of the speech. Father Peyton had asked his provincial in the United States for the services of a translator, and Father McGrath had been sent from Rome to Málaga for this assignment. Father McGrath had known Spanish from earliest childhood in his native Panama. He was later to become archbishop of Panama.

After several hours, Father Peyton came from his writing room and handed Father McGrath a sheaf of yellow paper. The writing on it was in longhand, with many words crossed out and corrections written in.

Archbishop McGrath later told the story, saying, "With care I labored for several hours over a translation that would be in the popular Spanish talk but that Father Peyton could, with some coaching, read in intelligible Spanish. It went over well. His spirit came through, even when the pronunciation did not.''

That rally attracted one hundred thousand Spaniards who crowded shoulder to shoulder along the tree-lined boulevards fanning out from one of the city's main plazas and the entrance to its port on the nearby Mediterranean. Father Peyton delivered

his speech from a platform before a tall altar erected for the occasion against a backdrop of palm and eucalyptus trees. As he read the unfamiliar Spanish words, the crowd did not mind the alien sounding Spanish spoken in an Irish brogue.

They understood him. He spoke to the feeling in their hearts, of the love they felt for the Blessed Mother Mary, their Santa Madre María.

Before the speech, as the Rosary was recited and the crowd gave the responses, the same rolling sound pounded the air as it had at Wembley Stadium and at other rallies. The Spanish words were different, but the rhythm and meaning were the same. After the first few *Hail Marys*, Father Peyton could pray fluently along with the assemblage.

After Málaga, Father Peyton went up to the mountain villages to appear at small rallies. He labored over every speech as hard as he had for the Málaga address.

A few days after the Málaga speech, Archbishop McGrath said as he related the story, "The same thing happened as before when Padre Peyton wrote another speech for another rally.

"Again the same worried prayer and writing. Again he handed me a bundle of freshly written and corrected yellow pages. I set to work, but as I read, I saw that my work was already done. It was exactly the same text as before: rewritten, re-experienced, re-prayed."

The first two texts Father Peyton handed him to translate, Archbishop McGrath reminisced, "were the same story he would later tell in fervor to millions."

His closing words were the same ones that ended all his rally speeches, only in Spanish:

"La familia que reza unida permanece unida."

The foreign-sounding words, to him, were a prologue, a practice, for what was to become the main part of his life's teachings and work. It was during that first Spanish Crusade that Father Peyton's next summit was revealed to him.

Concerned religious and lay leaders whom he met in Spain, and even his own associate Father Woods, were convinced that the greatest need for spiritual ministry in the Catholic countries of the world existed among the people of Latin America. The poor who dwelt in the villages and barrios had not even religious reassurance to enlighten the poverty of their lives. They were susceptible to the Red menace leaching out of Russia onto their lands, with its decoy of daily bread, not from God, but from the Communists.

There, providentially, among the Spaniards in Málaga, was the Rosary priest himself. He whose ancestors had preserved and defended their religion through the Rosary in the days when there were few priests in Ireland. It was only logical that the priest who had dedicated his life and priesthood to Mary and the spreading of the Rosary throughout the world should go to the aid of those beleagured Catholics in Latin America. It seemed logical also to Father Woods and others that Father Peyton should remain in Spain to learn the language.

At first, Father Peyton resisted all their arguments. He had already learned to say the Rosary in Spanish and to give his talk on daily family Rosary to Spaniards in their own language, but he still felt overwhelmed by the difficulties of the language barrier. But finally he overcame his fears and surrendered again to his destiny.

So it was that Father Peyton remained in Málaga to study Spanish while Father Woods and Father Murphy returned to the United States to prepare for the Crusade in Cleveland, Ohio.

Thus Father Peyton began preparation for the work that was to dominate seventeen years of his life. It was then 1953, and it would be seven years before he would arrive in Latin America.

An idea is born

Bing Crosby's voice came over the radio singing the eloquent "O Sanctissima." Father Peyton sat listening intently, alone in his room in Archbishop Edward F. Hoban's residence, where he was a guest during the Crusade in Cleveland, Ohio.

It was a warm June evening in 1953. The program was the debut of a new series of half-hour radio dramas produced on records by Family Theater of the Air in Hollywood, backed financially by the Catholic Daughters of America. The series, called "The Story of the Holy Rosary," dramatized in sequence the fifteen Mysteries. They were of the same high quality as the weekly radio shows and featured the donated talent of Hollywood film stars.

Father Peyton had flown from Málaga to Cleveland to conduct the rally. Father Woods had everything ready, but had not been able to get free time for the radio shows. Station managers had refused time because they considered the programs, each including the recitation of a decade of the Rosary, too denominational. Father Peyton had been looking forward to the premier airing of those programs as an innovative part of the media campaign for the crusades. His persuasiveness had won over the manager of one radio station and the programs were being broadcast on fifteen consecutive nights.

Father Peyton was elated as he listened night after night. He knew that the stories were reaching the ears and the minds and the hearts of people who had never heard them before.

By the end of the fifteenth broadcast, Father Peyton began to be dissatisfied. In his characteristic way, when he saw that something was good, he wanted to make it better.

The radio shows must have had their impact, for the Cleveland rally attracted eighty thousand people.

As Father Peyton pondered the fifteen Mystery radio dramas, an idea swept over him like a vision. People should be able to see, as well as hear. He would produce the fifteen Mysteries of the Rosary on film, with color and sound, in every major language of the world. The films would completely vitalize the Family Rosary Crusade. People all over the world, of every race and religion, would be able to see the Bible stories of Jesus and Mary played out before their eyes.

Production costs would be enormous, even with free talent of the stars, as he already knew from the television specials. He made a quick estimate of about twenty thousand dollars a film. He would need three hundred thousand dollars, an enormous amount of money.

What a time for such an idea to be born! The crusades were about to spread overseas. Dates had to be set without delay in response to invitations from the bishops of Ireland, and the Crusade team was due to begin work in Australia in a little more than a month. He had to get Father Woods to Ireland and back in the interim.

The idea burned in him. He had to do something about it

104

before leaving. He had one more date to keep, a speech before the Sisters of St. Dominic in Adrian, Michigan. Mother Gerald Barry, the superior general, was a great friend of Archbishop Hoban and a devotee of Our Blessed Mother. She had invited Father Peyton to speak before a conclave of more than five hundred teaching nuns gathered at the mother house for the summer.

He went to Adrian. As he was speaking before the nuns, a second inspiration struck him.

As he was leaving, he called Mother Gerald aside and proposed his idea to her. She told him she would think about it and asked him to come back the next day. The next day was July 2, the feast of the Visitation.

On that day, she gave him her answer as they stood in the open space outside the convent. It was "No."

"Look at that building," she ordered him, waving her hand toward the convent. "It still has to be paid for. Look at all those nuns that thronged the auditorium yesterday when you spoke. They have to be fed and clothed. I could not give you the kind of money you are asking for."

He was asking her for twenty thousand dollars to pay for the filming of one of the mysteries. He had, during his talk to the nuns, conceived the idea of asking the orders of nuns of the world to finance the films. He was offering Mother Gerald the privilege of financing *The Visitation*, on that very feast day. He had expected an easy acceptance as a sign of Our Lady's approval of his project, especially on this day, the anniversary of one of her most blessed days. Mother Gerald's refusal astounded him.

That early morning rejection began for Father Peyton a day that did not end until midnight. His next visit was to Detroit. There Mother Theresa McGivney, the mother superior of the Immaculate Heart Sisters of Monroe, was visiting one of her convents.

After explaining his idea to her, he said, "Now Mary is giving you the privilege to sponsor the film on the Visitation."

"The answer will be 'Yes,'" she replied without hesitation, observing only that she would have to get the approval of her council, "but that is assured."

One rejection, one acceptance, Father Peyton thought. He decided that the score of accomplishment of that day would be the omen for the success or failure of one of the most ambitious

105

projects he had ever conceived. He was booked on a flight to Chicago in an hour. He intended to take a train from Chicago to visit some nuns in Milwaukee. He would have to hurry to catch his plane.

"I will say a prayer of thanksgiving with you now before I leave you," Father Peyton said. And he knelt where he stood, in the convent hallway. Mother Theresa knelt with him. Together they prayed the *Hail Mary* and he spoke his words of gratitude. "Our Blessed Mother will thank you for the beautiful thing you are doing," he said as they rose from their knees. As he was leaving, he happened to ask about William Tenbush, one of his first benefactors, whose daughter was a nun of her order. Mother Theresa told him that he was in great sorrow because his daughter-in-law, a young mother, was critically ill in the hospital.

All thought of catching his plane, of the urgency of that day's goal, vanished from his mind.

"I will go to her and pray for her recovery," he said. "I will ask God to restore that blessed mother to her family, if it be His will." His response was not unusual. It was typical of his overriding concern for individuals. Each single soul in need had the most right and privilege to the benefits of his priesthood. He rushed to the young woman's hospital bedside.

He prayed for Mary's intercession for the life of this young mother. As he was ready to leave the hospital, a relative caught up with him with the report that the sick woman had said Our Lady had appeared to her and told her she would get well. He learned later that the young mother had been restored to health and to her family.

It did not matter that he missed his plane to Chicago. He caught a later flight. He checked in at a hotel. There was a message waiting for him to call Mother Gerald in Adrian. He had told her where he would be staying that night. He called her as soon as he reached his room.

"I've changed my mind. I'd like to sponsor one of the Mysteries, and I'd like to take *The Nativity*," Mother Gerald told him. The "No" to the day's first request had been changed to a "Yes" before the day ended.

The day was not yet over. There was just enough time, if all went well, before midnight of this feast day for one more trip, one more city, and one more plea. He telephoned Mother Mary

106

Andrina, superior general of the School Sisters of Notre Dame, headquartered in Milwaukee, and asked her to keep her council of nuns up and waiting for him. He took a train to Milwaukee.

Harry John, founder and president of the de Rance Foundation, met him at the station and drove him to the convent.

The council of nuns, sleepy and exhausted, up hours past their bedtime, came awake and excited as they listened to his idea and plea. They said "Yes,"—just minutes before midnight.

In just one day, Father Peyton had obtained pledges for sixty thousand dollars for three of the films.

The omen for success had been sent by the Blessed Mother Mary. She wanted those films.

In Cleveland Father Peyton had met a friend of his and an associate of Conrad Hilton, and had learned from him that the international hotel magnate was flying two planeloads of celebrities to Madrid for a party to mark the opening of a Hilton Hotel there. Although Father Peyton had never met the owner of the Hilton hotels, his friend invited him to join the party. Then with a heart full of joy and confidence in the days to come, he flew back to Albany to prepare for the trip to Spain.

Father Woods went with him to New York to bid him farewell. Father Peyton wanted to thank Mr. Hilton personally for this favor.

"Oh, dear Mr. Hilton, you are doing our Blessed Mother a great favor by taking me to Madrid and she will thank you and repay you for it."

Then Father Peyton told Hilton, "It is of the utmost necessity that Father Woods gets to Ireland right away. By taking him to Spain you can save him time in getting there. You can save Ireland."

Hilton looked up into the priest's blue eyes and saw that he was completely serious. Suddenly he burst into laughter and could not stop. The idea that he, Conrad Hilton, could singlehandedly save Ireland tickled him. In his glee he ushered both priests, one onto each plane.

Father Peyton prayed aloud for a safe flight as the plane leveled off in the air, and the other distinguished guests chorused their "amens."

Father Peyton, who was calling his new friend "dear Conrad" by the time they reached Madrid, went along to the hotel. He became the first person to cross the threshold, with the owner, for the official opening of the new hotel. So it was that the Madrid Hilton Hotel was blessed by Father Peyton.

As they took off for home in the early morning after the gala party, Father Peyton glanced around doubtfully at the groups of celebrities and listened to their laughter and chatter. He wondered how they would react, in their glow of enjoyment, to the seriousness of a prayer. They might consider it undesirably sobering. But he said the prayer for a safe landing anyway, and it was received with good-natured "amens" and several gleeful affirmations. Father Peyton chuckled to himself and relaxed. He had taken a pledge in his youth in Ireland never to let alcohol pass his lips and he was sometimes the only completely sober person at a gathering. He did not object to this. He did not judge people. He only loved them.

Crusades world-wide

Passengers with seatbelts tightly fastened clutched their seats as the plane shuddered in the violent storm, sometimes plummeting downward into air pockets in the turbulence. Stewardesses trying to reach frightened travelers with reassurance stood straddle-legged in the aisle clutching the backs of seats or were forced to sit.

Father Peyton and Father Woods both had their beads in hand and were praying. The flight to Australia on that August 15, 1953, was one of the roughest rides Father Peyton had ever experienced, on land, sea or in the air.

The plane flew out of the storm into blue sky and landed smoothly. They were welcomed to Melbourne by Archbishop Daniel Mannix, then in his nineties and still not popular with the British government. The meeting stirred Father Peyton's memory of his boyhood in Ireland, when the comments of that outspoken exponent of Irish independence had brought joy to the Irish and irritation to the English. Back at the turn of the decade that ended World War I, Bishop Mannix had been intercepted on the high seas by a British submarine and taken from a liner going from Australia to his native Ireland. He delighted all Ireland when put ashore in the south of England with his summation to the press of what he called "the greatest British naval victory since Jutland."

The invitation to bring the Family Rosary Crusade to Australia had been extended after Father Peyton had made an appearance preaching at a religious gathering of eighty thousand people in Melbourne in 1951. At that time, Archbishop Mannix had telephoned from Melbourne to Albany to ask Father Peyton to come. So great had been the response to Father Peyton that Archbishop Mannix had subsequently interested the bishops of other Australian dioceses in having the crusades.

In Australia, the Crusade team was able to set the continent in motion progressively, with a tempo never before achieved.

Father Peyton and Father Woods made the first contact with bishops in each diocese. They started in Brisbane, where they were received by Archbishop James Dubig, a bishop of more than fifty years then in his nineties, but still vigorous.

Father Murphy followed them to Australia and continued after their initial visits with the work of organizing the Crusade. Father Peyton returned to speak at the rallies, in some dioceses at a central site and in others at several places, depending upon population, distance, and transportation.

They conducted a whirlwind campaign in Australia, starting in Queensland and on to New South Wales, Victoria, Tasmania, South Australia, the Northern Territory and Western Australia. Attendance at rallies in twenty-six dioceses, including eighty five thousand at Brisbane and one hundred and ten thousand at Sydney, totaled well over half a million people.

Everywhere he went, Father Peyton talked about his dream of the films he wanted to produce on the fifteen Mysteries of the Rosary. Four communities of nuns each pledged to contribute twenty thousand dollars. These were the Good Shepherd nuns, the Sisters of Mercy, the Brown Sisters of St. Joseph and the Presentation Sisters. Cardinal Archbishop of Sydney Norman Thomas Gilroy pledged twenty thousand dollars in behalf of himself and other bishops in Australia. The total contribution from Australia was one hundred thousand dollars.

Money was not the only thing he needed for the films. He knew that two prices had to be paid—one price to men for the production and another to God to obtain His blessing for the spiritual fruits of the films. The latter also was given generously in Australia.

Whatever lingering doubts Father Peyton had about the success of the films vanished after his experience in Tasmania. There he spoke to an order of Carmelite nuns, so cloistered that even the priest who addressed them spoke through a curtain that hid them from view. The mother superior told him that she would have to curb their excesses of sacrifice for his project. Later, he received her definite answer at Archbishop Mannix's residence in Melbourne. Her letter stated the entire community would recite special prayers daily for the entire Marian year beginning the eighth of December and that each nun would perform a personal sacrifice. He felt that their prayers would be especially powerful coming from a land linked through suffering with the traditions of his birthplace. He felt in the soil of Tasmania the sweat and tears of the Irish patriots who had been exiled there long ago when it was the infamous British penal colony of Van Diemen's Land.

After Australia, the crusades went into the four dioceses of New Zealand. They finished there around St. Patrick's Day, and then it was time to go to Ireland, halfway around the world.

The organization set in motion by Father Woods on that quick trip aided by Conrad Hilton had prepared ten dioceses in Ireland for the crusades. The Irish bishops and more than one hundred thousand of his countrymen took Father Peyton to their hearts. The feeling was mutual as he looked upon those seas of Irish faces and listened again to their voices.

He had carried forth family Rosary from Ireland, and he brought it back with honor and acclaim. He thanked the Irish people for the tradition kept alive by their ancestors. He pleaded with them to hold fast to that custom that had given birth to the Family Rosary Crusade now spreading throughout the world. He smiled inwardly at the recollection of his youthful dream of a boastful return to his homeland.

In Ireland, too, he asked the orders of nuns to contribute money for the Rosary films. The joint contribution of the mother superiors of Irish nuns was thirty thousand dollars. For them, it was a very large amount. They chose the film of the fourth

Glorious Mystery, Our Lady's assumption into heaven, to sponsor. By that time, the original estimate of twenty thousand dollars per film had jumped to thirty thousand.

Return to Spain

The Málaga crusades had inspired other Spanish bishops to invite Father Peyton to their dioceses. He went back to Spain in the fall of 1954. Some controversy had arisen. There was some grumbling that Spain with its devotion to the Blessed Mother did not need a priest from materialistic America telling its people how to pray.

Among the journalists sent to interview Father Peyton during those next Spanish crusades was María Luisa Luca de Tena. Her assignment was to evaluate the priest.

"Dear María Luisa," Father Peyton greeted her, "Will you say a prayer with me before we talk?" After an *Ave María* prayed together in Spanish and Father Peyton's prayer for the success of her article, their interview in English went smoothly. The article she wrote was favorable to Father Peyton.

During the interview he asked her to take a message to her father, who was the owner of the Madrid daily newspaper, *ABC*. "Tell your father," he said, "that I want four pages in his newspaper to explain the Family Rosary Crusade to Spain." She demurred, explaining that the paper was for a sophisticated secular audience and was not of a religious character. Father Peyton then added, "Tell your blessed father, dear María Luisa, that Our Blessed Mother will be grateful to him for it." Everybody laughed when she spoke the first part of the message at dinner a few days later in her father's home in Madrid. They stopped laughing when she finished the message. Although Father Peyton did not get the four pages, he did get a feature story that was to help him later in Latin America.

María Luisa was a member of the Instituto de Misioneras Seculares. This was an organization of lay people throughout Spain who engaged in a wide variety of apostolic projects, always with the approval of the bishop of the diocese in which they worked. She introduced Father Peyton to other members and they became interested in his work. This institute became another finger pointing him in the direction of Latin America.

María Camino, the founder of the secular missionaries, became one of Father Peyton's most helpful supporters in Spain and elsewhere. Thirteen of her missionaries became members of the Family Rosary Crusade working in Latin America as well as in Spain.

Crusades were conducted that September and October in four dioceses of Spain, with several rallies in each diocese. A total of eighty thousand people attended the three rallies at Bilbao.

During those early years in Spain, Father Peyton made many friends who were to continue to support and follow him as he returned again and again to that country, for crusades and also to make the Rosary films.

Three high ranking government officials became champions of the family Rosary.

Luis Carrero Blanco, the prime minister of Spain and Franco's right hand man, frequently joined Father Peyton in praying the Rosary. Later, after the establishment in Madrid of the first satellite office of the Family Rosary Crusade in 1959, he made it a practice to go with his family to the office chapel at four o'clock every weekday afternoon to pray the Rosary. The Crusade quarters, in fact, were located in the same building at Hermanos Becguer 6, where Señor Blanco lived.

Antonio de Oriol, the minister of justice, was another friend who could not do enough for the Family Rosary Crusade in Spain. Still another was Antonio Garrigues, the ambassador from Spain in Washington during the Kennedy years and later ambassador to the Vatican.

One day Miguel Crescente González was riding in a taxi with Father Peyton to the Hotel Castellano in Madrid.

"Would you pray the Rosary with me?" Father Peyton asked him. Together they prayed five decades, finishing just as the taxi drew up to the hotel entrance.

Señor González lingered behind to pay the fare. The taxi driver asked him, "Who was that priest?"

"That is Padre Peyton," Señor González replied. "Have you heard of him?" "Si, señor. Who has not heard of Father Peyton?"

Señor González, who worked for two years with Father Peyton in Spain, agreed. "Yes," he said, "Everyone in Spain knows Padre Peyton as well as they know any bullfighter or artist. We need Our Lady to watch over Spain."

"Tell Padre Peyton," said the taxi driver," that now I will pray the Rosary every day with my family."

One nun who became a friend on the first day Father Peyton entered Spain and remained loyal and helpful all through the years was Mother Concepción of the Loretta Nuns, popularly known as the Irish Nuns because so many of them came from Ireland. She was director of the house and college in Madrid all during the filming of the Mysteries of the Rosary. She gave to all the Crusade members a hearty hospitality, support and a total dedication to the Crusade work.

As Father Peyton traveled from one distant land to another, he never lost his vision of the films he wanted to produce on the fifteen Mysteries of the Rosary. The more he tried to tell the story of Jesus and Mary to people who had never heard it before and in words foreign to them, the more he wanted those films.

While Father Peyton was draping the Rosary around the world, the Hollywood staff, by then under the direction of Father Lawyer, was at work on the films—getting the scripts written and overseeing other production details.

When Father Peyton had first taken his idea to Hollywood, the staff there had received it as they did all his fantastic ideas. Some had smiled; others had called it impossible; a few had just walked away.

After many meetings with some of the great idea men of Hollywood, and with much discussion and many outbursts of opposing views, the decision was finally made to dramatize the stories of the fifteen Mysteries authentically as they were told in the Bible. They were to be half-hour programs suitable for television, and re-editing as three major motion picture films.

One Mystery was assigned to each of fifteen Catholic film script writers. Joseph Breen Jr. was appointed as script editor to insure that the stories would have continuity and some consistency of format. Scripts were submitted, accepted, rejected, rewritten, revised, under his direction and coordination. Later, after he had lived with these writers and their scripts from February, 1953, to September, 1955, it was decided that he would become the director. Whenever there was conflict between drama and accuracy, as there often was in the scripts submitted, Father William Robinson, a Holy Cross Father assigned to the project, made sure scriptural accuracy won out. He would insist that the Bible was dramatic enough to be the world's all-time best seller.

Spain was chosen as the location for the filming because landscapes and architecture like those of ancient Palestine could still be found in southern Spain and the inhabitants bore the facial characteristics inherited from centuries of Arab occupation that would be needed in the crowd scenes. In addition, costs of production, zooming in Hollywood, would be lower in Spain. Also, Spain was a Catholic country, and its actors and people were familiar with religious plays and well informed on the subject matter.

Father Lawyer and John Kirby arrived in Madrid on September 27, 1955, and set up headquarters there for the production. The next six months they spent arranging details, getting the leading actors of Spain, the use of a studio, the technicians and the contractors for the sets, arranging for the wardrobes, the outside sites, and getting government permissions.

Ecumenical dimensions

The Family Rosary Crusade became ecumenical years before the word "ecumenism" emerged into the popular parlance. The crusades had spread over three continents, in countries with predominantly Christian populations. A fourth and a fifth continent where preparations were being made were mostly non-Christian. No one knew how Father Peyton's message would be received.

The rest of 1954 and nearly all of 1955 saw Father Peyton and his teams in Asia and Africa. The minority Catholic groups would respond. But what would happen if Father Peyton tried to hold rallies in the streets or large stadiums? How would people of other creeds and this Catholic priest react to each other?

The answer came in India, the next major campaign after Ireland. After a few preliminary crusades and rallies, plans were being made for a huge outdoor rally in Bombay.

It was providential that he arrived in Bombay in time for the Marian Congress organized by Valerian Cardinal Gracias of Bombay to coincide with the end of the Marian year. Father Peyton sought out Mother María del Rosario, superior of the Sisters of Jesus and Mary, who was attending the congress from Rome. She agreed to sponsor one of the Rosary films and would raise the money by asking all the nuns in all her convents and the children in their schools to make sacrifices.

As rally day approached, Father Peyton was undergoing his usual anguished worrying. Archbishop Angelo Fernandes, archbishop of Delhi, reported:

> It was before the great finale of the Rosary Crusade in Bombay. Father Peyton was pacing about in the corridor, his Rosary in his hands, wondering and asking me repeatedly, "Will they come? How many do you think will show up?" Anxious as he was to spread the message, he was all concerned to reach as many as possible.
>
> Knowing the Bombay people well, I had kept telling him that Our Lady will draw them and in strength.
>
> The massive crowd stirred Father Peyton to the depths and told on him emotionally. He just let himself go, not for the scheduled 15 minutes but for well-nigh an hour! What came through was his vibrant love of Our Lady which he sought to communicate by word and voice and gesture in his own inimitable way. The message certainly reached everybody, "The family that prays together stays together."

Cardinal Gracias, although enthusiastic, had some doubts. He related later:

> When Father Peyton was our guest here at Archbishop's House I was really doubting, coming as he did immediately after the National Marian Congress, whether the crowds would come. He asked me one morning to join him in reciting the Rosary in my private chapel. And what was the result?

In the evening the next day in a big park there came streams of people from the city and suburbs. The rally was a grand success. I attribute the success of that rally to the recitation of the Rosary that we did together. He always struck me as a man of deep convictions and fervent devotion to Our Lady.

News reports estimated the crowd at the Bombay rally at two hundred thousand people.

The crowds listened to his words and the prayers of the Rosary being translated into their various languages by interpreters.

Father Peyton noted among these peoples of Asia a deep respect for their own holy men and a mysticism and reverence for the spiritual that, he said later, "gave dignity to even the most wretched lives." This reverence was extended to the Catholic priests among them.

For his part, Father Peyton reacted to these peoples of Asia—Hindus, Moslems, Sikhs, Parsis—with growing ecumenism. He told them of the benefits of daily family prayer and urged them to gather their families together each day for prayer of their own religions. The important thing, he said, was to pray together. But he never failed to add, "especially the Rosary," and told them the story of the Rosary.

With Father Quinn and other team members doing advance work, the Family Rosary Crusade was conducted in thirty-three dioceses of India. Father Peyton preached at rallies to almost half a million people.

After India, the Crusade went on to thirteen dioceses in Burma, Malaya, Thailand, Ceylon and Pakistan.

While Father Peyton was finishing in Asia, the advance team was in Africa making arrangements for the crusades that would take up the rest of 1955.

Father Peyton reached Africa on March 17, 1955, when he landed at Nairobi, at the invitation of Archbishop John J. McCarthy and Archbishop J.R. Knox, apostolic delegate, and the other bishops in countries where crusades were to be conducted.

He then went to South Africa, where the crusades were to begin. Owen Cardinal McCann, archbishop of Cape Town, later gave this report:

I recall that I was anxious to have him visit South Africa, and to

117

preach the Rosary Crusade. He came to South Africa at the invitation of all the bishops and started here in Cape Town. We had a big rally attended by many thousands of people on a blazing hot Sunday. There were many distinguished people present including the mayor of Cape Town who was not a Catholic.

Father Peyton's message caught on, and the Family Rosary Crusade caught on. The pledges taken on that day to say the Family Rosary were renewed regularly every year. In one parish stickers stating "This is a Family Rosary Home" were affixed to the front windows of the houses.

The echoes of that Family Rosary Sunday are still heard in the archdiocese. I have no doubt that the Crusade had an impact on a very large number of families.

Every October in this archdiocese there is a Rosary rally and procession. It is organized by the Legion of Mary.

Father Peyton labored for seven months in Africa, from the tip, up the east coast and into the interior. He went into Kenya, Tanganyika, Rhodesia, Nyasaland, Uganda and the Sudan, conducting hundreds of rallies in every city, town, village and mission within reach.

He held the Rosary aloft and told the story of it before crowds of thousands—all blacks, all whites, and blacks and whites mingled, and before crowds of Arabs. He preached to the tiny minority of Catholics, other Christians, Moslems, and pagans. His slogan, "The Family That Prays Together Stays Together," waved on banners in many languages, including Arabic. He preached by the great Lake Victoria, by the rivers, on the veld and in the high mountains and by the sands of the desert.

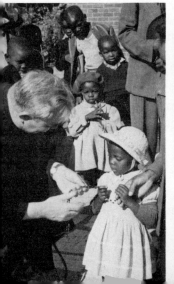

The people of Africa clogged the highways on their way to the rallies. They arrived in lorries and autos, on bicycles and on foot, with their baggage on their backs or on their heads. They welcomed him with native bands, singing children and processions. Everywhere the Crusade went, there went also the Pilgrim statue of Our Lady.

More than a million went to hear Father Peyton speaking from elaborate stages, from mission balconies and makeshift platforms. After the rallies, the native organizations collected hundreds of thousands of pledges for daily family Rosary from African families.

It gave Father Peyton great pleasure to tell the crowds of blacks about the God who so loved His Mother that He could refuse her nothing she asked. It gave him great pleasure to tell them also that they had the same mother in Heaven who loved them equally with all her children, and who would respond to all who called upon her.

He also found a common denominator with the followers of Islam in their great reverence for the Mother of Jesus, even though they looked upon Jesus as a great prophet rather than the only begotten Son of God.

Father Peyton was always aware of the political and social turmoil about him, but he continued to concentrate on what he felt was his mission—bringing spiritual meaning and hope to those in need, especially to those most deprived.

There were at the time in concentration compounds thousands of blacks suspected of complicity in the Mau Mau uprisings. At one of these compounds in Kenya where he spoke he found

several thousand prisoners assembled and under heavy guard when he arrived. After his talk, some 500 joined him in the recitation of the Rosary.

Father Peyton's faith in Mary's protection was put to a test later as the team returned home through a huge game preserve. The guards had said they could drive through and view the preserve by taking a short detour. Father Quinn later told the story:

As we entered the jungle area in our small Volkswagen we spotted a group of ten or fifteen giraffe grazing on the hillside. Father Peyton suggested we stop our car and take a closer look. While we were watching, four or five lions joined the giraffe and also a herd of wildebeests came across the hill. In the distance we could see a hyena darting towards a small cluster of gazelle. Since this was our first encounter with the wild animals that we had read about and heard about since childhood, Father Peyton and I especially were jumping with wonderment at the scene before our eyes.

As the sun began to set, we got back in the car and Father Collerton turned the key. Nothing happened. He turned it several more times and still the motor refused to turn over. We opened up the hood and since all of us were non-professional mechanics, the best we could do was tap a few parts with a screwdriver and kick the tires to see if they were full of air and then to honk the horn to make sure the battery wasn't dead. After all these attempts failed, Father Peyton suggested we get back in the car and say the Joyful Mysteries of the Rosary, asking Our Blessed Mother to help get the motor started.

After the Joyful Mysteries, Father Ned and I again got out and took a look at the motor. We found an old crank in the back seat and each of us took turns cranking the car to no avail. Again Father Peyton called us into the car to say the Sorrowful Mysteries of the Rosary. Instead of meditating on the Mysteries of the Rosary, since it was getting very dark, my mind was imagining an elephant drifting over our way and gently tipping our Volkswagen over or, I could hear in the distance, the lions growling before dashing off for their supper! I knew I was supposed to be prepared for death but it did not seem like this was the type of death I wanted to suffer. When we finished saying the Sorrowful Mysteries, Father Ned and I took turns on the crank again and on my final turn before my arm was about to fall out of its socket, the motor turned over and we were able to get the car going.

By now it was pitch dark and with nothing but the stars and the fearsome noises of the wild beasts we started back towards Nairobi.

After a few moments of driving, Father Peyton relieved us all by asking us to join with him in saying the Glorious Mysteries of the Rosary in thanksgiving for our escape from the jungle that night.

Father Peyton flew from one African country to another. He traveled the sometimes long distances from city to village by Land Rover, truck and car.

Attendance at the rallies varied greatly. Fifty thousand people gathered at each of two rallies in Uganda and forty-five thousand at one in Kenya. In other places where social unrest had made a low profile expedient, or where population was sparse, as few as a thousand attended.

During the five years the Crusade had been spreading worldwide, operations became streamlined. The teamwork between Crusade leaders and between native volunteers made the crusades fall into place like a well-known jigsaw puzzle.

When Father Peyton came, he too went to the bishops and asked their blessing and prayers, and to the clergy, begging their cooperation and thanking them, and to the meetings of the volunteers.

He went into the seminaries and asked the young students to pass on to future generations Our Lady's legacy to the world. He went to the nuns in the convents and asked their prayers and help. They stormed heaven with their entreaties for the acceptance of family Rosary and stormed their classrooms with teaching and entreaties to the children to tell their parents about the Rosary and the Crusade. The nuns went also into the field and spread the word of the Crusade. Many made sacrifices to help support it.

Father Peyton visited the schools, urging the children to use their influence as apostles for Mary and her Rosary in their homes. The children responded, building shrines, writing essays, drawing posters and doing many other creative works for the Mother Mary.

Father Peyton went to the sick and asked them to offer their sufferings for the goal of the Crusade.

He went into the prisons, and in many led prisoners on their knees in the Rosary.

The Family Rosary Crusade had spread over five continents. The diocesan campaigns and the weekly radio show still being produced by Family Theater of the Air had reached an audience of millions. Millions had pledged themselves to the daily family Rosary. The Crusade was a success. Its success had even surpassed Father Peyton's vision of thirteen summers before when his immediate superior in Washington, Father Christopher J. O'Toole, had helped him convince their Provincial Superior Father Steiner to let him undertake it.

The Crusade team had traveled millions of miles with the Rosary. Father Peyton had pushed himself tirelessly up and down and across Africa with no hint of failing health or energy except for the time he fell ill in Nairobi after preaching at a rally under the blazing equatorial sun.

Those two weeks, with Father Woods nursing him day and night, were a time of deep thought for Father Peyton. He had seen the cultures of five continents. He had taken the message of the Rosary to all the races of man and to people of many creeds. Witnessing first-hand the material inequities of mankind, he had told them of the equality of their souls in the eyes of God. He had brought hope and dignity to the oppressed and, he hoped, humility to the privileged. His massive endeavors had been undertaken at great personal risk.

He realized that, despite the success of the Crusade, he could fail. Every time he started a new diocesan crusade or a new project, he was putting himself on the line. He did not fear personal defeat. He would give life itself to honor Mary. But the thought that failure would be failing Our Blessed Mother overwhelmed him with anguish and fear. His love for the Mother of God might be the very thing that could mark him as a special target for the adversaries of God.

He prayed his Rosary with greater intensity than ever before, begging Mary to help him overcome any weakness of body or spirit. He recalled the words of Father John Maloney, who had said that Our Lady does not keep those who love her to herself, but leads them to her son Jesus. Like Peter, he begged her to tell Jesus he loved Him. He asked her to lead him to her son, the Son of God.

His Blessed Mother answered his pleas, with a little help from Father Woods.

"You have got to get up. The date for the next rally is near. And the people will be waiting for you," Father Woods insisted.

Father Peyton arose from his bed.

As he returned to activity his strength began to return. He knew the most ambitious work of his life was still ahead of him in Spain. Father Lawyer was already there working on details of the production of the films.

His anguished doubts began slowly to fade.

Film making in Spain

The search was on in Spain for the young Virgin Mary. She had to be a girl with purity of soul shining in a face of rare beauty to play the part of the young Mary of the Joyful Mysteries.

Father Lawyer, co-producer with Father Peyton, and Joe Breen looked at hundreds of photographs and interviewed more than five hundred young actresses—professionals and aspiring amateurs. Not one had the spiritual and physical beauty they sought.

Filming was ready to begin. The rest of the cast had been chosen. There was no problem with the Mary of the Sorrowful and Glorious Mysteries. One of Spain's leading actresses, Maruchi Fresno, was perfect for the part.

The rest of the cast had been chosen from Iberia's top talents.

Father Lawyer and Joe Breen turned to the streets and homes of Spain and the United States to find their young Mary.

They ran advertisements in the newspapers. Radio carried accounts of their search. They interviewed still more young girls and looked at even more photographs. They prayed. They were at a point of despair.

Father Peyton, then in South Africa, asked the Holy Cross Nuns there to help and assigned them the task, through prayer, of finding the girl to play the young Mary. One old nun dying of cancer said to him, "I will give the sufferings of my cancer, even to my death, to find the girl."

One day Father Lawyer and Joe Breen were having breakfast in

123

the convent of the Irish Nuns in Madrid when Mother Rosario told them, "In my mother's house in Murcia, I have seen a young girl sewing and I asked myself why God had given her such a beautiful face."

They begged Mother Rosario to have a photograph of the little seamstress rushed to Madrid. Then they sent for the girl. The train ride to the big city of Madrid was the first time Dolores Cantabella had been away from her home town. The casting director pushed her in front of the cameras under the bright lights of Madrid's largest movie studio. Timid and frightened, she would not raise her head; she would not speak. She could not walk properly, and she could not act. They sent her home.

In desperation, they chose a professional actress with a beautiful face who was not quite young enough, definitely not spiritual enough, who had been rejected before. In the meantime she had made other commitments. She held out for more money to play the part of Mary the Mother of God. Negotiations broke down. Then came the day before shooting was to begin. Still no young Mary. The movie makers, including the chosen actors and technicians, argued and prayed.

Finally Joe Breen said, "I am casting a face—a spiritual quality. This is it." He pointed to the picture of Dolores Cantabella.

"She can't act, can't even walk right, doesn't know how to use her hands, of course doesn't know a word of English. She'll cause me nothing but trouble. But Dolores will be the young Mary, Mother of God."

A telegram went to Murcia, and Dolores was in Madrid the next morning, on the Ain-Karim set. She asked, like the Mary of the Bible, "Why me?" Her own love for the Blessed Mother, added to the patient direction of Joe Breen, overcame the obstacles. Her nervousness and simplicity did not detract, but added to, a perfect performance. Her parents and her sweetheart wanted her to quit but, like the original Mary of

Nazareth, she had already said "Yes" and would not run out on God. After it was all over, she said, "I loved doing the part of Our Lady—to make others love her more." Although the producers of Spain and Hollywood became interested in her, she returned to the obscurity of Murcia and later married her sweetheart.

Father Lawyer and Father Peyton were sure that God had intervened to insure His choice of the girl to play His Mother. In this case, God had been the casting director, they insisted.

Elaborate sets had to be built reconstructing such places of biblical times as Pilate's palace and the temple at Jerusalem. An immense set of Calvary with twenty-five foot crosses began to sink after three weeks of filming of *The Crucifixion*. It was then they learned the set stood on a weak floor over an indoor swimming pool. A truck sank into the pool as it was hauling away some of the apparatus. Many scenes were filmed outdoors on sites chosen for their close resemblance to those of biblical Palestine.

The face of Christ was not shown, except in distant shots where features were indistinguishable. During *The Scourging at the Pillar* the whip hit the body by accident. The actor's comment was "Christ suffered more." The man was an inspiration to everyone else involved in the films.

One of the greatest problems in filming *The Crucifixion* was to get the crowds to rail against the figure of Jesus Christ. Joe Breen had to urge them to forget they were Catholics and to cry out for His death. Father Lawyer had to reassure the man who made the realistic crown of thorns that he would not be made a poor Christian by doing it, but rather a better Christian for realizing what his sins do to Christ.

All involved understood that they were engaged in a work of a divine nature in the reenactment of the life, death and Resurrection of Jesus and the joys and sorrows of Our Blessed Mother. Every day began and ended with a prayer and a blessing and thanks by a priest.

After the African campaigns Father Peyton had returned to the United States to pursue sources of funds for the films there. He combined his fund-raising with several crusades in Alaska and the northwestern states.

He went to Kansas City, Missouri, to conduct a Crusade, and it was there that a letter of great encouragement caught up with him. His heart filled with joy:

To Our beloved son
Patrick Peyton
Priest of the Congregation of Holy Cross

We have been pleased, beloved son, to learn of the encouraging spiritual results that have come from your cooperation with Our Venerable Brothers of the Episcopate, not only in the United States but also in distant lands, in the Crusade of the Family Rosary.

Among the apostolic tasks that have confronted Us in Our pontificate, of great significance and of constant concern to Us has been that of the integral preservation of the Christian Family, which is being tried so severely by the stress of our times and threatened on all sides by the harmful repercussions of current erroneous doctrines. As the building depends for its soundness on the foundation, so does civil society on its primary and essential cell—the Family, which draws, in turn, from the illuminated norms of Christianity, not only its greatest strength but also its highest sanction and perfection. To the end, therefore, of reenforcing the sacred unity of the domestic circle and of sanctifying the individual members through communal prayer and the fostering of a fervent love for the Blessed Mother of God, We have, on the occasion of the Marian Year, drawn upon the treasury of the Church to enrich with further indulgences the pious Catholic practice of the Family recitation of the Holy Rosary.

Consoling indeed, has been the response, throughout the Catholic world, to Our appeal for the ever wider extension of this devotion, so particularly adapted to serve as an antidote to the secularistic spirit of the present day. We renew Our words of paternal encouragement to the Ordinaries who are lending their zealous support to this most praiseworthy effort and, in like manner, to you beloved son, in your collaboration, when called upon by the Episcopal Shepherds of the Flock of Christ, to assist them in the conduct of the Family Rosary Crusade. In pledge of abundant celestial favours, We cordially impart to you Our Apostolic Blessing.

From the Vatican, November 2, 1955
Pius pp. XII

His travels in 1956 took him back to London, Ontario, to renew the Crusade in the cradle of its origin and to Greece for several diocesan campaigns. He returned as frequently as possible to Spain during the filming.

On one of Father Peyton's visits to the set, an altar was erected on the Ain-Karim set of Sevilla Studios, the largest studio in Spain, with the permission of the patriarch of Madrid. There Father Peyton said the first Mass ever said on a set in the history of the motion picture industry of Spain. Staff, cast, crew and friends were inspired by his words.

When the end of shooting finally came, another Mass was said in thanksgiving for the blessings and favors of God and His Blessed Mother—on the seventh of October, the feast of the Holy Rosary.

During the six months of filming, many things happened—births, accidents, even a death. The actress playing the Mary of the Sorrowful and Glorious Mysteries left once for Paris without permission. An amicable agreement without litigation precluded the sure headlines, "Family Rosary Sues Our Lady."

The last scenes were filmed on September 27, 1956, in Guacerma, a small pueblo in the Province of Murcia. There, permission was presumed for use of a small house for Mary's home in Nazareth, since the owner was away. The whole village turned out to watch. The only thing out of period was a small chimney. This was eliminated by a wicker basket commandeered from a passing donkey. The crew borrowed two burros and some red peppers from neighbors for decoration and filmed the house for a night scene. The interiors had been done on the studio set five months before.

The very last shot was one of Joseph walking away. They picked a street and a double for St. Joseph from the villagers.

In the end, the total cost including dubbing into many of the major languages of the world and several dialects was estimated by the Hollywood staff at almost one million dollars, or sixty-six thousand dollars a film. About sixty percent of the money collected came from countries other than the United States. Some of the orders of nuns who pledged the original estimate were able to increase their donations. Additional gifts came from other religious communities, cardinals, bishops, diocesan priests and lay people.

The films became an achievement of the Family Rosary Crusade that spread its work over the whole world.

Although Albany was home base, Father Peyton became an infrequent visitor more than a resident. He had a special reason for going there in November, 1957. He called upon Father Heinzer in his rectory at St. Madeleine Sophie Church.

"Will you come with me to the church? I have something very important I want to ask you, and I want to ask it there," Father Peyton said.

He led Father Heinzer to the statue of Our Lady, and they knelt. They prayed a *Hail Mary*, and asked her blessing and help through the beautiful prayer of the *Memorare*.

Then Father Peyton said, "I thought I'd ask you first before requesting permission for you to go to Hollywood, because we need a priest in that office." He wanted a priest who would continue the good relationship the Crusade and Family Theater of the Air had with Archbishop James F. McIntyre of Los Angeles, and he felt that Father Heinzer's deep devotion to Jesus and Mary and soft-spoken diplomacy would fill that need.

Debut in Brussels

Father Xavier Echenique was talking to Father Peyton one August day in 1957 in Madrid about the significance of the Vatican's decision some time before to participate in the World's Fair the following year in Brussels, Belgium. Father Echenique, secretary to the Society for the Propagation of the Faith in Spain, was one of the many friends Father Peyton had made during the filming in Spain.

"The Vatican exhibit will create a magnificent public relations image for the Church all over the world," Father Echenique said.

That set Father Peyton to thinking. It could do the same for the Rosary films—if only he could manage to show them there. They would be ready before then.

Never deterred by distance nor difficulty when he was inspired with an idea to honor Our Blessed Mother, Father Peyton set out immediately for Rome. He went to enlist the help of Count

Enrico Galeazzi, Governor of Vatican City, a friend of long standing whom he had met in Rome in 1949, when he had an audience with Pope Pius XII.

He quickly won his old friend as a collaborator. The count gave him a letter of introduction to Paul Heymans, the Vatican's commissioner general in Brussels. Heymans was to create the Vatican Pavilion at the fair. Father Peyton took the next plane to Brussels. He found Heymans and showed him the letter and an album of color stills from the Rosary movies.

Heymans was not impressed. He had never heard of Family Rosary Crusade or Family Theater or of Father Peyton. The architectural plans were all drawn, he pointed out, and some construction had already begun. There was no space even for a tiny theater. He also thought the kind of films a priest would make would not fit into the modern concept of the Vatican Pavilion, as he had planned it.

Father Ian Joos, ecclesiastical adviser for the Vatican Pavilion, had once visited Family Theater headquarters in Hollywood and knew Father Peyton and the quality of his productions. He arranged a luncheon appointment for Father Peyton and himself with Heymans and his assistant, Count de Monc eau de Bergendal.

Father Peyton presented his proposition in detail. He spoke with his usual conviction, describing the films, their authenticity, their wealth of talent and their quality. Heymans could not say "No" to Father Peyton's pleadings, and he said "Yes" to Our Blessed Mother.

But the architects could not change their plans. The only place Father Peyton's theater could go was underground. It would cost thirty thousand dollars, which he would have to provide. A telephone call and an explanation to Harry John, who had helped him before, got him the money. A theater to hold a hundred was built and furnished.

During the construction, reaction came from Pope Pius XII, who had been one of the first to view the completed films. In a letter dated April 4, 1958, he said:

> After years of laborious preparation and undaunted perseverance, always sustained by your whole-souled devotion to *Mary, Mother of God*, you have completed, beloved son, the fifteen Moving Pictures that tell the story of the fifteen *mysteries of*

the Rosary. It was indeed a massive undertaking that has been achieved with distinction.

Those films have an apostolic character and value quite beyond their technical and artistic perfection. They open up the book of God's revelation to man; they turn the pages of a divine love-story for those to read who will, and reading to understand the infinite yearning of God for the creature of His omnipotence.

Blessed will the faithful be who have the good fortune, let Us rather say the precious grace, to see these films. We sincerely hope their number will be legion...

The theater opened two months late, but the date of the premier pleased Father Peyton. It was 1958, May first, the first day of the month dedicated to Mary.

Hundreds of thousands of people streamed into the little theater to view the shows. Leaflets told the story in many languages of Family Rosary Crusade, Family Theater, and the films.

The immediate response to the films was intense. Priests upstairs hearing confessions reported that people were crowding the confessionals after viewing the films, including many who had neglected this duty for years.

Effects of the showings were also far-reaching. Many invitations to preach the Crusade were extended by bishops who saw the films. One of these was Archbishop Rufino I. Santos of Manila.

One day early in the fair, Auxiliary Bishop Leo Josef Suenens of Brussels came and saw the films. Bishop Suenens was then little known outside his own country. But Father Peyton had been warned to watch out for this man who took nothing for granted and asked penetrating questions.

Bishop Suenens liked the films, but did not give automatic endorsement to Father Peyton. He had heard of this Father Peyton and his activities and wanted to find out if he was a madman, a fanatic, or a truly holy priest with a divine mission. He invited Father Peyton to his home and there interrogated him.

But Bishop Suenens was not so easily satisfied by the answers. Under his cross-examination, Father Peyton formulated for the first time the distinction between the will of Our Lady and her personal honor.

Bishop Suenens was satisfied. He became a supporter of the Crusade. He wanted to organize a Crusade for Brussels, but his bishop thought such an undertaking would be too difficult in a diocese of almost two million Catholics. But Bishop Suenens introduced Father Peyton to his friend, Bishop Emile Josef de Smedt of Bruges.

The Crusade at Bruges was planned at that first meeting to take place the following year.

Father Peyton was at the fair one day when Peter Grace stopped and squeezed five minutes out of a packed schedule to view part of a film.

Mr. Grace's hurried first look at the films was of a scene in *The Crucifixion*. In the scene the centurion allowed Mary the Mother of Jesus to come forward from the crowd and stand under the cross.

Mr. Grace was deeply moved.

Peter Grace rearranged his schedule to spend half the next day viewing the films. Later he explained his reaction: "I had an idea that I was reasonably instructed in my faith. And I suppose I was—at the intellectual level. But what I never understood before was how Our Lady had suffered for me on Calvary.

His reaction to the reenactment of those world-shaking events was not an unusual one.

"You must saturate Latin America with these films," he told Father Peyton. "You have here the answer to the shortage of priests and catechists there."

Father Peyton's trans-Atlantic flights were frequent that year as he tried to be at the World's Fair as much as possible and at the same time appear at scheduled Crusade rallies. Most of them at the time were in the northwestern United States.

One of those trips was in February of 1959 for a private audience with Pope John XXIII, who had succeeded to the papacy the year before. Father DePrizio, fluent in Spanish and French in addition to his native American English, accompanied Father Peyton as his translator as well as his provincial. Pope John spoke French as well as his native Italian, and so the interview was conducted in French.

The Holy Father stressed to Father Peyton the importance of teaching the children. He said, "I know of your great work, and my blessing goes with you wherever you go. But I ask you especially to teach the children—teach the children everywhere the Mysteries of the Rosary—for in this way you will be teaching the life of Christ to the men and women of tomorrow."

Peter Grace's encouragement, backed up by a promise of financial help, convinced Father Peyton that it was time to move into Latin America. He chose Chile as the starting point—because his old friend and translator in Spain Father Mark McGrath was on the staff of St. George's College in Santiago. He flew there for a quick visit and happy reunion with his friend.

Auxiliary Bishop Emilio Tagle Covarrubias, in temporary charge of the archdiocese of Santiago, approved not only the Crusade there, but also setting up of headquarters in that city for all of Chile's dioceses.

Father Peyton returned to Belgium to prepare for the Bruges Crusade. As that campaign was beginning a letter reached him endorsing his move into Latin America. It was from Pope John XXIII and was dated May 1, the beginning of the month dedicated to Mary. Pope John wrote:

We have been informed that you are beginning a new stage in the apostolate which has so characteristically distinguished your life. With the technical help of motion pictures to show the meaning, value and excellence of the Mysteries of the Rosary, you wish to increase devotion to the Holy Rosary in the nations of Latin America.

The undertaking of such a step has given us paternal joy. Everything which tends to increase devotion to the Mother of God and at the same time makes more devout the faithful, reechoes in our soul feelings of joy.

You are carrying out this work on a continent where cathedrals, churches and shrines preserve the nation's deep love of the Blessed Virgin sculptured in stone. One day long ago there arrived in that continent a ship named "Mary" (Christopher Columbus's flagship, the *Santa María*); "Mary"—the same name which missionaries were to spread on the mountain tops, in the plains and in the jungles. Our spontaneous wish is that your mission today—wherever the bishops will call you—may in like manner penetrate the depths of hearts and the intimate circle of families and leave many lasting fruits of salvation.

Individuals, whatever their spiritual status may be, will undoubtedly find in the fervent recitation of the holy Rosary, an invitation to regulate their lives in conformity with Christian principles. They will, in truth, find the Rosary a spring of most abundant graces to help them in fulfilling faithfully their duties in life.

Souls lacking in faith and wavering for want of courage are in need of maternal help to overcome discouragement in their sad plight. This maternal help they can receive through devotion to the Blessed Virgin who has given a Redeeming God to the world...

When parents and children gather together at the end of the day in the recitation of the Rosary, together they meditate on the example of work, obedience, and charity which shone in the house of Nazareth; together they learn from the Mother of God to suffer serenely; to accept with dignity and courage the difficulties of life and to acquire the proper attitude to the daily events of life. It is certain that they will meet with greater facility the problems of family life. Homes will thereby be converted into sanctuaries of peace. Torrents of divine favors will come to them, even the inestimable favor of a priestly or religious vocation...

Most ardently we beg the Lord from our heart that souls, families and nations may derive abundant fruit from the holy Rosary and that our Lord may assist you, beloved son, with His grace in your enterprise. As a pledge of such favors, we are pleased to impart to you our apostolic blessing which we joyfully extend to all who aid you in these labors and to all who in their homes honor the Queen of Heaven and of Earth with the laudable practice of the Family Rosary.

End of a long journey

"I think he is just like Jesus," said the little girl perched atop her father's shoulder in the crowd surrounding Father Peyton.

Sister Marie Eymard was nearby and heard the child. She had watched as Father Peyton's big hand engulfed the child's little one. "How like him to give special attention to the children," she thought as she watched the men and women coming to speak to the priest who bent his head to hear their words.

The 1959 Crusade in Bruges had opened in May with the first showing of the Rosary films at a Crusade and continued to the climax of the rally in June.

Fifty thousand people jammed the streets leading to Father Peyton. They had heard his talk from the high platform through loudspeakers. Sister Marie Eymard had translated his talk, and some of the words still rang in her ears—"Mary is alive. She is here... She will help you if you ask her." She had seen the sea of upturned faces and heard the hush as though the crowd expected Our Blessed Mother to appear beside the black-robed priest as he raised his arms upward, Rosary waving from one hand.

Sister Marie Eymard had been Father Peyton's translator from the beginning of the showing of the films at the World's Fair in Brussels the year before. She had continued with him through the Bruges Crusade.

The films had added a new dimension to the Crusade. They had been shown indoors, in a small auditorium, but had been seen by thirty-five thousand viewers. After the Crusade, eight hundred thousand out of one million Catholics signed pledges for the daily family Rosary.

Sister Eymard saw that a plan could be built around the films for more extended teaching of the Bible to school children.

She had prepared a manual as a guide to this teaching. The manual contained a brief synopsis of each film and the citations for Scripture readings relevant to each. In it also were suggestions for various types of activities that could be carried on in conjunction with the films. Her manual became another bead in the chain of prayers being linked to guide Father Peyton's way and bolster his success in Latin America.

Bishop de Smedt wrote a detailed analysis of the Crusade after it ended and sent it to all his priests. It was the first thorough evaluation undertaken by anyone outside the Crusade team.

The success of the campaign "in the face of materialism, indifference and even opposition to family prayer," wrote the bishop, "proved that the Holy Spirit through the intercession of Mary poured down divine grace upon the people." He attributed the success to the faith and prayers of the clergy and the participation of the laity, especially the men. The Crusade crushed "with a sledgehammer blow," he wrote, the prejudice that men will not participate in religious activities and proved Father Peyton's rightness in employing men.

The Crusade itself, he concluded, proved that Christian life has a social dimension, and is not just a personal intimate contact with the Holy Spirit, as the opposition claimed. This it proved through the use of all media—newspapers, radio, television, the Rosary films, sermons of priests on the Rosary, teaching in the schools. Furthermore, the rally as a formulator of public opinion showed the influence came from Jesus and Mary, not from one's own person.

Bishop de Smedt urged all priests and the lay organization set up by the Crusade to continue work of promotion of devotion to the Rosary, reminding people of their commitments and by instituting new programs for the Rosary.

The Crusade had been criticized for its lack of follow-up. The Crusade team was aware of this weakness, but felt it was the responsibility of the diocese that had had the Crusade. Bishop de Smedt's evaluation was a good answer to later similar criticisms. In fact, the Crusade did not have the manpower or facilities to insure permanence. All it could do was to plant the seed, and then leave it to be nourished or neglected by the people there.

Although no one, especially Bishop de Smedt, questioned the premise of local responsibility for the follow-up, Father Peyton began to think of this as a weakness of the Crusade. He knew that crusades were too often followed by neglect. Elements had been added as the work had progressed. Why not permanence, he asked himself. The vision of post-crusade Family Rosary satellites all over the world sprang into his mind.

After the Bruges Crusade, Father Peyton returned in August to Santiago for the groundwork in Chile.

Father Peyton regarded the moment he boarded the plane in New York on August 15, 1959, the feast of the Assumption, bound for Santiago, as the beginning of his missionary work in Latin America. He was due to arrive August 16, but a brief stopover in Bogotá, Colombia, became a three-day delay when a changeover plane arrived late. Father Peyton used the time to visit CELAM (Conferencia Episcopal Latinoamericana), the secretariat of Latin American bishops. He wanted to enlist their support for the Crusade. They welcomed him and promised cooperation. So it was that he flew into Santiago's Los Cerrillos Airport on August 19. There waiting to welcome him he found Father Francis Provenzano, superior general of St. Joseph's College, where he would stay. Also there were seven other priests of the college, some seminarians and María Luisa Luca de Tena, the Spanish journalist who had become an ardent supporter and helper, and three of her secular missionary colleagues. They were Carmen Amann, Fuensanta Gonzalez and Begoña Díaz.

Father Peyton's old friend Mark McGrath smiled with amused remembrance when he heard Father Peyton's greeting to him in Spanish.

The next day, Father Peyton held a press conference for thirty representatives of the secular and religious media. The reporters felt the solemnity of the subject when Father Peyton knelt upon the floor and invited them to join him in a *Hail Mary*.

One skeptical reporter challenged the goal of bringing prayer to people with so many problems of poverty and social and political unrest. When the answer impressed him with Father Peyton's absolute confidence in the power and will of Mary to help the people, the reporter retreated to another subject and asked, "Of all the continents where you have been, where would you most like to live?"

Father Peyton replied, "In none of them. I wish to live only in heaven."

The next day the press, radio and television began spreading the image of the Rev. Patrick Peyton, C.S.C., and his apostolate to the Mother of God, throughout the dioceses of Chile.

Father Peyton remained in Chile for a month, spinning the many strands of the organization for the Crusade, visiting many of the country's religious and secular leaders. The first outdoor showings of the fifteen Rosary films began November 8.

As Father Peyton was beginning his apostolate in Latin America, the Vatican also was initiating an expansion of missionary service to that vast under-served Catholic continent.

Further impetus for the crusades came from Superior General of the Congregation of Holy Cross—none other than Father Christopher O'Toole, who had helped the newly ordained Father Peyton launch an impossible dream one long-ago summer on the campus of Holy Cross College.

Father O'Toole urged all Holy Cross provincials to support the work of the Family Rosary Crusade in Latin America.

A growing social consciousness awoke in the Catholic Church. The decade of the sixties was to see priests involved in social action and human rights in both Americas.

Father Quinn was the first to go to Manila—in August, 1959.

He was followed shortly by two secular missionaries from Spain, Tere Aguinaco and Margarita de Lecca. An Irish secretary from Dublin, Terry Fellowes, also went.

Father Peyton was still in Chile when he was summoned to the Philippines in October to finish preparations for the Manila rally.

He held a press conference. As usual with the beginning of an undertaking, he opened it with a *Hail Mary* and a plea for her intercession for the success of the Crusade. The reporters, although Catholic, were not used to press conferences that opened with a prayer. The result was a barrage of newspaper feature articles and radio and television announcements. Posters announcing the Crusade were put up everywhere, and a sound truck traveled through the streets blaring its message. A neon-lighted sign, "Rosary Rally," covered the wings of an airplane overhead.

Pastors, schools and churches cooperated practically one hundred percent. The pastors promised a daily Holy Hour for the forty days of the Crusade from November 1 to December 10, and sermons on the Rosary on the five Sundays. The teams of two lay leaders each built up an army of one hundred thousand door-to-door visitors to call on every family in an archdiocese of two and a half million people. They visited the sick to obtain their heroic pledges.

The archdiocese was divided into sites for four rallies, with the last and main one in Manila, where there was an estimated attendance of one-and-a-half million.

The press estimated the crowd at the rally at Cebu, the second largest city in the Philippines, at over a million people.

Cardinal Archbishop of Cebu Julio Rosales, who gave not only his blessing but his full cooperation to the Crusade, was deeply impressed by Father Peyton. He was especially moved when Father Peyton gave him a Rosary and a small statue of Mary, which he cherished. He later said, "This to me was very symbolic of his love of Our Lady, a love that he wants everyone to share."

When Father Peyton came to Cebu then and later, Cardinal Rosales observed, they always had to make a special bed for him because he was too tall to fit in the standard-size beds of the Filipinos. "We did not mind this extra effort because we are just too happy to have him with us," he added.

Cardinal Rosales summed up his impression of Father Peyton thus:

> I have observed that Father Peyton's Crusade rallies have always been the biggest gathering of people in every place they were held. I witnessed this in my own archdiocese of Cebu some fifteen years ago and, last year in Tacloban City, Leyte. Leyte's Governor Romualdez made the same observation. I believe that this is due to Father Peyton's way of preparing for these rallies. I have observed how he prays to Our Blessed Mother and puts everything in her hands.
>
> Father Peyton has been made instrument by God to save the world from destruction and the evils of communism since the Rosary is the strongest weapon to destroy our enemies.
>
> If Father Peyton will succeed to spread throughout the world the devotion to the Holy Rosary—and I am sure he will—then and only then Russia will be converted and real peace can be achieved.
>
> I have always observed that Father Peyton is a man of prayer and penance. He would accept any kind of suffering even if only one soul could be saved.

The Manila rally was scheduled for four-thirty in the afternoon on Sunday, December 6.

Masses of people were converging toward the spot in Luneta Park where the raised dais supported a backdrop with a color poster bearing the Crusade slogan, "The Family That Prays Together Stays Together." A huge chain of beads was strung between two large crosses at either end.

A quarter of a million people were already assembled when Father Bienvenido Lopez, the bishop's liaison with the Crusade, began leading the crowd in the Rosary. At that moment the skies

141

let loose a torrent of rain. The people did not run for shelter. Those coming kept on coming through the rain. The Rosary recitation continued.

The massive chorus of voices in prayer like a rythmic wind rose and fell against the sound of the rain. But the individual speakers would be scarcely audible in the torrent. The rest of the rally would have to be postponed.

As the time came for Father Peyton to appear, the rain stopped. The sun shone brilliantly as he mounted the platform. A steaming throng of a million and a half people listened spellbound to him.

Father Peyton's calmness in the storm impressed a man who later became the Archbishop of Manila, Jaime Cardinal L. Sin. He described it: "He was not the least perturbed by the threatening rain. He was very very confident that the people would not disperse during the rainstorm. They did not seek shelter. They stayed under the rain—drenched to the skin."

Summing up the effect of the Crusade upon the people and his own impressions, Cardinal Sin reflected:

> I was impressed on the preparations which underlined the role of prayer. This bespeaks of the spirituality of this man of God.
>
> His sermon was always the same, with some alterations, but the people were always spellbound, not by his eloquence, nor by the loftiness of the subject, but by the simplicity by which it was given. It was given with unction, coming from a priest with a cause—to bring Mary to the hearts of the people of God.

One of these devotees of Our Lady standing unobtrusively in the rain-drenched throng was a lady of one of the leading families of the Philippines—Josefina Madrigal Bayot. She afterward described the effect Father Peyton and the Crusade had upon her and others:

> It was my love for Mary and the Holy Rosary that led me to Father Peyton. It seems that Mary was very pleased and smiling on the faith of the Filipino people. After the heavy rain the sun appeared. Poor, rich, young and even the very old were present.
>
> The way Father Peyton talked and prayed, especially the way he said "Hail Mary" and "Holy Mary," slowly and with such genuine love and devotion, explaining the meaning of the words, touched my heart to the very core.

Because of this effect on me, I decided to go with Cardinal Santos's pilgrimage to the Holy Land, there to attend Father Peyton's Crusade rally. I went with my two sons and a friend. It was in Jerusalem that I came to know him well and he became my good friend. It was because of the way he prayed, talked and said the Holy Mass that I wished to become his friend—there was an aura of sanctity around him.

A family I met there told me they decided to join the pilgrimage after hearing Father Peyton speak in Manila just four days before its departure. This shows the effect on people. In the Family Rosary Crusade Rally at Nazareth, while speaking of Mary the Mother of God, Father Peyton said, "What is good for Jesus Christ is surely good enough for me." True is what Cardinal Sin of Manila once said to me, "Father Peyton loves our Blessed Mother very much."

I have a very close friend whom I have been trying to convince for years to say the Rosary every day. I used to see her very often and I would urge, coax and argue with her to pray the Rosary but to no avail. Father Peyton met her, became her friend and now she says the Rosary with her daughter and her entire household. In fact she told me she could not sleep without saying the Rosary.

In my own family, I am a widow with a daughter and two sons. There exists a bond of love, peace, unity and an awareness of God, with no generation gap, though my sons are in their early twenties. This I attribute to our praying together every night. As Father Peyton says, "The family that prays together stays together."

Father Quinn and the three secular missionaries had completed their work in the Philippines and left for Chile. Two other Holy Cross Fathers assigned to Chile were Father Philip Higgins and Father William Belyea, a Canadian.

Father Peyton, never one to let an inspiration cool nor a vision fade, told Cardinal Santos about his dream of establishing permanent Crusade offices. Cardinal Santos approved and appointed Father Lopez as director, a post he continued to hold even after he became auxiliary bishop of Manila thirteen years later. Manila became the distribution point for the films and Crusade literature, reaching out to the Far East. Earlier that same year, the office established for the film-making in Madrid gained the status of permanency with the move to a building owned by a friend of Luis Carrero Blanco.

The decade of the fifties had ended with the realization of a dream. Father Peyton prayed the Rosary in thanksgiving, ending each decade of "Hail Marys" with an especially joyful:

> Glory be to the Father, and to the Son, and to the Holy Spirit.
> As it was in the beginning, is now, and ever shall be, world without end. Amen.

Even as he was thanking Mary for her intercession in the establishment of permanent offices abroad, he heard from Father Heinzer that the Hollywood office was in jeopardy. The old building on Sunset Boulevard had been condemned, and the safety commission had ordered its demolition.

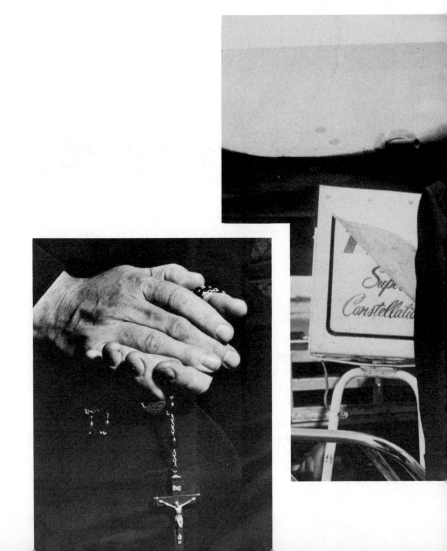

Part 4

Third decade—the sixties
Reaching Latin America

The challenge of Latin America

Padre Nuestro que estás en el cielo. Santificado sea tu nombre. Venga tu reino. Hágase tu voluntad en la tierra como en el cielo.

Father Peyton, in the front passenger seat of the car, fingered his chain of black beads reverently as he led the Rosary in Spanish. As the car rolled on through traffic, heading for downtown Santiago, the driver and the other passengers chorused the responses.

Danos hoy nuestro pan de cada dia. Perdona nuestras ofensas, como también nosotros perdonamos a los que nos ofenden. No nos dejes caer en tentación, y libranos del mal. Amén.

Father Peyton had flown back to Santiago that March 8, 1960, to stay. The Popular Mission built around the showing of the Rosary films was progressing in seven dioceses of central Chile directed by teams of trained local volunteers. It was time to begin his work toward the great rallies that would climax the campaigns. He also would prepare for other Latin American Crusades.

Father Quinn and the secular missionaries greeted him at Los Cerrillos Airport. They took him to the downtown Santiago office in Presidential Square. They were eager to tell him of their plans and preparations, but he had wanted to give thanks for this beginning of a new decade of his apostleship for Mary—in a new land and among new people.

"Will you say the Rosary with me first?" he had cut into their excited conversation as they got into the car. He knew he would need all the help he could get from heaven and earth.

He led the prayers in the Spanish he had learned seven years earlier in Malága preparing for this moment. It was the language he would be speaking. Most Latin Americans speak Spanish or, in Brazil, the very similar Portuguese. The Spanish conquerors and colonists from the sixteenth century had bestowed their religion and their language upon their new world. The Portuguese had done the same in Brazil.

When the group arrived at the office in the building next to the palace of Chile's President Jorge Allessandri, Father Peyton went immediately to the statue of Mary. He prayed for her help and intercession with her son Jesus to help overcome the difficulties of the Latin American crusades.

Father Quinn and the others explained their plans to Father Peyton as he studied their schedules and the circles drawn on the map of Chile. He looked over clippings of newspaper publicity already obtained. A map of Santiago, headquarters for the Chile campaigns, showed the parishes of the archdiocese. It also showed neighborhood sites in each parish for the film showings.

Latin America would present its own special challenge to the Crusade. The diversity of its land and its people would require more time for the preparation, with modifications in approach. The land, dominated by the spine of the Andes Mountains, that drop sharply on the west into the Pacific Ocean, would pose difficulty of travel.

The great Amazon River fed by the towering snow-capped peaks and draining the jungle basin and the Brazilian Highlands on its four-thousand-mile course eastward presented forbidding terrain. Vast areas of the basin averaged only two people per square mile. The whole South American mainland was sparsely populated for its vast area. Brazil, occupying almost half the continent, averaged at the time only twenty people for each of its more than three million square miles. Much jungle and mountain land was uninhabitable. Travel and transport would be difficult. Railway access was limited and most rivers non-navigable.

The Crusade teams would have to travel great distances. Centers of population around coastal cities were few and far apart and separated by mountain, rain forest and jungle. In most of South America, only half the people lived in cities. The other half lived in rural villages far apart in valleys, on mountain plateaus and in coastal oases. Many settlements were isolated by lack of telephone lines and roads. They could be reached only by ox-cart or riverboat along a few navigable stretches of rivers.

The difficulties did not worry the priest who had journeyed on troop trains, dog sleds and camel caravan.

"It's the people, not the place, we are interested in" he told his team. "We are bringing Our Blessed Mother's help to the people, and she will help us reach them."

The Crusade would have to appeal to people of widely differing economic and social status. The nations of Latin America were separated as much by cultural canyons as by physical barriers. Affluent and literate countries coexisted with impoverished and illiterate ones, sometimes side by side. The same disparity existed between the classes of people within each nation, to a greater or lesser extent.

The native Indians had not been annihilated as they had in North America. They were protected from enslavement in colonial days by Jesuit missionaries who believed they had souls. The colonists had been forced to import slaves captured from black African tribes, at that time lumped with the animals in the belief that they had no souls.

All of Latin America was trapped in a system of latifundia. It was an economic and social system inherited along with their holdings by the colonists who had taken over broad estates and developed them into huge plantations. Their wealthy descendants held a tight grip on the inheritance. It was a system in which a few wealthy families controlled the land and the power while the masses who worked for them lived in poverty and dependence. These poor inhabited slums with mushroom huts, made of salvaged junk and mud, rimming the cities, in poor shacks on vast plantations or in poor shelters in remote villages.

Most of the poor were of varied racial mixture, descended from the colonial settlers, the native Indians and imported black Africans.

Racial stigmas had not been created as in North America. Inter-mingling and inter-marriage among the races had been common. Descendants of black slaves and native Indians had been absorbed into the general population, although in some areas more of one or the other remained. Clusters of blacks had remained in the cities. Many Indians still lived in desperate need in rural villages, although droves had migrated from that poverty to that of city slums. Though race in itself was not an obstacle to upward mobility through marriage or personal ability, few of the masses ever escaped from the prison of their poverty.

When Father Peyton arrived, the governments of Latin America were all constitutional democracies—in theory. Some countries were closer than others to a semblance of democracy, but none followed completely the principles of self-government by the governed. Many were closer to dictatorships—some absolute, some despotic, some benevolent.

The wealthy aristocracy controlled the elections and the governments. The poor were disenfranchised by their illiteracy, and those who did vote found it expedient to vote for their employer's choice of candidate. The poor had no candidates of their own. Those who professed to represent their interests forgot their promises as soon as they won election.

The bishops were caught in a paradox. They were deeply concerned for the welfare of the people under their spiritual care. Some who were outspoken in their advocacy of land and social reforms incurred the displeasure of the ruling class, of which they themselves were members by virtue of property owned by their Church.

The pressure of such inequities was bound to erupt into political turmoil as the ruling classes sought to protect their holdings against the demands of the poor for a larger share. The result was periodic uprisings, civil war, revolution and counter-revolution. Advocates of reform were sometimes sincere patriots, but more often were foreign agents with detailed plans for fomenting chaos and bloody revolution as a route for their own takeover of power.

The world was still watching to see in which direction Fidel Castro would lead Cuba.

If Cuba went Communist, it would encourage agents already at work in Latin America.

Nearly all Latin Americans were baptized Roman Catholics. The wealthy ruling classes who sent their children abroad to be educated and the literate middle classes followed traditional religious practices of the Church.

The pre-colonial belief of the Indians in a hierarchy of gods had made the Christian idea of one God acceptable to them. The blacks too had adopted the religion of their masters. But their rudimentary knowledge of the Catholic religion was mixed with vestiges of aboriginal pagan superstition and spiritism.

The Catholic religion had been reinforced by later immigrants from Germany, Ireland and Italy. The only non-Catholics were minority pockets of Japanese and Christians of other denominations from Europe.

Priests were in critically short supply for the masses of poor

Catholics. Dioceses took in vast areas of cities and distant hinterlands and were very populous. All Latin America averaged only one priest for every six thousand people.

The conventional church could not reach the masses to teach religious knowledge and practices. As few as three hundred, mostly women, in a parish of thousands might attend church regularly. Some of the scattered villages saw a priest only once a year. Most of the poor knew little about God, less about the lives of Jesus and Mary and had never heard of the Rosary.

Father Peyton already knew from information sent him by his advance team and from background reading, news and interviews with people familiar with the land and its people, much of what his associates told him that evening as they explained their strategies.

He was prepared for the special challenges of Latin America. The years and experiences had brought him to the prime of his health and endurance. His faith in the power of daily family Rosary had been reinforced by the many times he had been forced to defend it. That faith had been confirmed millions of times over by testimonials of families of five continents. The Crusade organization had been worn to the smoothness of often prayed Rosary beads.

Alone later that night in the dimness of the chapel at St. George's College, where the Crusade priests were guests, Father Peyton prayed his own private prayers in communion with his Blessed Mother. He was suddenly overcome by a revelation. He recognized his frustration at the delays in reaching Latin America as evidence of his own blindness. His faith in Mary had always been confident and complete, but he felt at that moment that the Blessed Mother herself had removed his blinders and let him see even more of her will and power in her guidance of him.

The Rosary films, the secular missionaries, the legions of helpers, all the experiences and accomplishments needed for this place were Mary's doing and none of his. She had gently but firmly guided him from place to place, from person to person, from event to event, to this place and these people in her own time and according to her own plan. She had put each in its place until all fell together in a design like a constellation of stars. All his past life was just a novitiate to the new work. He, a mere instrument and particle of God's work, could not see God's design. But Mary had opened his eyes and shone her light a little further on the pathway to understanding of the existence of God's plan. With deep humility, he reflected that Mary was the driver and he was truly the donkey. Never again would he chafe at delays or what appeared to him as obstacles or failures. Such a driver well knew the way, and he had only to follow where she led him.

Beginning in Chile

Father Quinn and his crew had divided all Chile into three parts. They had mapped campaign dates for the most suitable weather for the rallies in each part. The Crusade was scheduled to begin in the center region, then move north to the tropics in winter, then south in the summer at the end of the rainy season.

Chile, a long ruffle tapering along the western edge of South America from the bottom of the hump to the very tip of the continent where Punta Arenas, the world's southernmost city, lies, promised the least difficulty of transition to a new land and people.

Large numbers of people could be reached at the same time. There were fewer obstacles. Three quarters of the country's population, compared with half in the rest of Latin America, lived in cities, all strung along the coastal plains. There were fewer scattered villages. Large areas of mountain, jungle and desert were uninhabited.

Chile offered a less volatile political and social system. The government at the time had been brought closer to a true democracy under President Alessandri.

The day after arriving in Santiago, Father Peyton held another press conference after spending most of the morning telephoning the media and promising the thanks of their Blessed Mother if they would send representatives. The publicity, along with letters of introduction from friends abroad, opened doors for him as he made courtesy visits upon religious, social and political leaders.

Father Peyton knew he had to work within the system. Nothing could be done in Latin America without the approval of the ruling class. He also visited the leaders of the poor in the slum neighborhoods. He opened each discussion with an appeal to the Blessed Mother for her favors upon his listeners and their families. He called each by name to her attention before asking them to help him convey her message to the people. They could not refuse the Mother of God.

The aristocracy welcomed him into their homes and offices. They greeted him as a messenger sent from Mary, Queen of Heaven, to reinforce and restore the blessings of their faith for themselves and their compatriots. No matter how unworthy of earthly bounties they considered their underlings, they viewed them as equal in the love of God the Father. They respected the equality of souls before God. They felt their station in life imposed upon them a responsibility for the spiritual welfare of their laborers. They saw in Father Peyton and the Rosary Crusade a heaven-sent opportunity to help them meet that obligation.

The leaders of the poor welcomed him. They agreed to help him because the masses were as starved for spiritual as for physical sustenance. Chile had more priests than most other Latin American countries, but still averaged only one priest to every three thousand people. Religion did not flourish in the miseries of lives of the poor. "They will not listen to you; they will not pray," one slum-dweller told Father Peyton.

The bishops of all twenty dioceses of Chile wanted the Crusade. They welcomed him, but pronounced as impossible his idea of recruiting an army of men volunteers. The men wanted no part in religious activities. The small percentage of parishioners who did go to church were mostly women.

The bishop of each diocese was asked to assign two priests familiar with its people to work full-time with the Crusade. One became Crusade director and the other directed the Popular Mission, preliminary to the Crusade.

The Popular Mission was built around the Rosary films. The plan, based by Begoña Díaz and her sister secular missionaries on Sister Marie Eymard's manual, used the films as basis for a course in Christian doctrine.

For the public film showings teams of local men volunteers were trained by Crusade priests and secular missionaries. One volunteer would operate the machinery and the other speak after each showing on the Scripture meaning and its relation to the people's lives. The speakers were taught Christian doctrine but not told what to say. Chosen as typical of their neighborhoods, they spoke in their own words and like their listeners. It was the pastor's job to recruit these teams. Many a pastor simply shook his head in dismay at the idea of getting men to volunteer.

Sites were chosen in all neighborhoods. They were no more than a fifteen-minute walk from anywhere in a neighborhood to make viewing available to all. Parish halls and schools were never chosen. This was to avoid identification with the Church so that all might feel free to attend. The films were shown outdoors in the streets, in public squares, at marketplaces on nine-by-seven foot portable screens or on the exterior walls of bars and other buildings.

Though every neighborhood was flooded with posters and other publicity, word-of-mouth was the only way to reach many of the poor who could not read and did not own radios or televisions. So, a corps of women was organized, like that of the men who worked the post-rally pledge week, to visit every home and invite all the family to attend the films.

The Crusade supplied equipment and training, but the plan called for operation and administration by local people.

The Popular Mission that evolved in Chile required the timely dispatch and transport, according to a complex schedule, of seventeen tons of equipment. That included more than forty projectors and screens, loudspeakers, more than sixty copies of the fifteen reels of the films, and portable generators. These had been purchased and shipped to Chile by wealthy friends. When the backstage work was completed, the equipment was moved into place in jeeps.

Two films were shown each of seven consecutive nights. On the eighth, with one film left, Mass or recitation of the Rosary or a procession to a shrine of Our Lady concluded the program. The films were shown as quickly as manpower permitted. They went from site to site as fast as possible. The shows were always free and no money was ever collected. Nor would Father Peyton permit the gatherings to be exploited for commercial gain by anyone.

For many of the poor, it was the first time they had ever seen a movie. And it was through this wondrous new experience that many first learned of those long-ago events that were the foundation of their religion. In movement and color they saw what had happened reenacted on the screen. They saw the people of the Bible come alive and heard them speak the words they had spoken twenty centuries ago. The dramatic portrayal of God's love and the love of Jesus and Mary for all made grown men and women weep. Priests reported that men as well as women who saw the films began coming to church in droves.

The favorable reaction was not unanimous, however. There were sometimes hecklers in the crowds. Anti-Crusade protests were spread by some who feared religion as a foe of their special interests, especially in the labor unions where men were made vulnerable by their material needs and in the universities where young idealists hoped to heal the ills of their world. Communists were especially vocal, although few in number, in courting the young students who were the future leaders of their country. Father Peyton wanted to court them for God and insisted on taking the Crusade to the campuses, in spite of sometimes angry and loud demonstrations.

It was seven months from Father Peyton's first arrival in Santiago to the first rally. Preparations were slowed by many obstacles—huge parishes, travel distances, apathy of the people, difficulty recruiting volunteers. But Father Peyton pressed ahead. He pushed himself and his team tirelessly to prepare for the May rallies. The team at the time consisted of Father Quinn and three secular missionaries and Terry Fellowes. The team went from place to place ahead of Father Peyton living out of suitcases. They became known as "Our Lady's gypsies."

The first rally was in San Felipe on the first of May. Father

Peyton told a gathering of ten thousand of the Blessed Mother's special love for the people of Latin America. He pleaded with them to love and honor her as the Mother of God, the mother of Jesus and the mother of them all, through daily family recitation of the Rosary.

Weekly rallies during the month of Mary took him next on May 8 to Valparaiso. No one could escape knowing of the rally. It came to them on television and radio. They read it in newspapers and magazines. Posters and banners heralded it everywhere. It was proclaimed from pulpits. It came from school with children's homework. Neighbor told neighbor. Fifty thousand awaited Father Peyton at Valparaiso.

He came in colorful pageantry with bishops, priests and lay participants. Dignitaries and families led the prayers in a mass recitation of the Rosary. Spectators told each other they had never before heard so many people praying all together. The people thronged around Father Peyton after the ceremonies, and he did not hurry away but stopped to talk with them.

Father Peyton brought more than his message of the Rosary to Chile. He brought the Rosary literally in the form of tons of Rosary beads. A simple but crucial obstacle the Crusade discovered during the first campaigns was that the poor had no Rosary beads. Two Canadian priests he met in Chile arranged for the Catholic Women's League of Canada to pay for the first million sets. A factory in Ireland supplied them at a discount price of fifty thousand dollars. Subsequently, supplying of Rosary beads to Latin America, Asia and Africa became an ongoing work of the Family Rosary Crusade. Other organizations followed the Canadian example. Used Rosaries were gathered and donated by organizations and individuals. Sorting, repair and shipping became a major work of the Albany headquarters office.

The church bells of Santiago rang for fifteen minutes as the procession led by the statue of Mary filled the cleared avenues of the city. People lined the streets and crowded balconies. Flowers were dropped from balconies upon Our Lady all along the way.

Cheers of more than half a million voices greeted Our Lady as she entered Cosimo Park and the crowd parted for the procession. Strong young men bore Mary up steps and placed her gently upon the raised platform, overlooking the carpet of people. The speakers took their places. Children in bright colors moved into an open area below to arrange themselves in a living Rosary. In reciting the Rosary, the bishop and four families each led a decade. The sound of the responses thundered into the air like the rhythmic pounding of huge breakers on a shore. Father Peyton's growing fame had preceded him to that third great rally on May 15. He spoke before five hundred and fifty thousand people. Loudspeakers carried his voice to the throng in the park and to even more spilling into the streets.

The last rally in May was on the twenty-second in Talca. Father Quinn was on the platform at one end of the park, making a final check of loudspeakers, flowers for the stage, chairs for the dignitaries and other details. A local priest was helping him.

The park was filling with people. About a half hour before the rally was set to begin the earth under their feet rumbled and shook. The people kept on coming, walking faster, some running. No one knew what was occurring or what danger they might be in.

"What's happening?" "I don't know." "It's the end of the world." "Let's get to the priest," they cried to one another. Mothers scooped little children into their arms. People rushed up to the two priests and grabbed them by the arm or the cassock, begging them to hear their confessions. "It's doomsday," they cried out.

The local priest signaled the leader of the band nearby. The band played and the muffled underground thunder shook the earth as people stumbled down the city streets toward the park.

Fearing the crowd might panic, Father Quinn grabbed the microphone and shouted, "We must ask Mary for help. We must pray the Rosary." He began the prayers. Forty thousand pairs of eyes implored heaven as the praying voices rose to a roar above the rumbling in intense new awareness of the meaning of the words, *"Holy Mary, Mother of God, pray for us now and at the hour of our death."*

Father Peyton was on his knees praying beside his bed in the bishop's house when the first tremor came.

He rushed outside and saw a lone little girl, about nine, running back and forth in a panic in the street, empty because the people had all gone to the rally. She was crying, frightened by the noise and the shaking of the earth and the absence of people. Father Peyton stopped to comfort her and told her the people were all in the park. Reassured, she ran off toward the park, and he followed swiftly with his long stride.

The First Sorrowful Mystery
The Agony in the Garden

Then he went out and made his way, as was his custom, to the Mount of Olives: his disciples accompanied him. On reaching the place he said to them, "Pray that you may not be put to the test." He withdrew from them about a stone's throw, then went down on his knees and prayed in these words: "Father, if it is your will, take this cup from me: yet

not my will but yours be done." An angel then appeared to him from heaven to strengthen him. In his anguish he prayed with all the greater intensity, and his sweat became like drops of blood falling to the ground. Then he rose from prayer and came to his disciples, only to find them asleep, exhausted with grief. He said to them, "Why are you sleeping? Wake up, and pray that you may not be subjected to the trial."

(Luke 22: 39-46)

Father Peyton's meditation
on The Agony in the Garden

When we pray the sorrowful mysteries of the Rosary, we take the hand of Mary to share with her the suffering inflicted on her Divine Son during the last hours of his life: fear, pain, humiliation and death.

More dreaded than any other human experience is suffering. It is the lot of all of us. It is life's great mystery. It raises seemingly unanswerable questions. Often we can't understand it. We lose our faith. We blame God, even hate Him. We ask why. "Why me?"

For millions of us living in a world of suffering, the Rosary is loved, fingered and prayed. Through its sorrowful mysteries it gives meaning to our misery. From it we get strength, courage and hope to endure our sufferings, to sanctify them, to make them serve as stepping stones for us to reach our destiny.

In the first sorrowful mystery, we gaze upon Our Savior in agony. We see how He comes to grips with this worst of all sufferings—fear. Fear is a terrible experience. It drives some of us to despair, even suicide. We grasp at any straw to help us escape impending suffering: ill health, the loss of a good name, bankruptcy, blackmail, violence, the break-up of a marriage, or death itself.

How mighty is the flood of fear that envelops Christ in the garden on the night of His agony! We understand why. He had a world to save and He alone could save it. "His hour" had come. It is the hour for Him to wrestle with evil. He stands alone as He enters that conflict with Satan. He takes our place. He assumes all our guilt, so that we might once again regain what we had lost—the love and friendship of God.

His sufferings are, as it were, the "red hot iron" that will purge us and make us whole, fit to be one with Him forever.

This and much more does the Rosary say to us as we, with so much love and devotion to Jesus and Mary, pray the first sorrowful mystery of the Rosary.

A great cheer arose from the throng as Father Peyton appeared on the platform. If it was the end of the world, there was no better place to be than in the presence of the priest who had spoken to them from the screen fifteen times—at the end of each Rosary film—promising them the protection of their Blessed Mother.

As he spoke, the shock waves continued. None knew it then, but they were on the periphery of the great earthquakes that shook southern Chile from May 21 through May 30, killing five thousand people and devastating whole towns, and measuring 8.3 on the Richter scale.

On the day of the Talca rally, Fidel Castro established diplomatic relations with the Union of Soviet Socialist Republics and the People's Republic of China. His route was beginning to be marked.

In mid-1960, after a year and a half of Castro's diatribes against the United States and confiscation of U.S.-owned property, an angry Congress empowered President Dwight D. Eisenhower to embargo exports to Cuba and cancel purchases of Cuban sugar. Castro lost not only his biggest market but also the price stability maintained by the U.S. sugar subsidy. He turned to the Communist countries for trade—manufactured goods and rice in exchange for Cuban sugar—at the lower free market price.

After Talca and a few more rallies in central Chile, Father Peyton followed the team to the far north of Chile for crusades in the winter months, then to the south.

When they reached Temuco, they saw for the first time the massive destruction left by the southern earthquakes.

The despair and discouragement was evident. Families shattered by the loss of loved ones sought to rebuild their lives in the rubble of flattened homes, churches, schools and chapels. These survivors, Father Peyton observed, knew the fragility of their earthly lives. Forty thousand flocked around him at the rally on September 25 as he told them that daily family Rosary would bring Mary's help in restoring their lives. Their expressions of courage as he talked with them after the rally gave him the courage to go on through this devastated land.

Conditions were worse in Valdivia. The inhabitants were still digging the city out of the mud of a second disaster. The work of rebuilding after the earthquakes and the huge tidal waves that came in their wake was progressing. Then two months later, rains poured down to overflow the riverbanks and flood the city with waist-high water. Mud and marsh covered the city. The cathedral was one of the already-weakened buildings leveled by the floods.

The bishop told Father Peyton the fifteen thousand gathered for the rally on October 2 was the largest assemblage he had ever seen in Valdivia. After the rally Father Peyton spoke with thousands of people. He looked into sorrowful faces as they thanked him for coming to them in a time of such great need. Some told him, "We have seen death and we have heard death. Only the spiritual can save us now."

In sharp contrast to the awakened spirituality of the people of Talca was the attitude toward religion found at the next Crusade in Concepción. Father Quinn headed the advance team. The bishop had told him that Concepción was a city cold to religion, that the steelworkers would only ridicule the Crusade and that the strong Communist influence there would disrupt it.

The laymen to run the Popular Mission were recruited with great difficulty, many motivated only by their interest in the strange projection equipment.

At the first film showing, as Father Quinn stood on the rim of the circle of light flickering from the screen over the constantly shifting small group in front of it, he began to agree with the bishop's appraisal.

The men uttered sharp wolf whistles when the young Mary first appeared on the screen. Father Quinn gasped as suddenly a rock ripped a gaping hole in the screen. More rocks flew as the magnificent drama of The Annunciation played over the screen. There was general noise and disorder.

During a scene of Mary's visit to the home of Zachary and Elizabeth in The Visitation, someone cut the electric cord to the projector, leaving the area in darkness.

Disruption continued the next night. The noise abated slightly during The Nativity scene when the ecstasy on the face of the new mother stilled even the men, and during The Presentation with old Simeon's prophecy of sorrow.

On the third night the disorderly men were hushed by the growing crowd as it watched in sympathy and suspense the search of the young parents for their lost child. One shrill whistle in the dark was the last of the brash mockery as those nearby shifted away from the whistler and he fled to the edge of the crowd. The second film that evening, beginning the five Sorrowful Mysteries, went without incident. Still no prayer was said. The concluding speech was not given.

Father Quinn, shocked and offended, reminded himself of

Christ's answer to His tormenters and persevered. After the third night the crowd began gradually to grow. The interested ones forced the disrupters to retreat. Order was restored. On the last two nights the Rosary was recited, and on the final night the speech was made to an enthralled fifteen hundred people.

When Father Peyton arrived and was shown newspaper articles of the mockery, he set his jaw in the hard lines characteristic of his conviction. The devil was trying to undo the Crusade. It was to be a battle between the devil and Our Lady. Father Peyton knew which way the battle would go because he knew the crusades were under the protection of Mary. He knew something was going to happen to those men.

It rained all that October 9 and was still pouring when Father Quinn went to pick up Father Peyton in a jeep and take him to the cathedral for the procession. The front of the cathedral shimmered through the rain. Our Lady stood on the roof, a Rosary draped in her hands and falling over the facade of the cathedral. Before the front door stood another huge statue of Our Lady. The Rosary beads, made of special shatter-proof lightbulbs for the Crusade in the likely event of rain, beamed mistily through the downpour. It had not been possible entirely to avoid the rainy season in the south.

Forty thousand spectators, including thousands from a particularly irreverent section, stood for two hours listening to the speeches and reciting the Rosary to the musical accompaniment of the storm.

Father Peyton was little protected under his large black umbrella as he shook hands for more than an hour after the rally.

The rally proved Father Quinn's perseverance and Mary's power and will triumphant. Water that was not rain flowed down the cheeks of the women as they expressed their love and gratitude for the new respect suddenly shown by the husbands. Ribald men were subdued and thanked Father Peyton solemnly for their new appreciation of their families. A few men in rough working clothes apologized for their initial irreverence.

Our Lady had not only drenched the hecklers, she had also converted them.

The techniques needed to meet the special challenges of Latin America evolved during the campaigns in Chile. The original organization was retained, new features added. Activities were carefully synchronized to make better use of the Crusade's limited manpower.

Fifteen months of hectic activity took the Crusade to the last scheduled stop in the southernmost city of the world. Fifteen thousand gathered for that rally in Punta Arenas on November 13. Father Peyton learned from the bishop that the inhabitants of the little village of Por Venir on the island of Tierra del Fuego south of the tip of South America had no way to travel to the mainland. He assented to the bishop's request to go there and so took the Crusade on a little side trip on November 15 to the most southern populated place in the world. He had traversed almost the entire earth's axis from the inhabited areas nearest the North Pole to those nearest the South Pole.

Bishop Manuel Larain of Talca called the effect of the Chilean Crusade "a great explosion of dormant faith." He saw great numbers of men as well as women flocking to the churches, families resuming devotion of family Rosary and many called to the priesthood.

His voice calling for social and land reforms was heard all over the continent in his capacity as vice president at that time and later as president of the secretariat of Latin American bishops. A working democracy, with land, capital, education and health care for all was his answer to those who espoused communism.

He said to Father Peyton, "Communism rides on the shoulders of a discontented peasantry. If every man is a property owner, it will lose its appeal."

President Alessandri visited the Santiago headquarters toward the end of the Crusade in Chile. The losses from the great earthquakes were still being counted.

The disaster so devastated Chile's economy that in later years the democratic faction was unable to bind the country and it fell to the Communist Salvador Allende. But the Crusade had brought such a revival of faith that President Alessandri wanted to thank Father Peyton personally. According to media and official sources, an estimated one million and one hundred and ten thousand people had attended the rallies.

By the end of 1960 when the Crusade was concluded, Father Peyton's slogans had inundated the environment. Nearly everyone in Chile had learned that *"La familia que reza unida, permanence unida."*

New building in Hollywood

Father Heinzer climbed the stairs from the first to the top floor, roaming from one room to another. He looked at empty rooms. The old wooden building had been the site of great activities. In the heart of mythical Hollywood, so close to major film studios, it had been visited by many of the most glamorous and famous movie stars. Father Heinzer went back downstairs and watched as the office staff and volunteers packed the last remnants of the accumulation of more than ten years. There were boxes and boxes of film reels, records, tapes, glossy print and color pictures and snapshots, press clippings, magazines, and books.

The old building had been pronounced unsafe and was condemned.

Memories of the people who had come to that building to help and of their dedication with their talents and time flooded over Father Heinzer. He was always amazed when he thought of the extraordinary accomplishments of Family Theater: the hundreds of Hollywood stars who had made the Family Theater of the Air weekly shows the most popular programs in America for years, the wealthy benefactors who had underwritten the costs, the free radio time. Father Peyton had indeed been the pioneer of the electronic pulpit for the spread of religion.

John Fuller was editing the Rosary films when Father Heinzer arrived in Hollywood. He could still see the tears running down Johnny's face as he viewed the Sorrowful Mysteries.

The old building was to be torn down and replaced by a modern new one. The architectural firm of Verge and Clatworthy had donated plans for the new structure. The contractor and others had agreed to work at cost.

Father Heinzer was very worried. Even with the discounts, the cost of construction would be great. He thought Father Peyton had exhausted his resources in the huge sums he had raised before and could not do it again. Besides, Father Peyton was busy in Latin America.

Father Heinzer went into the room that had been refurbished as a chapel. He knelt before the statue of the Madonna and Child to pray once more before the men came to move her into the dingy rented quarters that were to serve as a temporary home of Family Theater. He prayed for the help of Our Lady as he fingered his Rosary beads that one last time in the old building.

They moved out on March 25, the feast of The Annunciation.

Father Peyton returned to California from Chile briefly to prepare for a Crusade in San Francisco. He met Robert Raskob and asked for a $175,000 grant from the Raskob Foundation, which he got in two weeks. Other donations brought the fund for building and equipment to two hundred and twenty-five thousand dollars. Father Peyton and Father Heinzer said a lot of Masses and a lot of Rosaries for the success of the Latin American Crusades and the building.

The new building that rose on the site of the old at 7201 Sunset Boulevard was built of concrete and glass. It was a spacious street-level structure with a full basement. Special features were a theater, film-cutting room, film storage rooms, a recording studio and the chapel. It was built around an open courtyard, where the statue of Our Lady was placed to be viewed through sliding glass walls.

The staff moved into the new building on December 25, 1960, Christmas Day, the feast of The Nativity—exactly nine months after they had moved out of the old building.

Father Heinzer in Hollywood and Father Peyton in Chile said
as many Masses and Rosaries of thanksgiving as they had of supplication.

Father Peyton continued tirelessly on the move, crossing the
physical barriers of Latin America and bridging its cultural
canyons with the Rosary. Everywhere he went the media were
saturated with promotion of his message. His ''I know. I lived
it,'' brought his personal story to the audiences at every rally as
he spoke from the pulpit of makeshift platforms overlooking
vistas of peopled parks and plazas and city streets.

That story of family love and of faith gave conviction to his
pleas. The family got its origin from God. It's from God the man
got his house, his wife, his children. It's to him that God en-

trusted the innocent little child. But He leaves the training to the teacher, the priest, the minister, the nun.

It's in the home that the saints or the sinners are made. The first five years are when the adult is formed in the child. If the parents love the child, they will be the teacher.

They must teach the child that God is the giver of life.

The parents might say to God in the hearing of the children, "You could have made me the little animal that I fed today, or the little blade of grass, and that would have been great, just to have life. But out of the millions of things that I could have been, You chose to give me human life, with a soul, intelligence, willpower, freedom to find my own mission out of my own uniqueness."

The family together must thank God as the giver of its gifts, the love of parents and children each for the other, for the day, for the air we breathe, the food that's grown from the seed, the wheat that's made into bread to feed the children.

The Rosary is the discipline and training to build the strong will and the moral fiber the same as the discipline and training for the child learning the violin to play a concert someday in a great hall or the football player who is going to be a great star or the horse trainer who wants to win the derby. Praying the Rosary coordinates all the powers of a person—imagination, memory, mind, heart, soul, voice, lips, knees, hands, as we say the beads while contemplating the Mysteries.

The prayers of the Rosary are easy for the children to learn, especially when they say it with the family every day.

Marvels in Caracas

When Father Peyton finally caught up with his Crusade team in Caracas, Venezuela, he found them all helplessly discouraged. He walked into the makeshift headquarters and all eyes turned toward him. Agitated voices all spoke at once. He stood calmly, head slightly bent toward them to sort out the words. Begoña Díaz was particularly agitated. She was in charge of coordinating the program. She finally was able to explain the problem as the other voices subsided.

"We can't get the machinery to show the films," she told Father Peyton.

"Why not? Have they not arrived yet?" he asked.

"Oh, yes," she answered tartly. "They're here. They're sitting right out there, in the harbor. We can't get them out of customs unless we pay the two hundred thousand bolivares fee, and we don't have two hundred thousand bolivares. The banks are all closed because it's Saturday. It seems that nobody in the government of Caracas works on a Saturday who could give his guarantee for the payment." The projectors and other equipment were needed by Monday when the Popular Mission was to begin.

Father Peyton had just arrived in Caracas. He phoned Monsignor Cayetano del Duca, a priest assigned to help the Crusade, and begged him to contact someone in government who would give the money guarantee.

Father Cayetano was sure it would be impossible, but he did reach an important man in government who had stopped briefly in his office.

"My secretary is not here, and I am busy. I am going horseback riding. I cannot comply with your request," the man retorted.

A few minutes later, Father Cayetano arrived at the Crusade headquarters to report his failure and ask what else he might do to help.

"Oh, for heaven's sake, do something, do something," Begoña wailed to Father Peyton.

"Oh, dear Begoña, don't worry," he answered calmly, "the Blessed Mother Mary will take care of it all."

Begoña replied sharply, "Yes, I can see her coming, I suppose in a little truck to carry it all away and have it ready for Monday."

Looking up at her with a sidewise tilt of the head that left the blue of his eyes brightly unshadowed by their ledge of brow, he smiled, "Who knows, Begoña? Who knows? She may do just that."

He left them then to go to Walter Donnelly, former ambassador to Venezuela. In a short time, he returned to report that

Walter contacted the president who gave his guarantee to customs and they could go and get the equipment.

The tons of projectors, screens, generators and other equipment shipped halfway around the continent from Chile to Venezuela were unloaded that day and were soon on the way to their destinations. The Crusade began in Caracas with the film showings the following Monday as scheduled.

One evening the film on the Agony in the Garden was showing. It was the first in which Christ appears as a grown man, but never full-face because the producers did not attempt to show the face of divinity.

A man in the ragged clothes of a slum dweller arose and forced his way through the crowd seated on the ground, in the street, on steps, leaning tightly packed against walls of buildings. He went in back of the screen. The neighborhood volunteer waiting to give his speech at the end of the film followed to ask what the man wanted.

"I want to see the face of Jesus," the man replied.

An estimated six hundred thousand people viewed the films during the Popular Mission phase of the Crusade in Caracas in 1961.

Five hundred thousand showed up en masse for the rally on July 16, 1961.

Father Peyton told them about the life he had lived with the Rosary as his daily comfort and strength and about the debt he must constantly repay to his family and to Our Blessed Mother for their love and assistance to him. Then he told them about Mary, and about the role she must play in their own lives if they would only invite her into their homes.

God entrusted to Mary, that precious teenage girl, a role so unique that no one before or after would ever get that role.

When the angel He sent as His messenger said to her, "*Hail Mary, full of grace, the Lord is with thee,*" our sister of long ago did not say, "Give me a moment. I do not understand the consequences of it." No, she accepted without hesitation the role that God gave her that set in motion the events leading humankind to the hope of salvation. She answered in effect, "I do not understand what you're asking of me, but my heart is Yours; Your will is mine; I will do whatever you ask of me."

When we pray the Rosary, we are saying to that sensitive woman, "Mary, Mother of God, you know your Son better than any other human being could know Him. You gave birth to Him. You fed Him; you washed His clothes; you taught Him His prayers; you listened to His conversation. You were present at His growing to manhood, at His crucifixion.

"You know how He behaves, how He reacts. We saw that at Cana when you delicately and simply told Him that the family had no wine and then told the waiters serving the wedding guests to do what He tells you to do. And so through you, that newly-wed couple had its first problem as a family solved."

Mary knows her Son as a human being, and He loves her as a son loves a mother. She lived under the same roof with God incarnate. No other woman ever had that privilege.

Mary's Divine Son Jesus from the cross entrusted a second role to His mother when he said to her, "There is your son" and to his beloved disciple, "There is your mother." And we interpret that to mean that He asked her to be the mother of all mankind, of all of us, forever. It was the last gift He gave to us as He was finishing His mission. He was telling her to do for His brothers what she did for Him; be their mother, their counselor, their friend; believe in them; console them; comfort them; help them to perform their roles they also have got from God—each and every one of them. He didn't ask her to be the mother of just the saints, but of the most diabolical man, the most devilish woman, not to write them off, but to believe in them, be mother to all of the sinners for whom He died.

We don't pray to Mary. We ask her to pray with us. We pray to God. Only to God can we say, "Have mercy on us" or, "Forgive us our sins," or ask for favors.

When we pray the Rosary and say "Hail Mary" over and over, we are saying "We believe you are alive, Mary, and that you are somebody's daughter, a real woman with a name and a face and a memory and a capability to respond.

When we repeat all those "Hail Marys," we are calling and calling the Mother of God and asking her to help us because we are drowning in the currents of our needs. When a man is drowning, he doesn't shout for help just once. He's shouting "Help! Help! Help!" until somebody throws him a plank. So the family with the Rosary, aware of its needs and its sorrows, is shouting "Help! Help! Help!" to Mary, who has the power to help them be rescued.

Like any mother, she responds to her child's cry for help. And like any mother, she loves to hear her child call her "mother" and turn to her for help and want to be with her.

In the Rosary film *The Assumption*, there's a scene when Mary is dying, with Peter at her bedside. He is crying. He will miss her. He says to her, "Tell your Son that I love Him." She says, "Peter, he knows that already." But Peter answers, "Yes, but He'll like it better if it comes through your lips."

In the Mystery of The Assumption Mary was taken up to heaven body and soul, the first fruits of the passion and death of Jesus, and we can follow her. Her body and soul entered a new life, the mother to be with the Son, with her God forever. Mary is alive. She will come to us if we ask her. Like God, she does not force herself upon us, but must be asked. When we ask Mary to tell her Son that we love Him and beseech her, "*Holy Mary, Mother of God, pray for us sinners now and at the hour of our death,*" we follow the example of Peter. We say to her, "It will mean more coming from you."

If we go for a favor from an important man through his mother who is gracious and friendly or through his wife whom he loves and we ask her to help us, we have a good chance of getting the favor. Mary cannot refuse you when you ask her to pray with you.

She goes ahead of you and says to her son Jesus, "This family that I love, they are on the way to You my Son. I'm only telling you. They want something. They need something," the same way she did at Cana. Jesus hears His mother's voice supporting the voice of the family.

With Mary we have a good teacher, a good companion and a good counselor. With her eyes we see better; with her hands we knock louder; with her we will not be lost. She knows the way. Her faith becomes ours. Her adoration of God becomes ours. Her prayer becomes ours. Her purity, her peace, her sureness become ours.

If we entrust ourselves to her, she can do no less for us.

Innumerable incidents showing the effects of the Crusade upon families in Caracas were reported to Crusade workers. One mother was so moved by the action of her young daughter that she told Monsignor Cayetano about it.

This woman's older daughter had been enticed into a leftist group at the university she attended and had refused to take part in the family Rosary.

One day, the girl's little sister placed a doll in the center of the family prayer circle. "This is no time for playing with dolls," her mother rebuked her.

"Oh no, Mommy, Daddy," replied the child. "I am not here to play with the doll. I'm asking the doll to take my sister's place so that God and the Virgin Mary will protect her."

The thousands of volunteers visited the homes during pledge week after the rally. One day Father Peyton accompanied a group to a ghetto neighborhood.

As Father Peyton headed for one poor hut, the team captain exclaimed, "No, you cannot go in there," in Spanish, followed with such a barrage of words that Father Peyton could not understand half of them.

"Why can't I go in there?" he asked.

An English-speaking aide translated, "This is a Communist neighborhood. You would get a cold reception." The man might be, he explained, a leader of incitement against the Church and the government.

After listening reflectively to the aide's explanation, Father Peyton went and knocked on the door of the hut. A man opened the door and reluctantly stepped back and let him pass into the hut.

Half an hour later Father Peyton came out and called for a photographer from the group. The man came out, carrying in his arms a little child holding a Rosary and followed by his bedraggled wife, smiling timidly. They posed with Father Peyton for a picture.

"How did you do it? What did you say to them?" members of the group asked in astonishment as they turned away. The men knew the Communist leaders had become bolder in the past three months, since the failure of the Bay of Pigs invasion of Cuba supported by the United States. The arrest of priests and their flight from Cuba after their release had also emboldened these leaders to be more and more outspoken against the Church.

Father Peyton's answer was a radiant smile. "I just prayed with him," he said in a tone which bespoke the outcome inevitable, "for himself, for his wife, for his children. I invited Mary into the little home. She came and we all prayed together to her Beloved Son Jesus and thanked Him for saving us and thanked God for giving us life and for giving the man his beautiful wife and entrusting the beautiful souls of his little children to him. I did not change him. Mary's prayers did that."

A few weeks later, Father Peyton learned that the man had become a leader in promoting a Christian life.

President John F. Kennedy's response to the growing Communist influence in Latin America, sparked by the increasingly apparent Cuban-Russian affiliation, was to move swiftly in creating the Alliance for Progress. In August of 1961 the agreement was signed with specific provisions for aid and trade with Latin American countries.

Toward the end of that year there was no longer any doubt about Cuba's direction. The world had the answer it was waiting for: Fidel Castro said publicly on December 2, 1961, "I am a Marxist-Leninist, and I will be a Marxist-Leninist until the last day of my life."

A letter from Pope John XXIII dated the sixth of May, 1961, reached Father Peyton in Caracas. Reading Pope John's words, Father Peyton felt deep humility and gratitude for the role God had given him. He read:

> In the beginning of this month, which is dedicated in a very special way to devotion to the Most Holy Virgin, it is particularly gratifying to Us to reiterate to you Our expression of affection, to maintain your courage on the long journey which your zealous priestly ministry has undertaken to spread devotion to Mary, and which, after the fruitful days in Chile, you are now carrying out in Venezuela.

> We are convinced that the true piety to Mary, in which the recitation of the Holy Rosary takes precedence, besides contributing towards an intensification of the religious life of the faithful, can and should make them—as your own characteristic method of preaching shows and your experiences prove to be efficacious collaborators in the various branches of the Apostolate under the guidance of the Pastors of souls, who represent the authority of God, to Whom so fruitfully and humbly the Word Incarnate and the Virgin Mary submitted themselves.

174

In fact, whoever meditates on the Mysteries of the Rosary and contemplates the examples of total sacrifice and boundless charity proffered by Our Lord Jesus Christ and His Mother in their supreme ideal of glorifying God and saving the world, must feel impelled to orientate his life in such a way that the sublime message of the *Our Father* and the *Hail Mary*, as well as the benefits of the Annunciation, Calvary and Pentecost, may reach the greatest possible number of souls abundantly and rapidly.

Zeal is the natural consequence of a completely fulfilled devotion to Mary; a true Christian, conscious of the exigencies of this title and in love with the prerogatives and the triumph of Mary, must not content himself with a position of selfish piety in which he is concerned only with his own good, when his Faith tells him that there are others who are his brothers to whom perhaps it is necessary to teach the truths that are interwoven in the Gospel scenes of Nazareth, Bethlehem and Jerusalem, in order to impress upon them the neéd to know how to take advantage of the inexhaustible graces obtained there for the human race.

Multitude at the Golden Gate

Father Peyton had a date to keep in San Francisco. The Crusade team was busy preparing for the next Latin American Crusade in Bogotá, Colombia, and getting ready to move after that into the vast country of Brazil.

Word came from the Hollywood office that officials in San Francisco wanted the rally held in a small stadium. They believed the time was past when the Rosary priest could attract such huge crowds as he had done before. People were no longer interested in the Rosary, they said, and not many would come. They did not want Father Peyton to appear to fail. Even his own helpers advised against a large rally site for fear of embarrassment to him.

Father Peyton flew to San Francisco. He wanted the Golden Gate polo field which holds half a million people.

"I'm not thinking about myself. I'm thinking about Our Blessed Mother," he told the officials. "And she won't be satisfied with less than half a million."

More than half a million people spilled out of the polo fields into the park for the rally on October 7, 1961. It was reported by the newspapers as the largest crowd that had ever gathered in the park.

Father Peyton was flown to the rally site by helicopter, with the bishop's representative, the mayor and the governor of California.

The music, the pageantry, the speeches by dignitaries built an anticipation in the crowd for the main event. Then Father Peyton, waving Rosary beads in the air, began his eloquently simple plea for the unity and salvation of families through daily family prayer.

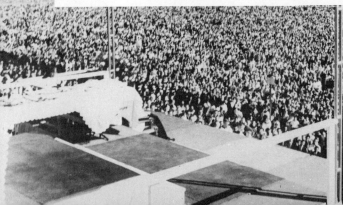

Conflict is everywhere today—between nation and nation, neighbor and neighbor, employer and worker. These conflicts bring so many pressures and problems into the homes that families cannot cope and are split and disunited by them.

Families are devastated. The husband and wife do not have the time or inclination to talk to each other. The husband does not respect the wife and sometimes even beats her and the children. The parents escape into alcoholism, unfaithfulness, separation and divorce.

The parents say, "We cannot live together. We will break up this union and be free of each other. We will break up our home. The little ones God has given us—let God be worried about them. They will not stop us from having our way."

Sometimes the parents try to cope with the children by giving them every material thing they can, and it seems the more they give, the more the children demand and the more problems arise. The children do not respect the parents. They turn to outside sources for the love that is lacking in the home—seeking an identity with a new breed of companions, in fad causes, untried values, drugs or even crime. The young people waste their time in asking, "Who am I? Who put me here? Where am I going?"

The parents seek outside solutions to the problems of the family—in pscychiatry, sociology, meetings for better family living, government commissions and agencies. And all of these do not solve the problems. They ignore the obvious answer—that is, God's answer. They do not give the children love and spirituality.

Families cannot exist without love. If the family breaks down, civilization as we know it cannot exist. The family is the basic unit of society. Society has to depend upon families to be fed and replaced. As families go, so goes society. Families must be saved.

It is the love of God as a family that is lacking in the home. The love of God strengthens the love of one for the other. Only God can save families.

Daily family prayer brings God back into the home. If you ask, He will be there. But you have to ask. God gave you the freedom to choose.

When a family prays as a family, they are pooling their spiritual resources to get God's attention. Together they are knocking on God's door and calling to him.

Two hands knocking on a door are stronger than one, and four are stronger than two. When two or more are knocking together on the door of a neighbor and crying out for a loaf of bread, the man inside is going to hear the din more than if it was one tiny little knock and one little voice. When it's the whole family knocking and the whole family asking, the man inside cannot help but answer. It works for prayer too.

When a family prays together, the whole family benefits. It doesn't mean there won't be conflicts because there will. But when you talk together to God, all of a sudden the troubles, differences, strains, annoyances disappear, and you begin to be a family again in love and unity.

Family prayer can help the unbeliever too. Even if you have to say to God, "We're not sure if You're alive and it isn't our fault. But if You're alive, will you help us because everything else has failed." That family has a good chance of winning because they're honest.

It's the beginning to pray together that's hard. The man would wonder, "What will my wife think of me, the great macho man, on his knees praying?" The mother would say, "My husband will laugh at me if I ask him to pray with me. We do a million and one things together, but God help us if we're seen together with our own children in our own home praying to the God who's given us everything we have. We're shy or embarrassed. But we can overcome the difficulty. Once we begin, family prayer can be an easy and normal part of family living."

You can pray in the position you are most comfortable. You can kneel down, stand or sit, whichever way you wish. It is the prayer that is important.

A structured prayer is best for the family praying together. Spontaneous prayer is becoming more popular today, and that is beautiful for it reveals the deepest yearning of the heart. It is not a question of one or the other. Indeed we need both. But for a family to attempt spontaneous prayer might not be as effective. Not everyone finds it easy to pray spontaneously, especially in a group. Some might impose their will upon the others, and some might not participate at all because they are shy or inhibited. The structured prayer is the staple for the soul as the bread is the staple for the body.

The Rosary is a Christian prayer, not just a Catholic monopoly. It is Christ-oriented and is scripturally inspired. The Rosary can be prayed by anybody that believes in Christ's divinity.

The "*Our Father*" prayed at the beginning of each decade is

Christ's own prayer, given by Him to His disciples when they asked Him how they should pray.

When we say, "*Hail Mary, full of grace, the Lord is with thee,*" we're speaking the words of the messenger of God. We're repeating her cousin Elizabeth's greeting when we say, "*Blessed art thou among women, and blessed is the fruit of thy womb.*" In "*Holy Mary, Mother of God,*" we tell Mary that we believe her Son is our God and we honor her for it. We admit our weaknesses and ask the Mother of God to "*pray for us now and at the hour of our death.*"

Non-Christians could not pray the Rosary, but they could pray the prayers of their faith. They can read Scripture. Anybody can read the Bible. Daily family prayer is not a luxury, but an absolute necessity, if families are to survive. God created a beautiful world but left the management to us and we have made a mess of it and brought down upon ourselves disorder and chaos. We can turn it around by saving families.

Soon after the San Francisco rally, Father Peyton was back in an airplane headed for Bogotá, where he would spend the rest of 1961 and half of 1962, with intermittent visits to Brazil to prepare for the Crusade there to begin in the fall of 1962.

A million people attended the rally in Bogotá, the one mass rally in Colombia, on March 25, 1962.

Anniversary in starlight

Father Germain-Marie Lalande stood in the receiving line between Father DePrizio and Father Peyton at the Beverly Hilton Hotel in Hollywood. He shook hands as the glittering parade of party-goers continued to file past into the international ballroom with leading ladies and men and other notables of the movie world, giants of industry, social and political and other leaders and many distinguished clergy.

Father Lalande watched in growing amazement as bejeweled and bedecked ladies greeted Father Peyton with hugs and some with light kisses. The superior general, who had only little more than a month earlier succeeded Father O'Toole as head of the Congregatio Sanctae Crucis, turned a face marked with bewilderment toward Father DePrizio.

Father DePrizio, who had been watching his superior's surprise in quiet amusement, shrugged his shoulders and explained, "*C'est la vie chez nous*—That's the way life is around here. It's the way Hollywood stars always act," he continued in French, to show their affection and gratitude toward those they love.

The dinner-party was a celebration given by his friends of the twentieth anniversary year of Father Peyton's Family Rosary Crusade. The actor Jack Haley, beloved "Tin Man" who wanted a heart in *The Wizard of Oz*, was the chairman. The glamorous Rosalind Russell was chairwoman. Danny Thomas was master of ceremonies, and many other film personalities added their talents to the event.

Father Peyton was surrounded by supporters who had played leading roles and bit parts in the events of those twenty years, and even before. The specific anniversary date he considered as the beginning of his work was the last Sunday in January, the day of his inspiration in 1942.

The ballroom seated fifteen hundred people and it was filled to capacity. The assemblage included fifteen hosts representing the fifteen Mysteries of the Rosary. Each had purchased one hundred tickets at one hundred dollars apiece. "I get The Annunciation," Jack Haley had said.

Father Lalande, seated at the head table, relaxed and enjoyed the entertainment by one Hollywood star after another. He was moved by the tributes to Father Peyton by one speaker after another as the evening grew old. Eleven o'clock came. A half hour later tributes were still being given. Father Peyton, billed as principal speaker, had not yet spoken.

It was twenty minutes to midnight when Father Peyton finally rose to speak. The crowded room grew quiet. Not a whisper or a rustle disturbed the sound of his voice. Even the waiters, anxious to end the night's work, stopped moving about to listen to the words giving new insights into God's plan, new meanings to family life and family prayer, a depth of understanding of the Rosary they had never known before, painting a vision of Mary the Mother of God as a real woman, giving them hope and inspiration.

"I know. I lived it." The oft-repeated words prefaced the story of the events that had led to his mission.

"God gave me the grace to know how I would respond to Our Blessed Mother's love, to her hopes of me, to her expectations that I would do my share.

"God has given me that beautiful grace to walk beside her and say everything I have is yours; you cannot do less for me; everything you have must be mine—your purity, your wisdom, your strength of prayer, your love of all mankind—to help me reach the destiny that God wants of me as he wanted of you. Total surrender to Mary is the secret of my happiness, my sureness, my security. It will be yours if you ask her.

"That is the grace that God has given me all these years—to have no other thought, no other purpose, but just to tell the world that Mary is a woman who could not say 'no' to God the Father when he gave her the first role as the Mother of God and who cannot say 'no' to Jesus Christ who gave her the second role as the Blessed Mother of all humanity.

"That is the mission that God gave me—to have the privilege of helping His Blessed Mother in fulfilling her second role by going among all people and bringing families to her to lead souls back to God."

When he finished speaking well after midnight, it was a full minute before the crowd reoriented itself and the waiters began their swift movements. The ballroom became bedlam as people crowded about the head table to speak to Father Peyton.

He was up early as usual the next morning saying his Mass and praying his gratitude. He got little rest as he visited with friends and benefactors and prepared to return to Latin America. The first rally in Brazil was just seven days away in Recife, the capital of the state of Pernambuco in the impoverished northeastern part of the country. Soon he and the copy of the Murillo Madonna that he always carried in his suitcase were again aboard a plane, bound for Brazil.

Crusade in Rio

"Even the army couldn't do it," one parish priest had remonstrated at Father Peyton's request during the preparatory work in Rio. "You couldn't get two men in the whole diocese to volunteer for anything religious."

"Maybe the army couldn't do it," Father Peyton smiled in response. "But you just watch Our Lady recruit an army for the Crusade." He had asked the priest and other parish priests to recruit hundreds of men from the various sections of their parishes to run the Popular Mission. As in Chile, the skeptical had been astonished at his request for technicians and speakers.

"They are simple workers," one had replied. "How can you get them to run machinery and preach? They have no skills."

But the system developed in Chile worked again. At the end of the training in Rio, one hundred and thirty-three technicians and three hundred and forty-nine speakers received diplomas.

Father Peyton had met even greater skepticism when he told the bishops he needed thousands of men to volunteer for pledge week to call upon every family in their diocese. He had adamantly refused suggestions that he try for women, because, he had said, "It is the men who practice no religion that we have got to get involved."

As usual the women had been easier to recruit. They did their task, visiting every home a few days before the films to invite families.

The Crusade team had been faced in the beginning with either limiting the film sites in Rio or obtaining more equipment. Father Peyton had done the only thing he considered logical. He approached a wealthy friend for a gift of a quarter of a million dollars. He obtained the money from his friend and others. Twenty tons of equipment, including sixty-four projectors, were used in Rio.

The publicity, the personal contacts and the school program all combined to attract people to the film showings. One mother told a Crusade worker about her little girl who had come home from school with her fist clenched about a piece of paper. She said she had a secret. The child refused to show the paper or go to bed until her daddy came home. Returning late, the father was so touched by his little girl's appeal that he knelt and said the words of the prayer on the paper that she had brought home from school to teach him. And he went to the church with his family the following Sunday. A Jewish lady attending the nightly movies reported she had been so moved by them that she had begun the practice of family recitation of the Psalms.

The fifteen thousand Masses and five thousand holy hour services of the Crusade in Rio had received their answer. Estimates placed attendance at the films at two million and one hundred and ninety-seven thousand, almost the total three million population of Rio. So powerful was the films' impact that the thousands of men needed volunteered to obtain the pledges for daily family Rosary.

Father DePrizio arrived in Rio a few days before the Crusade rally scheduled for December 16, 1962. Reports of the Crusade in Latin America had been so astounding that he wanted to see for himself what was going on.

As he hurried out of the airport building the first sight that greeted him was a huge billboard proclaiming in Portuguese, "The Family That Prays Together Stays Together." As he made his way to the residence of the priests, it was just one poster after another, billboards, electric signs—all repeating the slogan. It was inescapable. Rio was being told in plain words that the solution to family peace and family stability was family prayer.

Later in the evening he saw the famous statue of Christ high on Corcovado Mountain. There Father Phil Higgins and Father Joe Quinn had accomplished the impossible, placing an illuminated Rosary around the neck of the statue. The white and blue lights around the statue of the Sacred Heart might have raised liturgical eyebrows. But Father DePrizio was told Rio was awed by it—and loved it. It was the first time in Brazilian memory that anything had been hung from the statue.

Soon after his arrival, Father DePrizio was taken to the Crusade's headquarters in Rio. He later recalled his experiences there:

Since the staff for the Rio rally was so large, it was necessary to establish two offices in separate office buildings both located in the heart of this great city. Just visiting these offices and watching the teams of workers was in itself an unusual and quasi-exhausting experience.

Understand, of course, that it was the eleventh hour and all the last-minute preparations were being made. Our Lady's statue dominated the scene. And indeed she appeared like a great hostess arranging a grand party to which a million people had been invited. There was much to be done. The typewriters were going like mad, the telephones ringing in a curious symphony—and all the while there was a coming and going of reporters, clerics, lay workers, nuns, artists, electricians and a lot of uncategorized people bobbing in and out to offer their services. Now and then someone would proclaim, "I haven't had a bite to eat since breakfast." This would be followed by gulping down of coffee hastily proffered, and biting off a sandwich while continuing to work.

It seemed at first like a mad whirl. Yet it had rhyme and reason for it was clear that rising out of the multitude of details, the effect desired was being achieved. A great change was taking place in Rio. The city was literally being hypnotized into activity for Our Lady and her rally. From this office, strange and mysterious tentacles seemed to reach out encircling statesmen in government offices, police and firemen, politicians, society ladies and debutantes...no matter who they were or where, they were all responding to Father Peyton's inexorable rule that no talent, energy or skill should go unharnessed if it would serve Our Lady's cause.

And so it was that even a visiting provincial was summoned into duty. I found myself carrying armfuls of packages containing rally programs from one room to another where they were being prepared for distribution. One of Rio's outstanding citizens, a financier, was doing the same thing. And a small and humble monsignor had the piping on his robes all covered with dust as he, too, handed packages to secretaries and answered questions about some of the bishops expected for the rally.

One afternoon, at the height of all this labor, Father Peyton, who had been working away in his private office, suddenly appeared and announced that we would all make a holy hour. Instantly, everyone—priests, secular missionaries, laymen and laywomen, prelates and peasants, dropped whatever they were doing and proceeded to climb the stairs leading to the top story of this modern office building (owned by the diocese) where there was a small chapel. And as Father Pat saluted the Queen of Heaven with his fervent *Hail Marys* and we responded, tired but happy, one could reflect that here indeed was the real power of the Crusade rally—here in these moments of prayer...

On Friday afternoon preceding the rally a press conference was arranged by Father Joe Quinn. You may be sure this was no ordinary press conference. First of all, it was held in the large sacristy of the famous church called "Candelaria," one of the oldest and most beautiful in Rio. In a setting of handsome murals and sacred paintings reporters appeared from the best newspapers and magazines of Brazil, all anxious to interview Father Peyton. Then another unique feature. After a brief introduction by Father Quinn, Father Peyton took over. "I want to start with a Hail Mary," he told them. And suddenly the newsmen and journalists found themselves praying. That set the note for the entire conference.

Father Peyton spoke to them in Spanish, a tolerably good Spanish with overtones of County Mayo. He held these men and women enthralled as he told them of his life, the reason for his dedication to Our Lady and the aims of the Crusade. At one point he started to name the many Hollywood actors and actresses who had so generously responded to his appeal, giving their time and talent to Our Lady's cause. You could see the pencils flying and the startled faces registering degrees of amazement.

Immediately after the conference, we went outside to greet the crowd that had gathered. Four fire trucks with hook and ladder equipment had arrived during the conference to mount a huge banner of Our Lady which had been specially painted for the rally—to hang over the crowd during the program. Thousands gathered to watch men in mid-air unfolding Our Lady's image. All this had the thrill of a trapeze stunt and it didn't hurt the cause one bit. In the surrounding office buildings hundreds of workers left their duties to stare out of the windows. It was a miniature rally in itself—attracting the attention of a good part of the city, stopping traffic and building up enthusiasm for Sunday's event.

Sunday, the day of the rally started off like *dies illa, dies irae.*
There was a great heat and a multitude of new problems had
sprung up overnight. Father Joe Quinn and Father Phil Higgins
got no sleep that night. Father Pat himself spent most of the time
clutching his Rosary and praying for the success of the rally.

Early afternoon, as we rode to the rally grounds, we could not
help but remark the change in weather. From an intense
heat—suddenly we felt a cool breeze. When we reached the rally
area another fact hit us. The Brazilian sun had completely disappeared. What a great boon to have a cool breeze and no sun.
Otherwise the usual Brazilian heat would have smothered the
crowd. We echoed Father Peyton's joyful thanks to Our Lady for
providing just the right weather at the right time.

Almost two hours before the scheduled event and already a
great crowd had gathered. Perhaps a hundred thousand people
were waiting. Father Peyton went immediately into the nearby
church to pray. About three-thirty, a half hour or so before the

187

rally time, I went in to report to him. "There must be at least a half million people." "Thank God," he whispered between *Hail Mary's*, "that's good—Brazilians come late. We'll have a million, I'm sure, when the time comes."

And a million he did have—for by four o'clock the crowd was immense. When I mounted the high tribune erected on the main avenue of the city and looked out into the crowd, I felt that only on judgment day would I once again witness such a vast assembly. People—people—people. As far as the human eye could see. It seemed that all of Rio was there. A short distance away the famous Copacabana beach was almost deserted. And the huge city that a short time before was tingling with its *bosa nova* and doing its *samba*, quieted down and turned to Mary...turned to prayer as five representative families led the multitude in the five Glorious Mysteries of the Rosary...and turned to listen to Mary's apostle as he electrified the crowd. For forty minutes Father Pat pleaded Mary's cause for Family Prayer.

I shall never forget the image of this man of God and Mary holding a million and more people with his strong simple words. There were moments when it seemed his very heart would break and all his love and affection and tenderness for Our Lady would spill out and engulf that mob. There were moments, too, when he seemed like a great prophet, not a prophet of doom, but a prophet promising peace and blessing through Mary and family prayer.

All of a sudden it was over. The cardinal rose to express his gratitude and the crowd sang a hymn to Our Lady, and then the national anthem was sung as it has never been sung before...When Father Peyton descended from the high stage it was necessary to call the police to protect him. Thousands surged forward trying to touch his cassock, pleading for his blessing and prayer.

Minutes later, Father Peyton was in the church again before the high altar. I went to congratulate him. He said, "Tell the priests and missionaries to come at once for a holy hour of thanksgiving." And there in all the sweat and exhaustion of his massive frame he poured out his thanks to God and Our Lady. For the next three days the entire staff of priests and secular missionaries gathered with Father Pat for a holy hour at a church dedicated to Our Lady of Glory.

Newsmen described the Crusade as a religious awakening, a miracle of faith, a unifying force for all Brazilians and in other glowing terms. One report called it "not a religious revival, but a religious revolution."

Father Peyton had accomplished what most of the bishops and priests had told him couldn't be done.

During the Rio Crusade Father Peyton received an invitation to visit President João Goulart. He and Father Quinn made the journey to the presidential palace in the capital, Brasilia. Father Peyton gave a Rosary to Goulart as the government's official photographer's cameras clicked. The next day the picture appeared on the front pages of all of Brazil's major newspapers. Some leading Catholics protested to Father Peyton that Goulart cared nothing for the Rosary and was using him to mislead the public and promote himself, that Father Peyton had been led like a lamb to the slaughter.

Father Peyton assured them the Crusade was under the protection of Mary and that she would never allow its misuse. "Whoever uses the Crusade for selfish personal profit," he said to one Catholic leader, "will have to answer to Mary, not just to this naive Father Peyton, but to his boss."

That same December, on the eighth, the feast of the Immaculate Conception was celebrated as Family Day in Caracas and in Bogotá. These celebrations were planned and carried out by a post-Crusade organization formed by the trained leaders and personnel from the original organization.

The post-Crusade organization in Rio de Janeiro in 1963 asked President Goulart to proclaim the feast of the Immaculate Conception as a national celebration of "Family Day." With all the fervor generated by the Crusade, Goulart could not refuse. He proclaimed December 8 "Family Day" for all Brazil.

It featured an hour-long national television and radio broadcast, with a prominent family and individuals reciting the Rosary. In a unique and unprecedented appearance, Pope Paul VI gave a Christmas message on a national broadcast via previously prepared video and audio tape. That "Family Day" was a landmark in the history of the Crusade.

Father Peyton's dream of permanence for the Crusade was beginning to take shape.

He had a new inspiration to bring about this permanence by the establishment of satellite Crusade bases in key locations to serve all parts of the world as a Global Crusade. He dreamed of manning them with dedicated and devoted priests and nuns whom he would recruit. He dreamed of support for them by the cardinals and bishops and businessmen and other leaders. They would operate under the guidance of the Family Rosary Crusade and with materials furnished by Family Theater. The Rosary Films would be one of the most effective tools of the Crusade satellite bases.

The films were dubbed in other languages and eventually became available in English, Spanish, French, German, Portuguese, Italian, Flemish, Japanese, Korean and the Indian dialects of Quechua and Aymara.

Bubbling cauldrons of Brazil

Brazil was at a critical crossroads when the Family Rosary Crusade arrived there. The head of government was secretly planning the demise of the constitutional democracy.

Communists stirred the cauldrons of the nation's troubles brewing revolution. President João Goulart was an ambitious man. He schemed to use the radical left to destroy the legal democracy and replace it with dictatorship under his rule, through which he expected to grab personal wealth and total power. He made deals with Russia and fulfilled his part of the bargain by appointing undercover Communist agents to key government positions.

Goulart, nicknamed Jango, was not an elected president. He had been vice president, by a fluke, and had assumed the presidency in 1961 upon the resignation of his predecessor.

As in other Latin American countries, Brazil's large landowners controlled most of the power and the wealth and the poor worked for them. But latifundia was modified in Brazil by the existence of a growing middle class of business and professional men born of growing industrialization.

In late 1961 a group of middle class Rio businessmen, their suspicions aroused by rumor, got together and investigated Communist infiltration. They were alarmed at the previously unsuspected extent of it. They identified as Communists officials in positions to paralyze the country and take over the government. They uncovered corruption by government officials including Goulart. Businessmen from other cities joined the Rio investigators and formed affiliated groups in their own cities.

As owners of small businesses and property, the middle class favored a democratic system of government. They made alliances with other groups, including officers of the military. The officers, drawn from the upper and middle classes, were loyal to their own peer groups, to whom they owed their rank.

These respected citizens of Brazil had to work undercover against their government. When they tried to expose the Communists and Goulart's complicity, they met swift reprisals.

The country was torn by strikes, and the universities were already committed to the radicals. The country was in chaos.

The openness of the propaganda convinced Brazilians that it was only a matter of time before the outbreak of civil war. Terrorist attacks by guerrilla bands trained by Havana portended the imminence of the revolution. Brazilians expected it to be a bloody one, with strong Cuban leadership. They watched, helplessly fascinated, as their president played Russian roulette with their constitutional democracy.

The middle-class wives, feeling the security of their families threatened, took a hand in mid-1962. Less vulnerable to reprisal, they could operate openly. On June 15, five hundred women invaded the offices of *O Globo* to protest Goulart's appointment of Hermes Lima as prime minister. The next day the newspaper's headlines exposed Lima as a pro-Castro socialist.

The women's groups, growing in number throughout Brazil, concentrated on the working classes. They asked the wives of stevedores and other laborers to work on their husbands.

A washerwoman who asked help in organizing a group in her Rio slum told of Communists bringing pro-Communist primers and movies of Castro's guerrillas on the pretext of bringing education and recreation to the poor. The women's movement countered by establishing day care centers and classes in reading, nutrition, health care and other basic subjects among the poor.

When the media were forced to deny them publicity, the women substituted a letter-writing campaign to expose the identities of officials and candidates for congress who were Communist. When their mailings were refused, they turned to hand-delivery, using their own cars and cooperative drivers of taxis and buses and airplane pilots.

Father Peyton had not been long in Brazil before he discovered the truth of what one pastor told him: "We have four classes in Brazil—the wealthy, the middle class, the poor and the miserable." In Recife, in Rio, he found some of the economically and spiritually poorest people in the world. Around the Rio dumps he saw some of the "miserables" pawing through garbage for scraps of food. He visited them in their sheds of junk amidst the all-pervading stench. He told these wretches that they were as dear, as loved, by the same God, the same Jesus and the same Blessed Mother Mary as any others, that they had the same opportunity as any for eternal life. Some welcomed his words as they welcomed death as the only escape from their wretchedness.

To the poor, to the middle classes who were only a step above them with low incomes consumed by skyrocketing inflation, and to the aristocracy, Father Peyton brought the same message, in the same words and in the same loving manner. Their political affiliations did not concern him. There were no inequities among souls. He could not alter their material lives, but he could tell them how to appeal to their Blessed Mother for help.

Three cities of Brazil were scheduled to have the Crusade in

1963. Although the schedule would be a heavy one, Father Peyton had to take time for a quick visit to Spain. He had an important meeting there on January 29 to begin plans for a Crusade in Madrid. He decided to take Father Quinn along and leave him in Madrid to follow up on the meeting.

In the government building in the heart of downtown Madrid Luis Carrero Blanco spent the few free minutes before his next appointment looking over the timetable for the coming year of celebration in Spain. He was soon joined in his office by Antonio de Oriol y Urquijo.

"Father Peyton has arrived," the secretary announced a few minutes later, opening the door to admit the two black-suited priests. The old friends embraced one another affectionately. No sooner were the greetings over than Father Peyton said, "I want to say a little prayer for you before we talk." He launched at once into a *Memorare*, then asked Our Lady for her help in their joint venture and her continued protection for his dear friends Louis Carrero Blanco and Antonio de Oriol and their families and all the people of Spain. He asked the others to pray a *Hail Mary* with him. Seated around the large conference table, they all prayed together—Father Peyton, Father Quinn and the prime minister and the minister of justice of Spain.

As soon as the prayers were finished, Prime Minister Carrero Blanco told the others, "This is the second time today I have prayed for the success of the great Crusade in Madrid. I prayed for it also this morning at Mass." It was his practice to serve the Mass, which his family attended, each morning at the Church of San Francisco de Borja.

Father Peyton had some time previously accepted the invitation of the archbishop to bring the Crusade to Madrid. The Spanish officials wanted to do all they could to insure the full benefits of the Crusade, which they planned for 1964 to coincide with the year-long celebration of the twenty-fifth anniversary of Generalissimo Francisco Franco's victory in the Spanish civil war.

The two officials and the two priests agreed that a day in Mary's month of May would be an appropriate date for the rally. The officials would obtain the permissions to hold the rally in the Avenida Generalissimo Francisco Franco and to erect the stage over its broad concourse.

"How much money do you think you will need to conduct the Crusade here?" Antonio de Oriol asked. Father Peyton had no idea but made a quick guess and answered "Ten thousand dollars." The officials proposed that they would raise the money from among their wealthy friends. As it turned out later, de Oriol had to greatly intensify his fund-raising, for the expenses grew to several times Father Peyton's guess.

Father Peyton found an eager press awaiting him when he returned to Brazil. Reporters sought him out everywhere he stopped. This Rosary priest who was attracting larger crowds than had ever been seen before in Brazil and who was stirring up such a torrent of prayer was a unique personality. This Father Peyton was news.

Through press reports and accounts of individuals, the power and benefits of the Rosary circulated among the public and stirred people to prayer in many places even before the Crusade arrived. Devotion to the Blessed Mother was the one common denominator that could cut across all class lines in Latin America. But although all classes prayed the Rosary, many had never been taught the scriptural symbolism. Many, and not just the poor, learned these for the first time in their lives through the Crusade. Commentators credited the Crusade with uniting the Brazilian people in a massive awakening of faith.

Father Peyton had some months previous answered the invitations of the bishops with preliminary visits to them in the three cities separated by a total distance of about two thousand miles—in the eastern coastal city of Salvador de Bahia, south of it to Belo Horizonte, the capital of the state of Minas Gerais, and south again to Porto Alegre, in Rio Grande do Sul, where Leonel Brizola, Goulart's brother-in-law and chief spokesman, was governor. In February, 1963, shortly before the arrival of the Crusade team in Belo Horizonte, Brizola was scheduled to address a workers' union dominated by Communists. A couple of hours before the appointed time, the women of Belo Horizonte prevented the speech by marching with their Rosaries and filling the assembly hall with their prayers.

The advance Crusade team arrived shortly after these incidents. They found a populace eager to welcome them. Spacious rooms downtown were donated as an office and blessed and opened on March 14. The first task of recruitment of women to visit the homes before the film showings was made easy by the mood of the women.

After five weeks of preparation, the Crusade began with the

Popular Mission on April 8. One hundred and eighty five volunteer speakers and an equal number of volunteer technicians provided the manpower. Total attendance for all of the film showings was estimated by the press as almost two million.

"If I had such mechanical priests," said the pastor of a large parish to Father Peyton, speaking of the film equipment, "I would have no trouble teaching the faith to all my parish."

"I am hoping to have five hundred of them in your country," Father Peyton replied. He was even then working on a plan for a post-Crusade program in Brazil.

Ten days before the rally posters and banners went up all over the city. Six hundred thousand people attended the rally on June 16. Thousands of men worked as volunteers the following week to obtain pledges for daily family Rosary. The same efficient operation brought six hundred thousand to the rally at Salvador de Bahia and half a million at Porto Alegre.

During this period a letter came from Pope Paul VI, dated September 13, 1963, bringing much encouragement to Father Peyton. The Holy Father wrote:

As the month of October, dedicated to the Queen of the Most Holy Rosary, draws near, We desire to recall the exhortation given by Saint Bernard to the faithful, urging them to turn prayerfully to the Blessed Virgin, particularly in times of spiritual or material dangers (homil, 2, super "Missus est", circa finem). The counsel of this great Doctor of the Church was founded on a pious practice dating back to the first centuries, when the Christians would raise their hearts and minds to the Queen of heaven, by prayers and hymns, on festive occasions, as well as when they were exposed to trials and tribulations; and their supplications were never in vain.

You, beloved son, mindful of this ancient devotion to the Blessed Mother, and with great confidence in her powerful protection, founded the Family Rosary Crusade in 1942. Those were the days when the world was particularly afflicted not only by extreme material dangers but by moral evils as well. You strove to alleviate the sufferings of families, as you likewise do today, by making known to them the necessity, the power and the ease of prayer, especially that of the Rosary.

We are pleased to note that in the past twenty-one years, the Family Rosary Crusade has carried the message of family prayer to the peoples of thirty-two countries, bringing together approximately twenty million persons. To achieve the lofty aims of the

Crusade, you and your talented collaborators have used the mass media of communications effectively; and, the fifteen films and the radio series that tell the story of the fifteen Mysteries of the Rosary are indeed worthy of praise.

We cherish the prayerful hope that the zealous endeavours of the Family Rosary Crusade may be productive of ever more abundant spiritual fruits. In pledge thereof, We cordially impart to you, beloved son, and to all those who assist you in promoting devotion to the Queen of the Most Holy Rosary, Our special Apostolic Benediction.

Paulus P.P. VI

Redemption of Brazil

The Crusade team began work February 11, 1964, in the Archdiocese of São Paulo, the biggest archdiocese in the world with five million people in the city and another million in the suburbs and distant hinterlands.

In the city, the biggest in Brazil and the second largest in South America, they found an urban center of production and wealth and of sharp contrasts. Shopping centers, viaducts connecting main thoroughfares and the clean line of skyscrapers contrasted with ancient museums and churches. It was a city of business executives and street beggars, of pollution, crime and traffic congestion.

The shortage of priests was staggering. They could not even begin to reach their flocks with even the most basic religious teaching. One parish of one hundred and thirty thousand people, the largest in the world, was served by only one priest. Some parishes were without a priest. Only one hundred and twenty five priests served the entire diocese of six million people.

If the Crusade could be brought to these people, it would be the first religious movement most had ever experienced. It was obvious that only by recruiting many volunteers could the Crusade reach them at all.

The archdiocese was divided into six sectors and subdivided again and again into workable units for the Popular Mission. Despite difficulties, they were able to build the corps of laymen and women needed for the film showings.

The religious, business and social leaders whose help Father Peyton had enlisted were anxious to see the Crusade a success. They were acutely aware of the many problems of Brazil, with all of their moral, social and political implications.

The numbers of the poor were growing faster than any material aid could be brought to them. Their conditions were a blight upon and a danger to all Brazil. Some observers said it would be two or three generations before any improvement could be expected in the lives of the poor.

Listening to Father Peyton's view, the leaders began to see a ray of hope, that his mission could help. Some thought it could help solve the problems of the poor, while others, it is true, thought it might quiet the masses.

Father Peyton told them that these families were victims of poverty and its offspring of malnutrition and hunger, low morals, sickness, vice, high infant mortality and early death, juvenile and adult crime, illiteracy, lack of spirituality, irresponsibility and desertion by fathers, indifference and antagonism toward religion.

These shabby and disorganized families are the weak building blocks of their society. The sickness of one individual spread through the family in crowded unsanitary living conditions. The disease of families becomes the epidemics of communities. Moral decay is passed from individuals to society and back in the same way.

Since the basic problem of poor families was a moral one, Father Peyton told them, the basic solution was a religious one.

By strengthening the moral fiber of families, he said, we can strengthen their society to bring about their own improvement in self-help—cooperative learning and services. The poor, however, lacked the values for motivation to improve their own lives. Whatever leadership they had was either untrained and without resources or trained in fomenting chaos.

Father Peyton's answer was as old in its content as the missions of the apostles and as new in its approach as Vatican Council II, then in progress in Rome. Only a strong spiritual force could give the poor the spirituality and morality needed for the unity of families.

The daily family Rosary was that strong spiritual force. And Father Peyton had the organization to provide the resources and leadership to bring the desire for family unity and the means of obtaining it to families.

Father Peyton's sense of urgency was communicated to all who listened to him. Even in the midst of this great need, he was confronted by other tasks and worked with little rest to perform them. He dozed on all-night airplane journeys and in airport waiting rooms as he went back and forth to Rome to bring the importance of family Rosary to the attention of the fathers of Vatican Council II. It was during one of these sojourns in Rome in 1964 that Father Peyton received news of the death on February 25 of Father Woods, his beloved friend and devoted helper who had dedicated his life to the service of the Blessed Mother and family Rosary. He sorrowed for his earthly loss, but gained strength from his new friend in heaven. He did not go to the funeral, but remained at his work in Rome and Brazil, as he felt Father Woods would want him to do.

Space for a central office was donated in downtown São Paulo. The office was blessed and opened March 9. The same day the Crusade team began the series of assemblies with priests, educators and administrators for the parochial, school and institutional phase of the Crusade.

The blessing of the office was attended by businessmen and industrialists, government officials, social and community leaders and the Catholic hierarchy and religious organization leaders. Area media covered the event.

The office, in a new building owned by the Bank of Brazil, was a three-sided room with two sides of glass overlooking the streets. Space was abundant. It was the best office space ever obtained by the Crusade.

Because of the size of the archdiocese and the absence of Father Quinn, still in Spain, it was necessary to hire a small staff.

Funds for the Crusade came, as usual, from donations by wealthy benefactors. Other goods and services also were donated, including the best resources of several top advertising agencies of Brazil, especially Acar Propaganda, directed by Paulo Nascimento, who was assisted by Raquel Zuckerman.

The agency launched one of the biggest publicity campaigns the Family Rosary Crusade had ever had. Father Peyton, with Rosary beads in hand, looked out from the pages of practically every newspaper and periodical and was seen and heard in radio and television interviews.

Every form of mass media became a pulpit for his message. To Father Peyton, every radio program, TV, article in print, every poster and banner was a rock—not a pebble, but a rock—thrown into the stagnant pool of Christian value in the world.

Bishops exhorted the people to implore the help of Mary, especially Our Lady of Fatima, to save the country from a bloody and destructive war. Brazilians were devoted to Our Lady of Fatima, who had promised an end to war through prayer to her Immaculate Heart. Hardly a church or chapel lacked her statue.

Suddenly, unexpectedly, Brazil's President Goulart ridiculed the Rosary!

On nationwide television and radio on March 13, he said, "Why do you pray the Rosary? The Rosary can't save you now."

Goulart was now profaning the Rosary before all Brazil.

Brazilians listened in horror as he continued with the words that tolled the demise of their democratic form of government.

Goulart issued two decrees of confiscation, actually signing them before the cameras.

The decrees gave the six remaining privately owned oil refineries to the government monopoly and confiscated large tracts of land judged inadequately operated, allegedly for distribution to landless peasants. The president called the government and social order "outmoded" and demanded basic changes in the constitution.

His chief spokesman Brizola followed, demanding abolition of Congress and substitution of a governing body of peasants, workers and low-level military troops.

It was government by decree. It was modeled on Lenin and was a replay of Castro's scenario as he turned Cuba over to the Communists.

Brazil's middle class realized the crisis had arrived. There would be no turning back by this government. Goulart's actions were bound to bring on civil war, followed by Communist takeover.

To Father Peyton, denying the power of the Rosary was the same as denying Mary's role as the Mother of God. It was the same as denying her relationship with her Son Jesus and her role as mother of all mankind. It was the same as repudiating Christianity itself. Father Peyton's explanation of the Rosary as the embodiment of the tenets of Christianity had been spread throughout Brazil.

Three basic tenets of the Christian religion are kept in focus by meditation on the Mysteries of the Rosary. These are the incarnation of God as told in the Joyful Mysteries, the redemption of man, told in the Sorrowful Mysteries, and eternal life after death, as told in the Glorious Mysteries.

Christianity is based on the belief that Jesus is God incarnate. The Rosary tells us that we have a right to have hope—even in the worst tragedy and sorrow. It tells us we have hope of redemption because of Jesus. Despair is the opposite of hope, and so it is the worst sin of all because it denies the hope of eternal life.

Jesus conquered our two biggest problems—death and sin—at a terrible price to Himself.

The Rosary tells us we have hope of eternal life because of Jesus's resurrection. Christ had to go through Calvary to go ahead of us and show us the way and open the door, to show us that death is not an end but the threshold of a new life that will last forever. He rose from the dead and conquered the death that would have taken away the greatest gift, life, and separated us from the Father forever.

In praying the Rosary, we pick up the option we have to follow Jesus into eternal life with God the Father. That's the option we have that gives us the courage to live a life of integrity, of honesty, a life that is worthwhile, that gives our hearts joy and love and peace and the ability to cope with life's surprises whether for good or ill, the chance to fulfill our potential as families. God help the children when they grow up if we do not use it.

If you have to waste your life asking the questions, "Who am I? Who put me here? Where am I going?" or if you believe it is just yourself and then nothingness, a life that ends in the grave, then God help you.

A letter dated March 12 reached Father Peyton late that month from Pope Paul VI that read in part:

> The unity and sanctity of the family, today so gravely and so universally threatened and attacked, will find their sure defense and unfailing protection in the practice of family prayer. As the

motto of the Family Rosary Crusade succinctly asserts: "The family that prays together stays together;"and this unity will be a holy one, founded on the raising of the mind and heart to God in the meditation of the mysteries of the life, death and resurrection of Our Divine Redeemer and the life of His Immaculate Mother.

We therefore warmly recommend the Family Rosary Crusade, which inculcates the practice of daily prayer, of family prayer, and of prayer by means of the Rosary, in which, "meditating upon those mysteries...we may both imitate what they contain and obtain what they promise." We exhort all Catholic Families to introduce this devotion into their lives, and to encourage its propagation, in the assurance that "from this most salutary institution, innumerable good fruits will be poured forth upon Christendom."

To you, then, beloved son, to those who collaborate with you in the Family Rosary Crusade, to the Most Reverend Ordinaries who encourage its activities, as well as to all the faithful who undertake the pledge of daily family prayer together in the Rosary, We lovingly impart, as a pledge of abundant divine graces and richest heavenly favors, Our paternal Apostolic Benediction.

On March 19, the women of São Paulo swarmed out of their houses. They jammed the broad downtown boulevards of São Paulo, over a million women strong, carrying Rosary beads.

Newspapers headlining the women's "Proclamation" were being sold on the streets as they marched. The proclamation said the country was "in extreme danger" and had allowed "men of limitless ambition without Christian faith or scruples...to create hate and despair." It cited infiltration by "servants of totalitarianism, foreign to us and all-consuming." The proclamation concluded with "Mother of God, preserve us from the fate and suffering of the martyred women of Cuba, Poland, Hungary and other enslaved nations."

The women called their demonstration "The march of the Family with God toward Freedom." Similar demonstrations followed in other major cities despite police efforts to halt the crusading women.

Working in secret, the army generals, aided by navy officers and middle-class businessmen, organized a military takeover of the government. Their columns marched on March 31 and by mid-day of April 1 it was all over. Goulart fled to Uruguay and his conspirators fled or hid where they could.

Humberto Castello Branco, the army chief of staff who had

been most instrumental in engineering the bloodless counter-revolution, was named by the Chamber of Deputies to serve Goulart's unexpired term as president.

An editorial on the "Mysterious Force" Father Peyton had brought to Brazil said the Family Rosary Crusade had "released in Brazil a torrent of prayer" and continued that, "The Rosary brought about the miracle of the cohesion of all forces, brought their spirits together, unified their wills...And what we call revolution was a miracle of national unity. The people and the soldiers, in harmony with the same faith in God, and confidence in Brazil, were able to reach their ideal, without bloodshed, in the glow of the beads of the Rosary."

Everywhere Brazilians were giving thanks to the Virgin of Fatima for the miracle of revolution without bloodshed.

To a Crusade team member, the new President Castello Branco said, "I admire the Crusade. Since the great meeting in Rio de Janeiro, I give it credit for the formation of the public opinion of the Brazilian people in order to have the valor to bring about the revolution."

Many similar writings and observations attributed to the upsurge of prayers, especially the Rosary, the saving of Brazil from a civil war that would have cost many lives. They credited Father Peyton and the Family Rosary Crusade with awakening the people to the Rosary.

Father Peyton called it "a dubious credit." He said to Father Quinn and the team, "It will hurt me. It is not my mission to be concerned with politics. My mission is to save souls. My mission is to all people, no matter what their politics, from the highest to the lowest, the greatest of sinners. All are the children of God, and the Blessed Mother Mary is the mother of all."

Just how narrow was the escape from a bloodbath in Brazil emerged in the days following. A ship loaded with weapons turned back to Havana. A detailed plan for the assassination of anti-Communists and a list of hit men assigned to each were found. Also found were instruction manuals for terrorism and the fomenting of strikes and chaos, and communications systems were captured. An organization plan for five hundred thousand troops and caches of uniforms and shoes and hidden arsenals also were reportedly uncovered. Tons of Communist literature and huge amounts of counterfeit money with plans to use it to wreck the economy were discovered. Other proofs of conspiracy and corruption, including cancelled checks diverting government money to private use were found in Goulart's palace and in Brizola's home in Porto Alegre. The new government imposed political sanctions and/or jail sentences upon many, but no executions were ordered as would have been the case had the conspiracy succeeded.

When the August 16 date for the rally in São Paulo finally arrived, Father Peyton spoke with eloquent simplicity before a multitude who transformed the beautiful valley of Anhangabau, cut across with viaducts and serpentine highways, into a valley of prayer.

From the high platform overlooking that valley of two million upturned faces, Father Peyton told them about love. We express our love for one another in the daily encounters, in dialogue, in little remembrances, in being helped and helping when we are asked. God expresses His love in the millions of gifts we see around us every day. We express our love for God in dialogue with Him. Prayer is dialogue with God. Daily prayer, daily family prayer, daily family Rosary make that love for God grow.

The Rosary in itself has already proven its power. The family in itself is already a power. The family Rosary has a new power all its own. When a family united by the bond of love talks with one voice to God in Mary's way the power of the prayer is increased. The most powerful prayer said by the most powerful unit of society becomes an irresistible plea to God.

There remained one more Crusade in Brazil—in Curitiba. Plans were being made to take the Crusade to many other Central and South American countries. There was also the Crusade to begin immediately in Barcelona.

The Crusades were always in various overlapping phases in different countries.

Return to Spain

Sunday, May 31, 1964, dawned as a rainy day in Madrid. It was the day of the great outdoor Family Rosary celebration in honor of Our Blessed Mother. A million people were expected.

The long platform stretched over the broad lanes of the Avenida Generalissimo and into side streets on either edge. A canvas roof sheltered the chairs for the cardinal, the bishops and other participants. Father Quinn and Father Francis Grogan arrived about eight-thirty in the morning to check the arrangements. They stood under the canvas testing the microphone.

A great cloudburst drenched the air and ricocheted on the streets, pouring a curtain of water down all around the rim of the canvas roof. Suddenly, Father Quinn felt the hard slap of flaps of buckling and ripping canvas. Buckets of cold water poured over his head. The rain continued to pelt his back as he made his way out of the wet slippery mass. He had to call the fire department to remove the heavy covering.

Father Peyton was at the same time praying in the chapel, with all the faithful of Madrid praying with him, that the rain would stop before the afternoon rally.

About an hour and a half before the rally, the rain stopped and avenues dried. The minister of war sent army trucks with loudspeakers to help keep order and troops and marching military bands to join the procession. The sky shone blue above the multitude in the broad concourse.

Prince Juan Carlos, heir apparent to Franco as ruler of Spain, with his wife, was among the officials at the rally.

Officials estimated the crowd as one million and two hundred thousand people.

Father Peyton gave the Rosary beads he used for the rally to his friend Antonio de Oriol. It was his practice to bestow the Rosaries used at each rally upon individuals who had been extraordinarily helpful to the Crusade.

Father Peyton's prayers of gratitude were mixed with his petitions for what lay ahead as he boarded the airplane to return to Brazil to conclude the São Paulo Crusade.

Father Peyton returned to Spain the following year for a Crusade in Barcelona. The rally was on February 28, leaving the rest of the year free for the Crusades in the Dominican Republic.

Father Richard Sullivan went to the rally in Barcelona to view the Family Rosary Crusade in action.

Father Sullivan, by then Father Peyton's superior, had entered the seminary at Notre Dame in 1939, when the critically ill Patrick Peyton was in its infirmary praying for his life.

As he watched the throngs converging on the rally site, four hundred thousand strong, Father Sullivan recalled those early impressions, which he later described as follows:

> I was able to visit Pat and follow his progress of deterioration. He was the worst t.b. patient the world has ever seen. Complete rest and quiet meant for him that, far from being flat on his back, he was as restless as a feather in a hurricane—moving now on one elbow and now on the other. Nature didn't have a ghost of a chance to cure him. Then came the Novena on December 8, the feast of the Immaculate Conception. I visited him that day at the end of the Novena. He was certain that something had happened. He wanted to go to the clinic to see the doctor immediately. The superior, Father Thomas Irving, said, "Not today." He did get out to see the doctor in a few days. Pat told me the doctor examined him and found the fluid gone from his lungs. He was back in class in January. Pat immediately claimed that it was the Blessed Virgin who had cured him. It is certain that Pat did not help her.

With the same wry humor, Father Sullivan gave his report of what happened at the Barcelona rally, as follows:

> On the day of the rally—and this was generally true—Father Joseph Quinn and Father William Persia and the other associates were up before the crack of dawn to assure themselves that all details were taken care of. They worked feverishly up to the time of the rally. Meanwhile Father Pat rested, meditated and prepared himself for the great moment of his appearance and his address. The address was always powerful. At the end of the rally Father Pat had reached a peak of emotional exhilaration. His associates at the same moment reached the depth of exhaustion. Father Pat in his enthusiasm and in gratitude for the success of the day would ask his associates to join him in an Hour of Adoration during which he would thank the Lord and our Blessed Mother for all those persons and events who and which had made the day so memorable.
>
> In Barcelona one of the families which had recited or led a decade of the Rosary during the rally was a family of a soccer player by the name of Jesus. It so happened that on the evening of the rally an important game was to be played between Barcelona and Madrid. He invited us to attend. Then came the fatal moment: how to present this to Father Pat. Father Quinn and Father Persia asked me to be the intercessor. The intercession was very

simple and one which Father Pat could not refuse: "Father Pat, Jesus asked us to go to the soccer game tonight. I don't think that we can refuse Jesus." We went. It was a great game. Father Pat has never forgiven me.

Mary's lobbyist

Rumblings from Rome had been reaching Father Peyton's ears as he took his message up and down Brazil. Predictions of radical changes unfavorable to the Family Rosary Crusade had come at the very time the Crusade was awakening the dormant faith of millions of Latin Americans, when Father Peyton's message was pointing them toward the path where Mary waited with her all powerful intercession.

Vatican Council II was updating the teachings and practices of the Church to conform to the needs of the modern world. The thinking was that a better educated, more sophisticated populace was no longer satisfied with the old liturgies and that it wanted a more personal way of relating to the Creator. It was expected that some of the practices of the past would be sacrificed.

While the Council did not threaten the Family Rosary Crusade but on the contrary sought out ways to make it stronger in the Post Conciliar Church, the press misinterpreted the direction of the Council and predicted that the Rosary would be among the prayers outmoded and even went so far as to project a downgrading of devotion to Mary. These forebodings reached Father Peyton.

For years he had been strengthening his case in favor of daily family Rosary in answer to doubters and questioners—through his own experiences, through Scripture, theology, encyclicals of the popes, letters written to him by popes, and the testimonies of millions of people on six continents.

He saw Vatican Council II as an opportunity to strengthen

family prayer and family Rosary through its decrees. But he did not leave this to chance for the long-range goal of promoting his cause among the Council fathers.

It was apparent to him from the beginning that the Council was to be in the spirit of Pope John XXIII, who convened it in October, 1962. Father Peyton was well aware of that Pope's devotion to Mary.

One of the new friends he met in Rome was a Holy Cross seminarian, John J. Gurley. Father Peyton enlisted John's help in showing the Rosary films, in a little theater close by, to the fathers of the Council who wished to see them. After his ordination Father Gurley joined Father Peyton in the Family Rosary Crusade as an assistant.

While in Rome Father Peyton was successful in having notables of the Council write articles on the spirituality of the family in the modern world. The many such statements that were collected assured him of the bishops' awareness of the importance of family prayer.

Any words on family prayer or family Rosary that he could get, no matter how few, in the decrees of Vatican Council II, would be a triumph. Council decrees were made by all the bishops of the world in conjunction—debating, discussing, exploring every word. When a decree finally came, it was the result of exploration from a world point of view.

Father Peyton counted on many old friends, including bishops who had had the Crusade, to help him in his lobbying efforts.

One old friend in whom he found support was Cardinal Suenens, a noted leader in Council conclaves, the former bishop of Brussels who had so sharply interrogated him during the debut of the Rosary films. He met many new supporters at evening gatherings at the lodgings of Cardinal Suenens, where intimate discussions followed Mass and a simple supper.

For help in the intricate procedure of presenting proposals to the bishops for their statements, Father Peyton enlisted another old friend, Archbishop Mark McGrath, C.S.C., of Panama. Archbishop McGrath was a member of many drafting commissions. Cardinal Suenens was one of the noted speakers enlisted to present a statement on family prayer to the bishops. During the speeches, Father Peyton was cited for his devotion to the Family Rosary throughout the world. By then, there was hardly a cardinal or a bishop who had not been exposed, either directly or indirectly, to the Rosary priest's persuasion on behalf of family prayer and the Rosary.

Two statements on the value of family prayer were incorporated in the Council decrees as a result of Father Peyton's efforts. One edict was contained in the decree on the Apostolate of the Laity and the other in the decree on the Constitution of the Church in the Modern World.

These statements on family prayer, although small, were significant. Father Peyton, who had constantly searched for and used every bit of confirmation of his position he could find in Scripture and theology, was instrumental in creating them.

One of the Council documents most gratifying to Father Peyton, although he could claim no credit for it, was a chapter on Mary incorporated in the Constitution on the Nature of the Church.

It emphasized the role of the Mother of God as an integral part of the essential life of the Church. It also stressed the importance of devotion to Mary as a part of the prayer life of the Church. The document read in part: "The union of the Mother with the Son in the work of salvation is made manifest from the time of Christ's virginal conception up to His death. This maternity of Mary in the order of grace began with the consent which she gave in faith at The Annunciation and which she sustained without wavering beneath the cross, and lasts until the eternal fulfillment of all the elect. Taken up to heaven she did not lay aside this salvific duty, but by her constant intercession continued to bring us the gifts of eternal salvation. By her maternal charity, she cares for the brethren of her Son, who still journey on earth surrounded by dangers and difficulties, until they are led into the happiness of their true home."

The same statement, in a clear reference to the Rosary, urged that "...the cult, especially the liturgical cult, of the Blessed Virgin be generously fostered, and the practices and exercises of piety recommended by the magisterium of the Church towards her in the course of centuries be made of great moment."

Pope Paul VI, in proclaiming the decree on November 21, 1964, proclaimed in the same speech the role of Mary as "Mother of the Church." In that address, the pontiff renewed the consecration of the world, citing Russia in particular, to the Immaculate Heart of Mary. He promised to send a Golden Rose to Our Lady of Fatima with a delegation to that famous Portuguese shrine. The Golden Rose was a tradition of the Church to reward human royalty for its support. It had never before been bestowed upon a supernatural being, and the promise recognized the bodily presence of the Queen of Heaven and the Mother of God in Heaven and on earth.

In appearances at Fatima in 1917, Our Lady had implored devotion to her Immaculate Heart through the Rosary and prayer and penance as the only means of ending the world war and bringing lasting peace to the world.

She had warned that, unless men stopped offending the Lord, another and more terrible war would commence "precisely in the next Pontificate." That next Pontificate of Pope Pius XI was from 1922 until his death in February 1939.

Our Lady of Fatima had said that errors would be spread through the world that would give rise to wars, famine and persecutions. Different nations would be destroyed and the good would suffer. A night illumined by an unknown light would be God's signal that the castigation of the world for its many transgressions was at hand.

If mankind heeded her request, Russia would be converted, she foretold at a time when the world could not know why she singled out Russia, but was soon to discover it in the aftermath of revolution. She had given the world the terms of her peace plan. If devotion to the Immaculate Heart of Mary were established and men prayed and did penance for their sins, an era of peace would be granted to the world.

Father Peyton seized the opportunity presented by Vatican Council II to discuss with the bishops of Latin America the effects of the Family Rosary Crusade in their countries. The bishops were then planning their own programs of renewal. Although all had high praise for the Crusade, they complained that it diverted priests and other resources from their own pastoral programs. Father Peyton realized that the bishops were telling him that the Crusade was an outside activity that came with him and withered away when he left.

Other criticisms that Father Peyton had frequently heard were repeated: the Crusade brought no material aid to the poor; it offered prayer to calm them in their desperate needs, it had the potential for misuse by unscrupulous persons for personal profit. These criticisms were even more pronounced in the light of Vatican Council II's emphasis on social action.

If the Family Rosary Crusade was to survive, its critics had to be met head on. It had to be reevaluated in accordance with the decrees of the Council fathers. Solutions had to be found for the weaknesses that were constantly reiterated. Father Peyton not only listened astutely to the criticism; he sought it out.

He asked an eminent sociologist to make a comprehensive evaluation of the Latin American Crusades in their relation to the decrees of Vatican Council II. This was done over a period of several months by the Jesuit Father Renato Poblete of the Bellarmine Center for Sociological Research of Santiago, Chile. His report incorporated interviews with many bishops and leaders of Catholic thought and numerous statistical charts reflecting participation in the Crusades. The benefits of the Crusade were praised, but Father Poblete found a lack of follow-up a weakness. Another he stressed was that the Crusade depended too much upon Father Peyton himself.

Father Peyton next seized the opportunity of a week-long conference on the implications of Vatican Council II to conduct his own symposium on the implications of the Council to the Family Rosary Crusade. The conference, conducted by the Center for Continuing Education of Notre Dame University in March of 1966, was attended by leading theologians and religious scholars of the world. Father Peyton assembled the Crusade priests of Latin America at Notre Dame and invited the leaders of Catholic thought to join them in an evaluation of the Crusade. He also insured ecumenism in the discussions by inviting a leading Lutheran minister.

The symposium concluded that certain techniques of the Crusade were in accordance with the decrees of the Council because they were sociologically positive. These were: the census, the recruitment and training of the Crusade lay leaders, the free film showings on the Mysteries of the Rosary, the extensive use of the mass media of communications, house to house visitation and the rallies. It recommended that the Crusade be reformulated to reflect the social role of the family and that togetherness in prayer be extended to the wider family of the community.

Again, the dependence of the Crusade upon Father Peyton and the lack of follow-up were cited as weaknesses. These were problems Father Peyton had been working on for a long time. An experimental project was then in progress in Manila in which one priest supplied with the Rosary films and the equipment for showing them was organizing the follow-up to the Manila Rosary Crusade. This pilot project was to serve as a model for other countries.

The Crusade techniques were reorganized to maximize use of manpower. A plan was devised by which one Crusade leader with a do-it-yourself kit could take the Crusade into a country.

In some countries dedicated local priests were recruited as Crusade leaders. They received Crusade funds for necessary expenditures, which they augmented with their own ingenuity. In some countries these local priests and in other countries lay volunteers were the personnel to direct Crusade and post-Crusade programs.

Father Peyton entered the decade of the seventies with Crusades being operated simultaneously in several different countries by Holy Cross priests and priests of other orders whom he had inspired and recruited, using the Rosary films as a basis. As excellent as these films were, Father Peyton began to dream of producing other films of a biblical nature for showing on television and outdoor screens.

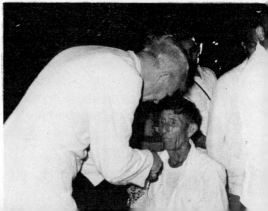

Part 5

Fourth decade—the seventies
Cross of sorrows

Called 'saint'

Father Luis Valdivieso Armijos resigned in 1969 his position in Rome as a member of his order's General Council of Dominicans to join Father Peyton's cause. He trained in Guatemala with Father John Gurley, who had kept his promise given in Rome and accepted assignment to the Crusade in 1967. Father Armijos had a lasting commitment to the Crusade and, after Guatemala, continued working with Father Gurley in Honduras and El Salvador and other Latin American countries.

Father Heinzer was in Hollywood tending to business matters, while Harvey Bernhard of later *Omen* fame served as volunteer director of production.

In the Albany office, Patricia Spanbauer could be found doing almost anything—from computer to cooking to washing the dishes, to ordering and receiving supplies, taking dictation, writing letters, directing clerical help and tending to countless details. She had traveled with some of the Crusades and enjoyed the variety of the work to the extent that she had refused other jobs. Father Pat had by then given up praying for her to fall in love and get married—and establish a family Rosary home—as it had become apparent her destiny was to remain with Family Rosary. Father J. Robert Rioux was winding up his eight years with the Crusade as priest in charge of the Albany office.

A new provincial, Father William Hogan, was installed as superior of the Eastern Province in 1970.

The Albany office remained world headquarters for Family Rosary Crusade. A computer and other modern equipment produced the voluminous mailings. A second building next door had been acquired. The Popular Mission—or Mobile Crusade—with the Rosary films, was being conducted simultaneously in many countries. Production and distribution of the Rosary films and other television and radio specials kept the Hollywood staff busy. New productions and projects were constantly being introduced.

The Albany building was theoretically his home, but he returned to it seldom. He had substitute homes in many parts of the world. The Little Sisters of the Poor in San Pedro, California, kept a room for him. A room in Peter Grace's home was "Father Peyton's room" to come and go as he willed, the same with Josefina Bayot in Manila and Hugh Tunney in Dublin. Bud Denihan and Arthur Keller of the Southgate Towers welcomed him whenever he was in New York City. Bishops' residences, rectories, monasteries and convents in innumerable cities were always open to his visits. Friends welcomed him. He had many homes, but not one.

Income was never far ahead of expenditures. Fund-raising was one of the essential occupations of Father Peyton's time. He continued begging among millionaires to finance his projects. Small donations that poured in daily to the Albany office also meant success of a project.

People called him "saint" and attributed miracles to him. To the former he said, "We are all saints, if we are in the service of God." To the latter he demurred, saying, "It is through prayer that miracles are performed. Only God can perform miracles. You praise Him when you say 'Our Father, who art in heaven, hallowed be your name; Your kingdom come; Your will be done on earth as it is in heaven.' And you pray for miracles every time you say, 'Give us this day our daily bread; and forgive us our trespasses as we forgive those who trespass against us; and lead us not into temptation, but deliver us from evil.'"

Language of tears

Father Armijos, short, brown-eyed and dark, and Father Peyton, tall, blue-eyed and by then with hair as white as the collar at his neck, strolled past the small shops in low buildings that walled both sides of the narrow San Salvador street.

"Look! There!" exclaimed Father Armijos, pointing to five or six young people with a large Family Rosary Crusade poster. Their shaggy grooming and attire marked them as non-traditionalist teenagers.

As the two priests drew near, they heard the young people urging their peers to attend the rally.

"God bless you," and "Our Blessed Mother will thank you," Father Peyton reiterated as he bent his head toward them and enveloped each extended hand in both his large hands.

"Would you stop for a while and talk with me? I would like to ask you something," he said. Their answers, sprinkled with "Si, Padre Peyton, si," showed they recognized him.

They stood under the hot sun, pressed close together by the pedestrians passing from either direction on the narrow sidewalk.

"I can see by your appearance that you are not of the conformist type," Father Peyton began. The young people laughed and shook their heads from side to side. He continued, "You are interested in breaking with present-day structures. You look down upon traditional programs." The young people assented with emphatic nods of their heads. "How is it then," Father Peyton asked, "that you are interested in and taking such an active part in this program of prayer which is precisely an outgrowth of traditional Christianity?"

"We have been looking for something real," a boy answered. "Something that is true."

"We have always dreamt of bringing Jesus Christ to our brothers and sisters in the city streets and the squares," said another.

"But a Christ who is authentic," another joined in, "a Christ who has no prejudices, no odor of money about Him, no talk of politics, the Christ of the gospel."

As they struggled to express what they felt, one young man's voice rose above the others, "You, Padre Peyton, have given us the opportunity we have dreamt of to bring a real Christ to our people. In you we have found an authentic witness of that Christ."

That dialogue went on with the young people commenting, "You are sincere." "We find in you no pride or arrogance, but the true humility of a man of God." "You do not wait for us to come to you. You come to us in the streets. You come among the poor." "You ask only for our prayers, for peace and unity and the salvation of our souls." "You show the love you speak about, the love of God and of brother and brother." "You collect no money, and you ask nothing for yourself. You speak only of God." "We follow you because we find you a truly holy man." Interspersed among these comments was Father Peyton's frequent "God bless you."

After the talk was ended, Father Peyton blessed the group and he and Father Armijos continued down the street.

"Those street children," said Father Armijos, "are all searching for something, and they do not know what they are searching for. You, Padre Peyton, are a powerful instrument of God to bring these children to Him."

"Yes, I am the instrument." replied Father Peyton, "but it is not I, but Mary our mother who leads them to God." After a short distance, the two parted to go their separate ways.

Father Peyton was on his way to visit José Dutriz, publisher of *La Prensa*, one of Central America's leading newspapers.

Upon being ushered into the publisher's office, Father Peyton, in one swift movement, dropped to his knees and drew his Rosary beads from his pocket, saying, "I'll say a little prayer before we talk." The man seated behind the desk followed his example.

The Irish-accented English "*Hail Mary, full of grace. The Lord is with you; blessed are you among women and blessed is the fruit of your womb Jesus,*" answered by the Spanish-accented English, "*Holy Mary, Mother of God, pray for us sinners, now and at the hour of our death,*" became the prologue to a deep and lasting friendship. Father Peyton's request for publicity was granted.

Father Peyton gave a set of Rosary beads to Señor Dutriz, with a prayer that it would protect him always. Father Peyton said to his new friend, "There is no one capable of doing harm to you because you will always be protected by our mother, our Holy Blessed Virgin." José Dutriz carried the Rosary with him everywhere he went and at a later time assured Father Peyton that it had protected him from perils many times.

Father Armijos was working in the Crusade office when Father Peyton returned. They discussed plans for the Crusade to take place mostly in and around the city of San Salvador, and for the rally scheduled for the following year, 1971, on March 6.

The Crusade was fortunate, they agreed, that it was able to have as director and liaison Bishop Oscar A. Romero, auxiliary bishop of the Archdiocese of San Salvador. He was a deeply religious man and much loved by his followers. They needed such a strong leader, for many of the people of El Salvador did not follow the practices of their religion and some had abandoned their faith. They would have to be brought back into the fold if the Crusade were to be a success. It would be harder also to bring them to God in the midst of the unrest current there. The injustices of latifundia in tiny El Salvador made it clear that trouble was coming.

Bishop Romero from his pulpit and Señor Dutriz from his newspaper pages aroused enthusiasm and cooperation for the Crusade. Donations of needed goods and services of all kinds ranged from promotion to cloth for banners, from printing to paper for posters.

During the Popular Mission one entire parish on the outskirts of San Salvador gathered nightly to view the Rosary films. Hanging from the belts of all the men were the machetes they used for the day's work of cutting sugar cane.

On the evening of the two Sorrowful Mysteries of The Scourging and The Crowning with Thorns, the sufferings of Christ overpowered one man. He drew his machete and, waving it above his head, charged toward the figures of those tormenting and mocking Christ.

A friend plunged after him and tackled him. It was some minutes before the man, angry and weeping, could be convinced what he saw was only the image of reality.

"Tears," said Father Armijos, "are the one language common to all who answer Father Peyton's message."

The Second Sorrowful Mystery
The Scourging of Christ

Jesus was arrested and brought before the Sanhedrin for questioning. When they asked Him if He were the Messiah, Jesus answered, "It is you who say it. But I tell you this: Soon you will see the Son of Man seated at the right hand of the Power and coming on the clouds of heaven." (Matthew 26: 64)

For this He was declared guilty of blasphemy. The chief priests, the elders and the scribes bound Him and took Him before Pilate. Pilate could find no fault in Jesus and sent Him to Herod. Herod, angry when Jesus would not perform a miracle for him, sent Him back to Pilate. There was another prisoner, Barabbas, convicted of murder and inciting to riot. According to law, the crowd could choose one prisoner to be released.

So when the procurator asked them, "Which one do you wish me to release for you?" they said, "Barabbas." Pilate said to them, "Then what am I to do with Jesus, the so-called Messiah?" "Crucify him!" they all cried. He said, "Why, what crime has he committed?" But they only shouted the louder, "Crucify him!" Pilate finally realized that he was making no impression and that a riot was breaking out instead. He called for water and washed his hands in front of the crowd, declaring as he did so, "I am innocent of the blood of this just man. The responsibility is yours." The whole people said in reply, "Let his blood be on us and on our children." At that, he released Barabbas to them. Jesus, however, he first had scourged; then he handed him over to be crucified.

(Matthew 27: 21-26)

Father Peyton's meditation
on The Scourging of Christ

With the Rosary in hand we move from the garden of Gethsemane to the courtyard of Pilate's palace for the Second Sorrowful Mystery. There we witness the trial, the accusations, the judgment and the brutal scourging of Jesus as ordered by Pilate even though he found no wrong in Him. The form Christ's suffering takes now is pain, searing pain...excruciating pain.

We see the brutal soldiers of Rome lash His naked body. His flesh tears, His blood flows from a thousand wounds. His sacred and innocent body is one gaping wound. He bears it all in silence and with dignity. Why?

He has to atone for the sins of our bodies—the sins of our flesh—the sins we commit through and with and against the "Temple of God" that our bodies were created to be. These sins are legion. They make the headlines of our newspapers. They cheapen women, they make brutes of men. They have names: abuse of sex, abortion, euthanasia, adultery, fornication, violence, murder, child abuse, wife-beating, drunkenness, drugs and the rest.

We see what it cost Jesus to get all this ugly, hideous desecration of our bodies cleansed and purified. It's no wonder we love Him and worship Him with all our hearts and souls.

Thanks to the holy Rosary for all the love and gratitude for Christ it awakens in its devotees when meditating and praying with Our Lady the Second Sorrowful Mystery.

The Third Sorrowful Mystery
The Crowning of Christ With Thorns

The procurator's soldiers took Jesus inside the praetorium and collected the whole cohort around him. They stripped off his clothes and wrapped him in a scarlet military cloak.

Weaving a crown out of thorns they fixed it on his head, and stuck a reed in his right hand. Then they began to mock him by dropping to their knees before him, saying, "All hail, king of the Jews!" They also spat at him. Afterward they took hold of the reed and kept striking him on the head. Finally, when they had finished making a fool of him, they stripped him of the cloak, dressed him in his own clothes, and led him off to crucifixion.

(Matthew 27: 27-31)

Father Peyton's meditation
on The Crowning of Christ With Thorns

The suffering of Christ in this Third Sorrowful Mystery takes the form of humiliation. The scourging isn't enough. There is another and more hideous crime or sin of ours to be forgiven and atoned for. It is what we call "pride." Satan played on this weakness when he told Eve, "God knows well that the moment you eat of this fruit, you will be like gods." She listened. She liked what she heard. She fell.

Unlike the sins of the body, the sin of pride is the sin of the mind. Some of us are not satisfied with how God made us. We can do better. We make ourselves other than what we are. We become arrogant, haughty, selfish, disdainful of others. We can even make hell upon earth for all around us.

It takes some doing to atone for the living lie that is pride. The Third Sorrowful Mystery of the Rosary tells what humiliation was inflicted upon Christ to wipe clean our slates of this sin.

The soldiers have finished the scourging. They have time on their hands. The final decision of Pilate is not yet made. Their brutish minds are aware of His claim of kingship and kingdom. They will mock Him as a king. They throw a scarlet cloak upon His shoulders. They thrust a reed into His hand. They plait a crown of thorns to crush down upon His head. All the trappings of royalty! They bow before Him. They blindfold Him. They slap His face. They make Him a fool, an idiot, a caricature of a king and a man.

What our sins of pride have taken out of Jesus! But in His holy love for us He knows it is all worthwhile. And indeed through meditating on the Third Sorrowful Mystery, God alone knows how pride has died, replaced by humility and truth, in countless friends of the most holy Rosary.

Eclipse of Mary

A young priest shuffled disconsolately past the shacks and the apathetic eyes that followed his progress down the street. It was hot and dusty and the stench of poverty was sour in the air. Little had changed despite his efforts to improve the living conditions of these people.

A commotion ahead caught his attention. As he drew nearer, he saw the skinny arms of children stretched toward a tall, white-haired priest in their midst. The priest was handing out something to the children.

He has something to give them—that's more than I have, the young priest thought. Then he saw what it was. Lifting a face contorted with pain, he blurted, "These people need rice and wheat and you give them Rosaries."

"Oh, Father," the tall priest answered with a smile, "they need the Rosaries too, to learn how to get Our blessed Mother to help them."

The children, who had ceased their clamoring to listen, began again stretching out their arms and the priest tenderly placed a set of beads in each empty hand. Then he blessed them and, gathering them around him, went down on one knee to their height and touched and talked with each one.

The young priest, who had stood watching, exclaimed, "I can show you people even worse off than these. Then you tell me if even you—oh yes, I recognize you and I know of your following—but I do not believe that even you can hand these people only a set of beads and a prayer."

"I have already done so," Father Peyton replied, "and they accepted them gratefully."

He recognized the young priest, not by name, but by the mission his words professed. He had seen him many times in the years since Vatican Council II, with a different face, a different voice, but nearly always young. It did not matter what city they were in, for he had seen his counterpart in many cities. He was a priest with a mission of social reform that had sprung from the councils of Vatican II.

"I do not criticize you for your social work," Father Peyton told his young critic. "Why do you castigate me for my prayer? These people need both."

Although Father Peyton recognized the need for a social mission, he did not believe it should abrogate the power of prayer. He saw in the shift to social action a corollary of the neglect of spirituality.

Reports were coming back to Father Peyton from pastors that the Rosary was no longer popular with their parishioners. They wanted something more up-to-date. Devotion to Mary was outmoded.

Moreover, the statement on Mary as part of a decree, rather than as a separate document, was interpreted by many priests as an intent of the Vatican Council fathers to diminish the role of Mary.

For this and other reasons, less emphasis was placed on devotion to Mary and teaching the Rosary. Some priests barely mentioned the name of Mary and it began sinking into oblivion in some parts of the world. The Mother of God was being obscured by an eclipse.

"What happens when the mother is banished from the home?" he asked rhetorically as he went about pleading for the restoration of devotion to Mary. "When the mother is sent away," he answered his question, "the home soon becomes a mess, untidy, in disorder. The children cry out, 'Where is our mother? Bring her home.' As soon as she comes back, the family home is in order, clean and livable.

"So too in our spiritual home, we need our mother. She is being shut out, and we her children see the chaos, disorder and confusion. The family is vulnerable to evil and beset with all kinds of disasters. We cry out, 'Where is our mother? Bring Mary home.'"

In his daily prayer for an end to the eclipse, Father Peyton addressed himself directly to God, bypassing Mary's help since the prayers were for and about her. He pleaded with Jesus to give him the power and the wisdom to help keep Mary alive in the hearts of her children.

If such an eclipse were to become total, it would plunge the world into a darkness of faith and the wars, famine and persecution she had warned of at Fatima.

An eclipse of Mary would mean an end to the Family Rosary Crusade and failure of Father Peyton's mission.

Father Peyton felt himself bent under the burden of a cross that he must carry.

The Fourth Sorrowful Mystery
The Carrying of the Cross

As they led him away, they laid hold of one Simon the Cyrenean who was coming in from the fields. They put a crossbeam on Simon's shoulder for him to carry along behind Jesus. A great crowd of people followed him, including women who beat their breasts and lamented over him. Jesus turned to them and said: "Daughters of Jerusalem, do not weep for me. Weep for yourselves and for your children. The days are coming when they will say, 'Happy are the sterile, the wombs that never bore and the

breasts that never nursed.' Then they will begin saying to the mountains, 'Fall on us,' and to the hills, 'Cover us.' If they do these things in the green wood, what will happen in the dry?''

(Luke 23: 26-31)

Father Peyton's meditation on The Carrying of the Cross

Endurance is the kind of suffering this Fourth Sorrowful Mystery of the Rosary helps us understand.

Jesus is a condemned man. The sentence has just been passed. ''Take Him you and crucify Him'' wasn't sufficient. Pilate had to be more definite. He was. He released Jesus to be crucified. Now there is no more doubt. He must die.

Fear, pain, humiliation, hunger, thirst, a night without sleep, have drained Him of every ounce of energy and strength. Yet in all His pain and suffering He shouldered the cross with dignity and struggles with it to the place of His execution.

With the Rosary in our hands we take our place in the crowd and watch the sorrowful and pitiful procession—Our Savior struggling and staggering on the way—the cross heavy on His shoulders—the two condemned thieves following, with their crosses. His Mother and His friends not too visible in the midst of such anger, hatred and hostility. He carries the cross until His energy is drained. He can't go on. His executioners press Simon the Cyrene to help. He does, and Our Savior reaches Calvary.

What does all this say to us as we cope with the demands, the surprises and the day-to-day sufferings that are our lot? We take courage and example from Jesus and from His Mother. We bear what has to be borne. We take up our cross and follow after falling, rising and falling again—accepting the help to carry our crosses and arriving like Him at our final hour.

The inspiration we get from this mystery of the Rosary helps us to have the courage, like Christ, to carry our cross with patience and endurance. It deepens our faith. It serves as an example to our children. It insures that we too, like our ancestors, will be remembered for handing down this precious inheritance.

Prisoners on their knees

"What can we do to help?" one of the prisoners asked Father Armijos. Following Father Peyton's enjoinder to take the message everywhere, to all classes, to the highest and the lowest, to all the institutions, he had gone to the Mexican prison at Guadalajara. About a hundred prisoners had seen the Rosary films and heard him tell them about the Crusade and the power of the Rosary to help them.

"What can we do?" they asked each other. After many nods and murmurs of assent, the answer came, "While Padre Peyton is speaking at the great rally, we will be on our knees praying for its success."

The rally in June of 1974 was a great success. Father Peyton spoke for about an hour and a half before an estimated one hundred thousand people who had come from miles around, from the city, the mountains, and the villages.

During all that time the prisoners, with the secular missionaries there to help, knelt in their cells and prayed.

Father Armijos and three priests in training from Puerto Rico—the fourth diocese of Puerto Rico had been unable to spare a priest—took the Popular Mission up and down and across Mexico to the cities and villages and mountain settlements. With the tons of equipment for showing the films packed in trucks, they rumbled up and down the narrow rocky roads spiraling around the mountains, unprotected except by Mary from the headlong dropoffs to canyons below. They rattled along lowland roads where sometimes bridges over streams flowing to the sea were only clanking planks. For three months in 1974, they swept through Mexico showing the religious films on the street corners of cities and sometimes on sheets roped between two trees in the little hamlets of shacks of sticks roofed with thick, woody palm fronds. Their route trailed from diocese to diocese where Father Peyton had been invited by the bishops to bring the Crusade.

The four priests helped Father Peyton when he arrived to speak at the rallies. The Mexicans, ninety-three percent of them Catholics, converged in the hundreds of thousands for these rare public religious gatherings with the appearance of priests in clerical garb.

Even in Mexico, traditionally and constitutionally not noted for its encouragement of public practice of the religion of its devout populace, Father Peyton's persuasiveness had prevailed upon the officials. They had granted him the necessary permissions to conduct public religious processions and ceremonies otherwise disallowed by federal law and make prohibited public appearances in clerical attire.

Despite Mexico's constitutional bans on activities of the Church, Father Peyton had managed to arrange Crusades in 16 dioceses, including such centers of population as Mexico City, Guadalajara, Oaxaca, Puebla and the Yucatan.

Sister Mary J. in Hollywood

The freeway with its lanes of steady traffic led Sister Mary J. Buckley into the cloud of smog over bustling Los Angeles and to Sunset Boulevard, studded with tall straight palm trees under the hot California sun. She found a warm welcome from Father Heinzer and the staff when she arrived at the modern building to take up her new position as manager of Family Theater, Inc.

Not only was the environment in complete contrast to small Albany, New York, with its snowy winters, but it was also a challenging new life for Sister Mary J. Many changes had taken place in the thirty-one years since she answered a knock on her classroom door and looked up for the first time at the face of Father Peyton. For one thing, she had changed her name from Sister Magdalena back to her given name, in accordance with changed rules of the Sisters of Mercy. For another, she wore contemporary dresses, reserving the neat black habit for formal religious occasions. After twenty-three years of teaching at Vincentian Institute, she had been assigned to her mother house in Albany as "mother general," a title changed to "president" during her service.

Sister Mary J. had followed the career of Father Peyton and had attended several of his rallies and other appearances. When her ten-year term as president was completed in 1972, Father Peyton had asked her to join him. Permission, surprisingly, had been granted. At age sixty-five, she found herself in charge of an organization equal to any in the great movie capital for its productions and utilization of top entertainment talents.

It was not long before she and the key professionals who worked with Family Theater became fast friends. There was Joseph Russell, who had come in the early years as a volunteer and remained as a member of the staff. He had worked on most of the radio dramas, taking pictures and grinding out publicity. He had become known in the trade as "Mr. Family Theater."

Two of the regular volunteers were John Fuller, Oscar nominee and film editor, and Joseph Finneran, Disney sound engineer. Both had given their talents over many years to the award-winning productions.

Those glamorous days of stars and the writers coming and going and directors and technicians of Hollywood engaging in hectic creation were gone. The years of weekly radio productions were past and the motion picture and television specials had all been made. No new ones were in progress. Except for publicity campaigns with public service spot performances, the work consisted mainly of reproduction and distribution of those major audio and video productions of the past.

The Hollywood glamor was still there, though. And the friendships of the past were still alive, evidenced by visits of Hollywood celebrities from time to time. Sister Mary J. quickly became attuned to her new life, especially as she listened to Joe Russell's anecdotes of the past.

He himself had been driving along Sunset Boulevard on August 15, 1949, when he saw the Family Theater sign. He had gone in and volunteered his help.

Irene Dunne always showed up to do her parts driven in a black Cadillac by a chauffeur.

Jeff Chandler, although Jewish, had called every week asking to be on a radio program. When he got a part, he was told to be there in ten minutes. He showed up wearing a baseball cap, bedroom slippers and jeans. He was to co-star with Rosalind

Russell. A newspaper photographer sent to get a picture of Chandler and Russell snapped his shot and went away, but was back soon. Rosalind had been late. He had photographed the wrong Russell. Joe Russell was not exactly the glamorous Rosalind the city editor had in mind.

Ethel and Lionel Barrymore spoke to each other for the first time on a Family Theater set after a feud of silence that had lasted three years.

One day the queen of the theater, Ethel Barrymore, had stormed into the studio angrily demanding, "Why the hell wasn't my name mentioned in that newspaper story yesterday?" The language from that majestic lady had shocked Father Lawyer.

While recording the first hour-long radio special, "The Joyful Hour," Father Peyton was to do his part and was told it would take twenty minutes. Gregory Peck also was recording. At the end of three hours it was finished. Gregory Peck said, "Those twenty minutes were the shortest three hours I ever spent in my life."

Raymond Burr fell off a horse and broke his arm while shooting the Family Theater movie The Search. He was back on location in a week and all who saw him said he did an excellent portrayal of a man in pain.

Sister Mary J. wondered if such exciting times would ever return to Family Theater. Father Peyton assured her he had plans to involve a new generation of stars and talent of Hollywood in future endeavors.

Sister Mary J. had her instructions from Father Peyton, "Make the Hollywood operation financially self-sufficient." One of the ways she set about doing this was by a creative approach to the sale and rental of the filmed specials, audio cassettes and publications.

She published promotional material, including a high-quality booklet cataloguing the productions, replete with pictures and color cover pages.

The fifteen Mysteries of the Rosary were offered as a series entitled The Life of Christ to bishops, priests and schools as a teaching aid. There were many other hour and half-hour productions, made for movie and television, both in color and black and white. They featured leading Hollywood actors and actresses. All had received high praise in reviews and many had won top awards.

Also completed by then were twenty-one five-minute films of current episodic stories based on the *Psalms* of the *Old Testament*. Other productions included half-hour filmed interviews with leading personalities and a series of twelve one-minute inspirational films and cassettes on what great men of history said about prayer. These inspirational messages of faith became particularly popular among schools, groups and institutions.

A documentary film in color made by Harvey Bernhard showed Father Peyton at rallies and among throngs in many of the distant places of the world.

Among audio cassettes, the one in constant demand and selling in the thousands was a recitation of the Rosary led by Father Peyton with group responses. Hundreds of letters were received by Family Theater telling of introducing family Rosary into homes by the cassette.

A typical story came from a mother of three. She wrote, "Every evening whether anybody is home or not I turn on the cassette, and I hear Father Peyton leading the Rosary. If I'm alone, I find it so much easier to pray with him. But usually my daughter arrives or my sons will drop in just at that time, and they all join in. It's so easy, so natural. No one feels forced into prayer."

Small books on the Rosary, including *Father Peyton's Rosary Prayer Book* soon became best-sellers. Among the publications was Father Peyton's own autobiography, *All For Her*.

Continual production and distribution of these mass media efforts spread the message of family prayer and family Rosary to hundreds of thousands throughout the world. It kept the Hollywood staff busy, along with planning new projects. Many of the TV specials also were shown repeatedly on television with donated time.

The films and cassettes were priced for sale and rental at a minimum to cover operational costs, with no profit. The primary goal was always the spreading of the message. The Rosary films and others were sent free to many countries for the Popular Mission and Crusade, and others were given to those who could benefit but could not pay, thanks to the many donors to Family Rosary and Family Theater.

Sister Mary J. was well immersed in the work when, later that year, tragedy struck one of the greatest friends of Father Peyton and the Crusade.

On December 20, 1973, Father Peyton and his staff were

stunned by the news. Luis Carrero Blanco, the prime minister of Spain, was assassinated by terrorists. He was blown up by a bomb exploding under his car as he left Mass in the morning.

Father Peyton so well remembered his last meeting with the prime minister. As Father Peyton was bidding him goodbye at the end of that meeting, Señor Carrero Blanco pulled his Rosary out of his pocket. It was the one given to him years before by Father Peyton. He said, "I never forget to pray for you on this Rosary." They were the last words spoken to Father Peyton by his good friend.

Anguish and triumph—the charred statue

The recruitment and training of local priests was Father Peyton's answer to the twin dilemmas of manpower shortage and the need for self-sustaining Crusade organizations in Latin America. The goal of recruiting these priests expanded from merely conducting the Crusades to remaining with them permanently.

Some of these priests who remained, like Father Armijos, relieved the Crusade of the charge that it depended too greatly upon Father Peyton himself. Others who came for awhile and then left for other work nevertheless contributed greatly to the Crusades. Such a one was Father Pablo Straub, on loan from his Redemptorist order for two years for the Crusades in Puerto Rico.

Father Pablo, one of the three priests trained in Mexico, was full of zeal when he returned to conduct the Crusade in Puerto Rico in January of 1975.

Father Pablo saw and heard of many souls awakened to faith in Puerto Rico. Typical was one incident related to him by the principal of a school. The schools were having Bible study and contests and other activities in connection with the Crusades.

The nun teaching one class had a picture of the Blessed Virgin which she gave to each child in turn to take home for a night and ask their parents to pray the Rosary before it.

Finally it was seven-year-old Juan's turn to have the picture. He carried it home tenderly and, with great excitement and pride, showed it to his mother, saying "We have to pray together when Daddy gets home."

Juan's mother, much disturbed by the idea of her husband's almost certain brusque refusal, made the excuse that "Daddy will not be home until late."

"Oh, Mommy," cried the little boy, "I cannot go to sleep until we pray together. I will wait up until midnight."

Hours later, when the father got home and was told what he must do, he barked, "I don't want any part of that nonsense." Juan began to cry. His mother begged her husband to join them, at least briefly. He agreed reluctantly. At first he had to repeat the words of the prayers after his wife, for he had forgotten them. But in a little while the father was leading the prayers in the way the boy said was Father Peyton's way.

Later after Juan was asleep, his father said to his mother, "I was overcome with great peace during that prayer. Something came over me that I haven't felt in years. It was beautiful. Why don't we continue to do it?"

A few days later the mother visited the school. She told the principal, "My husband hasn't prayed or gone to church for years. Now every night he comes home right after work and we pray together. My home has been transformed in such a short time I want to give the Sister my personal thanks." Similar reports came from many families.

Father Pablo, in an ongoing analysis of the effects of the Crusade, noted that the crime rate dropped fourteen percent in cities where the Crusade had been and not at all where it had not yet arrived. In one city slum area characterized by the popular name "Vicious Hole" the people after the Crusade renamed the place "Los Angeles"—the Angels.

Father Pablo also noted an increase in the demand for Communion breads—in one place from two thousand to nine thousand—and requests for millions of Rosaries.

The Crusade census, the first ever taken in the area where the vast majority of people lived in the mountains and countryside around the small urban core of San Sebastian, counted nine thousand, two hundred families, whereas the pastor had estimated only eight thousand. After the Crusade, four new chapels were built and three others refurbished.

The demand for new chapels was growing in Puerto Rico faster than it could be met. After the Crusade in Rio Abajo, a rural river valley in the town of Cidra, the people raised money to build a church by bake sales and through choral groups that traveled great distances singing door-to-door for donations. A priest who had visited regularly there for several years before the Crusade had been unable to get a handful of people for Mass. Afterward the new chapel, seating two hundred, was filled every Sunday to capacity and it became the activity center for the area.

The Crusade also justified the labors of a man called Ismael who was called "stupid" by his neighbors in rural Sabana. Ismael had got a group of laymen to work with the local priest from nearby Bayamon and they had built the huge Chapel of St. Gerard Magella, measuring forty by eighty feet. Only a tiny group of people had converged regularly in its vast interior before the Crusade. After the Crusade, even the standing room was filled and people stood outside looking in through the windows.

Father Peyton's message, Father Pablo wrote, "is limited in its scope to Our Lord's and Our Lady's life in family prayer, but its appeal is universal. Father Peyton is not concerned, as so many are these days, with his image of himself. He is dedicated to only one thing—getting his message across."

Father Peyton continued to receive the encouragement and support of his superiors in Holy Cross—new ones by that time. Father Thomas O. Barrosse had succeeded Father Lalande as superior general of the order in July, 1974. Also in 1974, Father William Ribando had become provincial of the Eastern Province.

In June of 1976 Father Peyton went to the Philippines to speak at a rally at Tacloban, Leyte. A multitude arrived from far and near by every kind of transport imaginable—by fishing boat, old wooden carts, rusty jeeps, on foot and children in baby buggies, in slings at their mothers' sides and on their fathers' shoulders.

As Father Peyton looked out upon the faces of these poor simple and humblest of people the idea struck him to buy one hundred movie projectors and make one hundred sets of the films to show the Rosary films to everyone in the Philippines.

In August of 1976 Father Peyton attended the International Eucharistic Congress in Philadelphia and brought the other Crusade priests there for the week of religious events to renew themselves in the Eucharist. Because of an occurrence there that prevented his return to Puerto Rico, he was not present when one of the most emotional events of the Puerto Rican rallies happened. This was an act of vandalism that, ironically, awakened the greatest religious fervor of all the Puerto Rican Crusades.

It was decided to have the rally at San Juan on December 10, 1976, two days after the feast of the Immaculate Conception. The rally was planned to coincide with the consecration of Puerto Rico to Our Lady of Providence as patron. It was also the last day of the annual meeting in San Juan of CELAM, the Latin American bishops' conference, attended by bishops of all Latin America. Since the ballpark of San Juan, the Roberto Clemente Coliseum, could not hold the anticipated half a million people, it was decided to have the rally in its huge parking lot.

The carved wooden statue of Our Lady of Providence that was to be crowned in the coronation ceremony and rally was kept in a church near the coliseum the night before the celebration. Our Lady of Providence looks down upon her Infant Jesus, lying face up, in His Mother's lap.

When the priests went to the church early in the morning to carry Our Lady to the coliseum, they found her knocked flat on the floor. One side of her face and body were charred and blackened by fire, but the body of the Infant Jesus was unscathed by the flames.

The priests lifted her up in their arms and spoke in shocked whispers of what to do, After consultation with the bishop and those in charge, it was decided to go ahead with the crowning of the desecrated and burned Our Lady of Providence. The priests carried her to the coliseum long before the crowd began to arrive.

When the statue was carried out of the coliseum held on high by a group of priests, the many other priests came running. Half a million people gathered in the huge parking lot gasped and wept in great anguish when they saw the charred and blackened Blessed Mother.

Luis Cardinal Aponte, the archbishop of San Juan, in his address said, "The hand that struck the match that burned the statue has also set aflame the hearts of the people of Puerto Rico with renewed love for Jesus Our Saviour."

Father Pablo, who was on the schedule to speak, could not even talk. Instead, he directed the singing which rose loud and fervent in half a million voices. The burning of the statue served to stimulate devotion to Mary, which had been diminishing also in Puerto Rico in the past few years.

Cross of sorrow

The Messiah, an epic movie made by the Italian producer Roberto Rossellini at the urging of Father Peyton and with the financial backing of Family Rosary Crusade, was shown in Italy. But an altercation arose and it was not dubbed in English for release by Family Theater.

Father Peyton and his associates wanted to change some of the scenes to depict to a greater degree the divinity of Christ, whose life as a man was the focus of the movie.

The great Rossellini would not allow changes in his creation.

He refused to honor the agreement that gave Family Theater the rights of distribution of an English version to be dubbed by Family Theater.

The case was taken to the Italian courts. Assuming the responsibility and the expense of the litigation was the benefactor who had donated a large share of the two million dollars contributed to the production costs.

The suit against Rossellini dragged on in the courts for a number of years and continued after his death against his estate. It was not to be settled until the late seventies—when the verdict was to go against the Rossellini estate in favor of the claimant.

Meanwhile, the long litigation caused Father Peyton much pain.

The film was vitally needed for his message, particularly at that time of dwindling devotion to Our Lady and the Rosary. The failure to bring the dynamic message of the life of Christ as portrayed in this religious masterpiece to families everywhere, even though it might be only a temporary delay, added to his anguish. He felt himself stretched out on a mental cross.

The Fifth Sorrowful Mystery
The Crucifixion

Two others who were criminals were led along with him to be crucified. When they came to Skull Place, as it was called, they crucified him there and the criminals as well, one on his right and the other on his left. Jesus said, "Father, forgive them; they do not know what they are doing." They divided his garments, rolling dice for them.

The people stood there watching, and the leaders kept jeering at him, saying, "He saved others; let him save himself if he is the Messiah of God, the chosen one."

The soldiers also made fun of him, coming forward to offer him their sour wine and saying, "If you are the king of the Jews, save yourself." There was an inscription over his head:

"THIS IS THE KING OF THE JEWS."

One of the criminals hanging in crucifixion blasphemed him: "Aren't you the Messiah? Then save yourself and us." But the other one rebuked him: "Have you no fear of God, seeing you are under the same sentence? We deserve it, after all. We are only paying the price for what we've done, but this man has done nothing wrong." He then said, "Jesus, remember me when you enter upon your reign." And Jesus replied, "I assure you: this day you will be with me in paradise."

It was now around midday, and darkness came over the whole land until midafternoon with an eclipse of the sun. The curtain in the sanctuary was torn in two. Jesus uttered a loud cry and said, "Father, into your hands, I commend my spirit." After he said this, he expired. The centurion, upon seeing what had happened, gave glory to God by saying, "Surely this was an innocent man." When the crowd which had assembled for this spectacle saw what had happened, they went home beating their breasts. All his friends and the women who had accompanied him from Galilee were standing at a distance watching everything.

(Luke 23: 32-49)

Father Peyton's meditation
on The Crucifixion

Death is the ultimate form of suffering. Each of us in one form or another must meet and experience death.

Jesus, remarkable in life, is still more so in His dying. Trusting to the end, loving to the end, dying that we might live, bearing the sin and misery of us all, He unites us with Himself at that hour of redemption.

Who, but Jesus, could say what He said from the Cross? To His executioners: "Father, forgive them..." To the criminal crucified beside Him: "I assure you, this day you will be with me in paradise." To His disciple and apostle John: "This is your mother." and to Mary, His Mother: "This is your son." To His Father: "My God, My God, why have you forsaken me?" For Himself and His need: "I thirst." Closer to His death: "Father, into your hands I commend my spirit." and finally: "It is finished."

He spoke for us. He asked pardon for us. He suffered for us. He made us inseparable from Himself so that the Father could look upon each of us as one with His most beloved son—worthy of love, pardon, forgiveness, life eternal and the bliss of heaven itself.

How dear and precious is the Rosary through which we pray such thoughts, not lightly, but in union with Christ who is the only one who made meaning out of life and lived its gifts and surprises to the fullest.

Heart attack

It was Christmas night, 1976. The huge Christmas tree in Grand Central Station sparkled with welcome to the lonely travelers. Stragglers on the streets issued in and out of the open mouths of subway entrances.

In a hotel suite high above the city street five women knelt before a picture of the Madonna and Child hanging on the wall.

Sister Gail Waring led the prayers, counting them off on her beads, and the others spoke the responses. Then each of the women in turn led a decade of the Rosary.

Father Peyton, resting in a large chair, moved his lips silently in the words of the prayers. He was too weak to speak aloud or to move about for more than a short time. His face was pale and sunken and his large frame was thinner.

Sister Gail had come from Albany to New York to spend the Christmas holidays with Sister Mary J. Buckley, who had come from Hollywood to help Father Peyton with correspondence he would not defer despite his weakened condition. The two Sisters of Mercy stayed in the same hotel and joined Father Peyton and the other three women each evening for supper and prayers.

Josefina Madrigal Bayot had flown from the Philippines as soon as she heard of the heart attack that had stricken Father Peyton in August in Philadelphia, where he was attending the International Eucharistic Congress. She had found him restless and impatient to be out of the hospital and at work and had moved him into the suite she rented for him at the Southgate Towers. There she and the nurse and secretary she brought with her, Esperanza Manlapid, and Benita Balangue, tended to his daily care and helped with the work he felt he must do.

As Mrs. Bayot led a decade of prayers, Sister Gail, listening to the words, thought of the people around the world who were that day celebrating the birth of Christ in their own special ways.

When the prayers of the last of the five Joyful Mysteries were finished, Father Peyton rose from his chair and knelt before the picture that was with him wherever he went. He prayed aloud the *Memorare*.

Remember, O most gracious Virgin Mary, that never was it known that anyone who fled to your protection, implored your help, or sought your intercession, was left unaided. Inspired with this confidence, I fly to you, O Virgin of virgins, my Mother! To you I come; before you I stand, sinful and sorrowful. O Mother of the Word incarnate, despise not my petitions, but in your mercy, hear and answer me. Amen.

Then he added, as usual, "And what we petition, dear Mary, is this," and went on with his requests for all present, naming each by name. With expressions of deep sorrow and pain, he asked Mary to beg forgiveness for those who had burned her statue, knowing she would do even this.

Then each of the women in turn followed with her own praise and prayer. Sister Gail, with a sensitive inner privacy, was not at ease praying thus aloud in a group. But in Father Peyton's presence, she could speak her innermost thoughts freely to God. She felt herself a novice at prayer being led by Father Peyton's prayer into another, barely glimpsed dimension of deepest spirituality.

Father Peyton concluded the prayers with one last request of great import. He stressed every word, "And we are begging you, dearest Mary, humbly on our knees before you, to pray with us for the safety of Antonio de Oriol, who is at this very moment held hostage by terrorists somewhere in Spain."

Solace in bondage

In the small room darkened by drawn shades, the man tied to the bed prayed for his life. He felt the cord tighten around his bound wrists as his thumb counted out the prayers of the Rosary on the tiny beads on the Rosary ring on his finger. One of his captors lounged nearby pointing a gun at him.

Antonio de Oriol had been snatched inside his office in Madrid on December 11, 1976, and taken blindfolded and gagged to the house a few miles away. He did not know where he was.

When his armed guard brought an evening meal on a tray and freed his hands from their bindings, he was able to reach the Rosary beads in his pocket. He kept these draped over his hands as he ate and after his wrists were rebound.

After a few days, his hands were no longer tied and he was

allowed to move about the small house, always at the point of a gun. The Rosary beads he prayed on constantly were those used by Father Peyton at the Madrid rally and given to him afterward.

Spain and the world waited to see whether the terrorists would carry out their threat to shoot him if their demands for the release of certain leftist prisoners were not met.

He could not help but think of the fate of his friend Luis Carrero Blanco a few years before. But the sure knowledge that Father Peyton was also praying for his, Antonio's, life, heartened him and gave him hope.

One day the terrorist guarding him said, "My mother prays more Rosaries than you do."

Señor de Oriol was more fortunate than other victims of terrorist assassins. The capture of some of the gang calling itself the October One Group led Spanish police to the hideout on the edge of Madrid. Police burst into the house and rescued him after sixty-two days of captivity on February 11, 1977, the feast of Our Lady of Lourdes.

A short time after de Oriol's liberation, he received a letter from the mother of that guard. She wrote that she had been praying the Rosary constantly during all the time of his captivity and afterward.

Describing the role of the Rosary during his ordeal, Señor de Oriol wrote to Father Peyton, "I can assure you that the Rosary was my greatest consolation and comfort during those days and hours of anguish, anxiety and fear. But at the time I experienced peace and serenity thanks to the protection of the Holy Virgin. I would invite all to pray faithfully for the conversion of such unfortunate men and for the situation that leads them to engage in such terrorist activities. Through the Rosary and meditation upon its Mysteries one experiences in a living and indescribable manner that divine friendship which makes us children of God and coheirs with Christ."

Private prayers

The depth of Father Peyton's private prayer life was often observed by the Franciscan Capuchin Friars at St. John's. St. John's had been a home to him in New York before his illness. After long months of recuperation, when he was finally allowed to go outside, he walked the short distance each morning to St. John's Friars' Chapel. There he said his private Mass and his Rosary and spent long periods of meditation long before the friars assembled for morning prayer at nine o'clock. The friars always welcomed his visits when he stayed to have bread and margarine and tea with them. They were inspired by his humility, his kindness to everyone and his gratefulness for the smallest favor. "He is probably busier than most of us," commented Father Dacian Dee, one of the friars, "but he gives priority to his personal prayer, which is clearly the source of the overwhelming power that people recognize in him."

Father Peyton's appetite for food was almost as large as his appetite for work, but under Josefina Bayot's strict guidance, he adhered to his diet. Between periods of rest advised by his physician, he continued his work by mail and telephone.

A new project that had begun that year was a three-year outdoor advertising campaign. The large billboards had been donated in years past by the Outdoor Advertising Association for the message that "The family that prays together stays together." The three-year campaign began with hundreds of billboards proclaiming, "God Makes House Calls." The following year would be featured, "God Listens" and, in 1978, "God Answers." The Hollywood office was in charge of the project.

Father Peyton kept in touch with the staffs in Hollywood and Albany and dictated letters by telephone to Pat Spanbauer. He felt he had to thank all who had helped him, and he continued to seek help from others for other programs.

The initiation of new Crusades abroad had slowed during Father Peyton's absorption in other projects. His long convalescence further slowed the momentum of his activities. This provided him with a much-needed respite to lay the groundwork for the perpetuation of the Family Rosary Crusade. Reminded by his heart attack of his own mortality, he began to focus more intently upon the creation of an organization that would survive after his death.

He faced his own approaching death with peace and faith; sometimes even with longing. In a rare moment of discouragement with the results of his work, he said to one of the women, "It's very hard to get people to pray. I want to die. I want to be with my Blessed Mother in heaven." But the discouragement was only momentary.

As in the illness of his earlier years, he was restless, and no one could slow him down. Finally his doctor released him to travel again.

Father Peyton went home to Ireland in August of 1977 to visit his sister Sarah, who was ill. It was not a vacation from his work. It was an opportunity to revitalize his message to his countrymen, and he made the most of it with interviews in all the media and by renewing old friendships with bishops who became interested in bringing the Crusade back.

He had a press conference in the Gresham Hotel in Dublin, then owned by Hugh Tunney, who afterward became a great friend and a leader in the Crusade. Father Peyton opened the conference with a *Hail Mary*, to the surprise of the reporters who had ordered and were being served drinks.

In the interviews, he spoke about the subject that had brought him such great anguish, indicating by his words that it was passing—the eclipse of Mary.

"An eclipse," he said "is a temporary thing. When it is over the light is more brilliant."

In another interview, when he was asked about the effect of the changes in the Church, he said, "The changes in the Church were marvelous although the Rosary and our mother Mary suffered an eclipse. But it wasn't the theologians of the changes who caused that. It was God Himself.

"We had grown too careless of His gift and He eclipsed it for a time to prove how much we'd miss our mother. And the chaos of some of the modern world proves it.

"But now we know better and the multitude of people turning to prayer and the Rosary tells us the eclipse is over."

During that visit in Ireland he met Sister Teresa McEntee who was just finishing her term as superior of a large convent and school of the Sisters of Mercy. In response to his invitation, she sandwiched in a quick trip on a busy day to visit him at his hotel. They prayed together and he asked her to join the Crusade as part of his global effort.

Sister Teresa was a very proper Irish nun used to the atmosphere of an orderly academic life. She came away from the meeting with Father Peyton convinced that she must endure any sacrifice or hardship entailed in carrying the Rosary to the poor in distant lands. Although she expected that permission was sure to be refused, she asked. Father Peyton and Sister Teresa were astonished at the answer. It was "Yes."

Father Peyton returned to Albany in the fall of 1977 for further rest. But the days were interspersed with directors' meetings, correspondence and trips to other cities.

On clear fall days he could be seen early in the morning walking up and down the broad cement sidewalk in front of his house at 773 Madison Avenue, with Rosary beads in hand, praying. People walking or driving by who were familiar with his work from years past knew Father Peyton was back in town.

One of his trips was to visit a group of friends and supporters in Washington, D.C. Another was to the Cleveland Friends of Father Peyton. They were one of the groups engaged in events to raise money for an "All for Her Fund," a trust fund of five million dollars Father Peyton was trying to accumulate to perpetuate his work.

Still another trip was to Detroit, Michigan, for a celebration of the thirty-fifth anniversary of his work. That event brought congratulatory messages from, among others, the President of the United States, the governor of Michigan, the mayor of Detroit and the archbishop of Detroit. President Jimmy Carter sent his personal representative to speak.

Father Peyton met Sister Teresa at Kennedy Airport in November, just before he was scheduled to take off for Manila, and sent her to Puerto Rico for training for the Crusade in the Philippines.

After arriving in Manila, Father Peyton met with leading businessmen and benefactors who would support the Crusade in the Philippines. The numbers of projectors and generators he had envisioned while speaking at Leyte was reduced from a goal of one hundred to a more practical thirty to begin the Popular Mission. The money to supply these came entirely from local sources.

This was unusual, for nowhere else except in Spain had any country completely financed its Crusade. Most of the Crusades had had considerable money from wealthy donors of the United States.

Bishop Bienvenido Lopez was named the national director of the Crusade, assisted by Señor Carmelo Gomez, placed in charge of the central office of the Pius XII Center with the approval and blessing of Cardinal Sin.

As an associate of the Crusade in the Philippines Father Peyton recruited the gentle and soft-spoken Franciscan priest, Father Eugene Kwiatkowski, who was then working for his order in the Philippines and had been for many years a missionary. Sister Teresa from Ireland would join Father Eugene after her training in Puerto Rico.

The seven-year campaign in the Philippines would establish a base in Manila that would be the springboard for spreading the Crusade throughout Asia.

Father Peyton celebrated his sixty-ninth birthday with friends in the Philippines on January 9, 1978. Late that month a letter was sent to him from the Vatican on behalf of the ailing Holy Father, Pope Paul VI. Monsignor G. Coppa of the Secretariat of State wrote on January 28:

> As you are so well aware, with the publication of *Marialis Cultus* four years ago, the Holy Father issued his exhortation for the right ordering and development of Marian devotion, in which the Rosary found once again a privileged papal recommendation. Subsequently, with the publication of his *Family Prayer Book* he has given new encouragement to the great practice of family prayer. He is hopeful that both initiatives on his part will continue to provide inspiration for you in your personal apostolate. At the same time he prays that all your priestly activities exercised in the communion of the universal Church and with the support of local bishops will help to build up the Body of Christ in faith and love.
>
> Commending you to the intercession of Mary Mother of God and Mother of the Church, His Holiness cordially renews to you his Apostolic Blessing.

That letter reinforced Father Peyton's conviction that the eclipse of Mary was passing and that she would be restored in full to her role as the mother of mankind at that time of man's desperate need of her.

He continued to preach the necessity of bringing Mary and the daily family Rosary into every home, saying:

"The society we live in is a ripoff society. Might is right. Do your own thing no matter who gets hurt. The ethic we live on is sand. Danger signals are all around us that our way of civilization is at an end. It's not coming to an end. It's at an end. But few are listening to the omens.

"Families are in greater upheaval today than ever before. Deep unhappiness, dissatisfaction, drug addiction, runaway and rebellious and lost children add to the growing problem.

"Conflict is everywhere today—between nation and nation, neighbor and neighbor, employer and worker. These conflicts bring so many pressures and problems into the homes that families cannot cope with them and are split and disunited.

"I foresee a time when the Church might be forced underground, either by necessity or indifference.

"People had better start preparing for their grandchildren to face a new style of living, a new way of survival that's based on faith, the faith of Jesus Christ—the way He managed life, how He helped individuals and society to cope with the dangers.

"Jesus conquered our two biggest problems—death and sin—at a terrible price to Himself." Father Peyton often explained the redemption of man in human terms: The Redeemer was like a brother who saves a big family. This oldest brother says to them, "Evil personified is outside, right outside, to do harm to us. But I love you so much that I want you to guard yourselves. Go under the bed. Go behind the doors. Turn out the lights, I want you to be careful while I will go outside to confront that evil personified for your sake. I'll get killed in doing it, but I love you that much."

Then he told them of the voice of the Mother reminding them of their debt to her Son Jesus and of the Rosary and the love and sacrifice of their Brother. Then he described the Rosary in families as millions of tiny lights being lit by those in whose memories the oft-repeated prayers still lingered. The lights would grow in number like the stars of a cloudless sky and in brilliance to light the continents of the world. Father Peyton had dedicated his life to Mary's service as the son, the brother, helping the mother to remind the family of man of the Rosary that she had promised would bring her to them to lead them in their troubles to their Brother Jesus who loved and helped them.

249

"Only families can bring civilization back and save the Church," he told them, " A way has to be found to bring Christian values to the family, in large gatherings and into the home itself. The Rosary can bring families through all dangers and evils.

"That is why I say it is the Rosary above all that must be taught," Father Peyton said frequently to his listeners. "Prayer is wonderful. All prayer is wonderful. All family prayer, no matter what is prayed, all group prayer is wonderful. But it is the Rosary prayed by families that will keep the lights of faith glowing in the days of darkness of faith, as it has done in the past. We must hold fast to the treasure of the Rosary, the gift of Our Blessed Mother, the role of Our Blessed Mother that was the last gift that Jesus gave us before he died. We must never forget the Rosary and its meaning, the very embodiment of our Christianity."

It was Father Peyton's resolution of the questions, the questioners, the anguish over compromise that had plagued his entire life.

It did not mean that he rejected ecumenism. On the contrary, he would continue to preach the value of all family prayer to solve the problems of the family.

But it did mean a primary emphasis upon the Rosary for Christians and that all the work he did must lead to Mary and the Rosary. It was no change from the position he had held and defended for years. It was a strong declaration and reaffirmation of his position, his message and his mission.

By April, too weak and ill to continue, Father Peyton was back in California. In early May he underwent bypass heart surgery in a hospital in Los Angeles. He did not fear death; he welcomed it. But he continued to pray to be allowed to finish his earthly mission.

During Father Peyton's convalescense at the Little Sisters of the Poor home in San Pedro, California, a letter came from Poland that further reassured him about the role of Mary in the Church.

Carol Cardinal Wojtyla, the archbishop of Cracow, wrote on June 26, 1978, in answer to a mailing Father Peyton had sent to the bishops of the world:

Here in Poland we are well acquainted with the power of the Rosary. You speak of an eclipse overshadowing Our Lady in recent years; we have not experienced it yet, perhaps owing to flourishing centers of pilgrimages, of which the greatest is the shrine of Our Lady in Czestochowa. There she has been venerated by all Poland for six centuries, and recently perhaps more than ever. Every year a special Rosary celebration is held daily in our churches during all October, "the Rosary month", with an exposition of the Blessed Sacrament and reciting one part of the Rosary.

We should certainly be happy if it could be daily recited in all our families!

Hoping your Crusade might soon embrace all the world and bring yet more spiritual fruit, I wish you the choicest of God's blessings on you and your movement.

The thought of the Polish people's continued veneration of Our Lady brought reassurance of the resurgence of devotion to her everywhere and comfort to Father Peyton in that time of his recuperation. Also, he discovered that worldwide demand for Rosary beads was on the increase. The Rosary and Father Peyton were both recovering.

Admissio

Almost fully recovered from heart surgery, Father Peyton made the journey to Rome for the pre-arranged audience with Pope John Paul II, on February 17, 1979.

Seated beside the Holy Father at a table the Pontiff had indicated, Father Peyton repeated, "I know. I lived it," and told Pope John Paul II of the heritage of the Rosary that had been passed on by his parents in his childhood home, of his illness in America and the debt he owed to Mary the Mother of God and how he had tried to repay that debt. He spoke only briefly of the performance and techniques of the Family Rosary Crusade, noting that they "are impressive but are history."

He did not dwell upon the past in detail, but on his hopes for the future.

"My time here is not to be much longer," Father Peyton said. "I do not wish the Crusade to die with me. His Holiness is my hope that it won't."

Pope John Paul II did not interrupt Father Peyton, but listened intently. When Father Peyton finished and mentioned his companion in the waiting room, His Holiness rang a bell and asked that Mr. Peter Grace be ushered in.

After a few words of greeting and posing for a photographer, the Holy Father thanked Peter Grace profusely for all the help he had given to Father Peyton—"this holy man." Peter Grace told Pope John Paul II how beautiful he thought the letter the Pontiff had written to Father Peyton from Poland while he was the archbishop of Cracow.

"I remember," replied Pope John Paul II, adding a few words about his own devotion to the Mother of God.

As they were leaving, Pope John Paul II embraced Father Peyton and a second time called him "a man of faith."

When the two men came out of the Holy Father's private meeting room, they encountered a group of about thirty people awaiting an audience. They recognized the first lady of the Philippines, Imelda Marcos, and an entourage of distinguished-looking ladies, all wearing black veils.

On the plane returning home from the Vatican, Father Peyton and Peter Grace reconstructed for one another's better remembrance the words that had been spoken and the events that had transpired.

It very soon became apparent from Pope John Paul II's words and actions that he was dedicated to devotion to Our Lady and that he was a devotee of the Rosary. In March the Pope began saying the Rosary in Latin over Vatican Radio on the first Saturday of every month.

His public discourses called for devotion to the Blessed Virgin Mary.

Father Peyton said later of his audience, "I passed the torch I had carried all my life into His Holiness's hands."

As later events evidenced, however, Father Peyton continued to carry the torch of his devotion to Mary in an upsurge of activity to enlist more and more people under her banner in the Crusade for daily family Rosary.

Returning from Rome, Father Peyton was hospitalized for three weeks with a recurring heart problem that the doctors resolved satisfactorily with new medication.

After weeks of activity in the New York and Albany areas, he journeyed to San Francisco in June to receive a special award from the Knights of Malta.

On July 26, the feast of Saints Joachim and Anne, the parents of Mary, Father Peyton was the speaker for Parents' Day, part of the centenary celebration of the pilgrim shrine of Our Lady of Knock, just thirty miles from his birthplace.

The families that prayed with Father Peyton in that pilgrim town, journeying from near and far even on a weekday, filled the church with an overflow outside.

When he finished speaking the applause was loud and long.

The throng pressed so hard to be near him that he was in danger of being hurt. Those close to him began to try to tear off bits of his cassock. The police brought an ambulance through the crowd and Father Peyton, still reaching out to the extended hands, was pushed into it and whisked away.

During the seventies, the Crusades expanded to Argentina, the Mexican Yucatan, Costa Rica, Bolivia, as well as Providence, Rhode Island; Joliet, Illinois, and St. Louis, Missouri.

The pendulum of religious activity had begun to swing back toward spirituality. Signs were all around of a resurgence of devotion to the Blessed Mother. Avant garde priests such as Jesuit Father Daniel Berrigan, who had gained national prominence a few years before for his opposition to the Vietnam war, were calling for a return to the Rosary. Rosary sales were on the upswing. The recovery of the Rosary hastened Father Peyton's recovery.

The "outmoded" Rosary was coming back into style, even though reports were still coming to Father Peyton that some priests and parishes still questioned its values.

Father Peyton could not understand how anyone could have the faith to say, "*Glory be to the Father, and to the Son, and to the Holy Spirit. As it was in the beginning, is now, and ever shall be, world without end,*" without having the faith to acknowledge and honor the Blessed Virgin Mary for her mission as Mother of the Incarnate God of that Blessed Trinity.

In November, 1979, Father Peyton received a letter dated November 8, from the Vatican Secretary of State on behalf of Pope John Paul II saying in part:

> His Holiness wishes to encourage you in your efforts to promote that devotion to the Virgin Mary which is appropriate for all who are faithful followers of her Son. He prays that through your labors on behalf of family prayer and the daily recitation of the Rosary Christ may be more deeply loved and joyfully praised.

The Most Joyful Mystery

"Roll it."

The telephone rang in the small office of the huge loft studio where the only light came from the floodlights beamed on the small group of actors.

"Cut," ordered Jack Shea, the director. One of the crew shouted, "Take that phone off the hook."

"Roll it," Jack Shea said again. Once again the actors performed and repeated their lines.

"Cut," the order came again. Then, "Okay, print it." A cheer went up from the small knots of crew members who had been silently and intently performing their tasks or watching the action.

Justin Henry ran away from the set to play, like any nine-year-old boy, on the big boom. Barnard Hughes walked from the shooting set to sit in one of the folding chairs. "My feet hurt," he said. "The hardest part of acting is on the feet."

Frank O'Connor, the producer, came by and told him he thought the scene was good.

Then Jason Miller and Diana Muldaur were called for a scene as the parents with Justin, playing their son Paul, and Barney, playing Paul's grandfather. The scene was played under the giant eye of the big boom camera. H. Austin Peterson, television consultant for Family Theater, continued to skip silently and unobtrusively around the set with his still camera snapping pictures.

After a couple of retakes for minor adjustments of position, the scene was completed and the order given to "Print it." The assistants, including Charles Pomerantz and Eddy Jo Bernel, began moving about and talking again.

Father Peyton could not have been better suited for his part as the priest in the half-hour television drama they were shooting. He walked among the crew with words of encouragement and thanks and many a "God bless you" and "Our Blessed Mother will be pleased." His expression of gratitude to the girl who brought him a glass of water was as profuse as his thanks to the stars.

Father Peyton was at home among these stars and talents of the movie and television world. It was like the old days. Some of the older members of the crew had even worked on his programs in those days. Most of the performers and crew were of a new generation, but they gave their talents as freely as those of old.

The exciting times of Hollywood productions of the past that Sister Mary J. Buckley had only heard about were finally back for Family Theater, but she was not there to see its culmination. She had been a part of the preparations but had been recalled by her order to Albany in July. Her assistant, Dennis Roverato, had taken her place as Family Theater manager just a few weeks before the actual shooting. Father Peyton planned to offer "The Most Joyful Mystery," as a free Christmas show to all the television stations throughout the country that would give it free broadcast time.

It was good timing for the production. Most of the artists were available because the actors' strike was on. Every day of the shooting, a mile or so of cars waited in the parking lane of the Los Angeles Freeway to add to the jam of traffic of onlookers driving through Universal City in hopes of catching sight of a celebrity on the picket line.

Father Peyton bent down to Justin Henry's height to talk to him. The little blond boy's blue eyes were startling in their unblinking eye contact with others. Father Peyton repeated again his thanks to Justin's mother standing nearby. The decision to accept Father Peyton's invitation to join the volunteer cast of stars for Family Theater's first production in years had been the child's, and he had said "Yes." It was his first part since two years before when he had been singled out at Midland Public School in the Henrys' home town of Rye, New York, from among thousands of first graders in many schools, to play the role of the child in the movie *Kramer vs. Kramer*.

Father Peyton was at the studio every day of the shooting thanking all who took part and waiting to be called for his own part. He accompanied the crew to outside locations for some shots, notably to Las Vegas, where Frank Sinatra recorded his part after one o'clock in the morning when he had just finished a performance at Caesar's Palace.

The story tells of the elderly grandfather disgruntled with the commercialism of Christmas. He takes his grandchild to church to learn the true meaning of Christmas. The child's parents have other plans for that Christmas eve and cannot accompany them to church.

The many-tapestried drama switches to a Christmas crèche where the roles of Joseph and Mary with her newborn babe come alive in a reenactment of the Nativity, the third Joyful Mystery of the Rosary, played by Don Galloway and Anne Lockhart.

The parents show up at the last minute in the church for a happy reunion, complete with the blessings and beneficent words of Father Peyton as the priest.

Appearing in cameo performances in a recitation of a decade of the Rosary are such familiar faces as Bob Newhart, Danny Thomas, Pat O'Brien, Ricardo Montalban, Kevin Dobson, Isabel Sanford, Dennis Day, Ray Bolger, Mary McDonough, Regis Philbin and Anne Lockhart.

Carols are sung by the Paulist Choristers of California and Frank Sinatra, who also introduces the narrative. In the finale, Father Peyton gives his brief message, closing with "God love you forever."

Father Peyton saw a potential for wider distribution of the Christmas special by having Family Theater syndicate it to individual stations, rather than give it to one network. It meant a great deal more work for him and he began it before the production was finished, working out of Hollywood and New York. He called for help upon his many friends in the fields of entertainment and industry. Over and over he prayed his Rosary.

Our Father who are in heaven, hallowed be Your name; Your kingdom come; Your will be done on earth as it is in heaven. Give us this day our daily bread; and forgive us our trespasses as we forgive those who trespass against us; and lead us not into temptation, but deliver us from evil. Amen.

They worked right up until a few days before Christmas. More than one hundred television stations agreed to donate free time to the broadcast.

This meant more than one hundred duplications of the film and sound track.

"The Most Joyful Mystery" was aired on Christmas eve and Christmas day, mostly in good time slots, across the United States and Canada. Reviewers acclaimed it. Requests began coming from TV stations and from individuals for a repeat performance.

The Christmas show was hardly aired before Father Peyton began work on an Easter program centered around the Resurrection.

The Greatest Mystery

Father Peyton flew to Paris to meet Her Serene Highness Princess Grace of Monaco and ask her to play a part in his Easter television special.

They had something in common. Princess Grace growing up as Grace Kelly in Philadelphia had listened to the weekly radio dramas of Father Peyton's Family Theater of the Air. Besides, her father had been born in County Mayo, Ireland, Father Peyton's ancestral home. She, like Father Peyton, also had a great love of the Rosary. Princess Grace said "Yes" to Father Peyton's request.

The sequence with Princess Grace in the principal role of narrator was filmed in London under the direction of Michael Gill. Barry Chattington directed the rest of the program, which was shot in many places around the world. Frank O'Connor again was the producer.

The half-hour program, "The Greatest Mystery," tells the story of the Resurrection, with the London Players in the Bible scenes of the first Easter, and of Easter celebrations in native traditions around the world. A decade of the Rosary is recited in the various languages. Petula Clark sings with the Chichester Cathedral Choir and the Oscar-winning Chieftains provide the hymns. The spiritual message is given by Father Peyton.

Distribution was the same as for the Christmas special. The show received a "Golden Halo" award from the Southern

California Motion Picture Council. The council also created a special award for Princess Grace for her performance.

Father Peyton had originally planned a trilogy of productions based on the Nativity, the Crucifixion and the Resurrection. The success of the first two programs and his own continuing strength in spite of his serious heart ailment convinced him that he could produce shows based on all fifteen mysteries.

In his thirties he had been hailed as the pioneer in religious programming for mass media. As much a visionary in his seventies, with his genius for the use of mass communications, he familiarized himself with the new electronic advances that provided the technology for individual television viewing. He envisioned a future with this capability in every home. The many audio-visual cassettes made for individual stations would provide a bank for duplication in the thousands.

This was the key to the future of getting the message of Family Rosary Crusade into every home. They could be distributed by Family Theater to individual families. Parents could use them to teach their children. Little children could learn about Jesus and Mary and the Rosary in their own homes, taught by their parents, long before they could be reached by the teachings of the priests and the nuns.

Father Peyton faced the decade of the eighties—the fifth decade of his work—in a spirit of hope and optimism.

His plan for a global Crusade was well on the way to being implemented with permanent bases in central locations to serve every continent of the world.

In Ireland he had the backing of Archbishop Dermot J. Ryan of Dublin for the establishment of a Crusade base there. Leading laymen, prominent among them Hugh Tunney, were interested. He also had a promise from Archbishop Joseph Cunnane of Tuam, and in Sligo from Bishop Dominic Conway of the diocese of Elphin, of two priests to help the work in Ireland. One of his goals for the Irish base was to recruit priests and nuns willing to work full-time for the Family Rosary Crusade and Our Lady. His hope was that in the coming years Crusade teams would multiply to serve the continents of Europe and Africa from the two bases in Ireland and Spain.

In Spain a permanent base was firmly established and operated by three Dominican priests dedicated full-time to directing diocesan crusades. It was financed in most part by that great

Spanish friend of Our Lady Antonio de Oriol and the ingenuity of the priests to acquire money for operational expenses in the dioceses where they worked.

In Latin America the base had been established in Rio de Janeiro twenty-one years before by a team that pioneered the pattern of a permanent base. The Latin American bishops were, for the most part, eager and willing to sponsor the Crusade programs. In Bolivia, the ongoing Crusade made available religious films for hundreds of thousands to view for the first time in their native languages by supplying the Rosary films in two native Indian languages of Quechua and Aymara. Additional crusades were being planned for Argentina, Colombia and Peru. The German bishops, through their charitable organization, Adveniat, gave a grant of eighty thousand dollars to help Family Rosary Crusade continue its work in Latin America.

In the United States, the offices in Albany and Hollywood continued to serve the North American continent and to support the bases serving the other continents of the world.

The main thrust of the crusades for the 1980s was in the Philippines. Father Pat planned the base already established in Manila as headquarters for a "sweep through Asia" and as a permanent base to carry on the mission in Asia. Enough money had been raised to begin since his last visit there in 1977 when he and the Filipino "giants" had organized the Family Rosary Crusade Foundation, Inc.

Along with making the films and establishing the world bases, Father Peyton was already at work on crusades in the Philippines, with several dates scheduled for rally talks. He also took advantage of assemblies of bishops and priests to attend and implore them to spread the message of Mary and daily family Rosary. One such gathering of utmost importance to him was the triennial Synod of Bishops in Rome in October, 1980. He was at the time restructuring the Crusade to continue on a permanent global basis, where, he said, "They will not need rallies—they will not need me." In his seventies and with recurring health problems, he knew that the end of his earthly mission was not far off. He spent every precious moment of his time insuring that his message of Mary and the Rosary would live on, his legacy to the world, after his death. The pace of his activities quickened.

He implored Mary's help with continual "Hail Marys" and petitions. It was from her that he got the strength to go on.

The First Glorious Mystery
The Resurrection

After the sabbath, as the first day of the week was dawning, Mary Magdalene came with the other Mary to inspect the tomb. Suddenly there was a mighty earthquake as the

angel of the Lord descended from heaven. He came to the stone, rolled it back, and sat on it. In appearance he resembled a flash of lightning while his garments were as dazzling as snow. The guards grew paralyzed with fear of him and fell down like dead men. Then the angel spoke, addressing the women: "Do not be frightened, I know you are looking for Jesus the crucified, but he is not here. He has been raised, exactly as he promised. Come and see the place where he was laid. Then go quickly and tell his disciples: 'He has been raised from the dead and now goes ahead of you to Galilee, where you will see him.' That is the message I have for you."

(Matthew 28: 1-7)

The women ran in fear and joy from the tomb to tell the disciples the news. Suddenly Jesus appeared before them and they embraced his feet. Jesus told them to tell His disciples to go to Galilee, where they would see Him.

The disciples refused to believe the women, but Peter and John ran to the tomb to see for themselves. Later Jesus appeared to two men on the road to Emmaus and revealed Himself to them. He appeared to the apostles where they were gathered, all except Thomas, in Jerusalem in a room with a locked door, and later to Thomas, who doubted, and told him to touch His wounds. His disciples no longer had any doubt that He had risen from the dead.

Father Peyton's meditation
on The Resurrection

The Resurrection is an awesome event. The apostles are bewildered, fearful, skeptical—like little children wishing that what they are hearing could be true, but fearing that it is but a fantasy, a fairytale. But all their misgivings finally give way to belief, certainty, and great joy. Now they can hope that everything He said and promised, He will fulfill. Now they are on safe ground to love Him, worship Him, and adore Him as their Lord and God. He has conquered death. Death has now lost its power. We are the inheritors of this same belief and faith.

Alone of all mankind, Jesus confronted death head-on and won. The Risen Christ is the heart and soul of our believing, our hoping and our loving. The Risen Christ is the reason for our optimism, our love for life, and our option for living it His way, the Christian way. He died that we might live. He arose from the dead—so shall we.

His claim for our total belief in Him, our unwavering hope and trust in Him, and our unreserved and life-long love for Him, is *His Resurrection*—the first glorious mystery of the Rosary.

Reflections on the Rosary

In a 1980 interview, Father Peyton described the origins, evolution and meaning of the Rosary.

Of the beginning of the Rosary, he said:

"Very few realize that the Rosary—with fifteen decades and each decade dedicated to a mystery in the life of Jesus and Mary—just didn't happen overnight. It evolved through a long prayer experience beginning with the early Christians. And it took a number of centuries before people began to pray it as we do today.

"Think of the early Christians. Who were they? The followers and friends of Jesus—the Apostles, early disciples, His mother and relatives. They were all Jews. And they followed the Jewish tradition of prayer and worship very carefully. Now as Jews they had an age-old beautiful practice—every week they prayed the psalms of David—one hundred and fifty of them during the course of the week.

"The fifteen decades total one hundred and fifty *Hail Marys*.

"The relationship is indirect but it's surely there. As time went on and the Church developed its own customs and practices as a Christian church, those psalms were taken and structured into what was called the psalter—or the divine office. That was really the official prayer book of the priests and the monks. But there were many in those early monasteries who couldn't read or write, They were allowed to substitute the Lord's prayer—the *Our Father*—for each of the one hundred and fifty psalms."

The Gentiles who joined the first Jewish Christians brought with them many of their own prayer practices. One of these was the repetition of one and the same prayer. And they counted it out by using what we might call a simple prayer counter. Sometimes they used ribbons or beads—even fish bones—or pebbles that they shifted from one pocket to the other. They were simple folk—and you can hear them praying away with steady, sometimes monotonous sounds—like the beat of drums or the rise and fall of waves on the seashore. Sometimes I think of the falling rain, or the blowing wind. All this creates an inner emotional mood that helps the mind and heart to feel the presence of God and sense the sacred.

"Hindus, Buddhists, some branches of Islam and many other religions use this method of repeating and counting the same prayer to help them in their prayer life. The newly founded Christian communities, in adopting this method of prayer, were in the groundwork of what much later became the Rosary.

"The Rosary itself, as we know it today, really came about in three stages. The first stage is the *Our Father*. The simple people were illiterate and they were not capable of reading the psalms, so they were permitted to pray an *Our Father* for each of the one hundred and fifty psalms."

The Lord's prayer was used as substitute for the Psalms prayed in the Jewish practice.

"Because that was the prayer that emphasized for them the Fatherhood of God. That was the prayer that brought them into the great new dimension taught to them by Jesus—that they were not slaves or servants but were children of God. And this concept, new to them, of being children of God, generated within them a powerful spiritual force that enabled many of them to accept martyrdom. The Lord's prayer became the most widely used prayer in the history of all mankind.

"Each decade of the Rosary begins with the praying of the *Our Father*. In the second stage we arrive at the prayer we know today as the *Hail Mary*. The first centuries of Christianity were much involved in controversies about Christ. The great question was how to look upon Him—as God or man or both? There were many discussions in the early councils of the Church. But a final and definite solution was given at a great Council known as the Council of Ephesus in the fifth century. And that Council proclaimed that Christ was both divine and human. In insisting upon the divinity of Christ, they gave Mary the title "Mother of God." And really that was nothing new. What they decreed simply echoed what the Christians had already recognized and believed that Jesus Christ is God and Mary is His mother. That caused joy and jubilation throughout the Christian world. In their inmost hearts people felt that the Council Fathers had spoken through the Holy Spirit in proclaiming a great truth: that Jesus is our brother because of His human nature, but He is also Son of God, and because He comes to us through Mary she can rightly be called "Mother of God." That was good news and they began to preach it everywhere. For instance, St. Patrick arrived in Ireland right after the Council. He brought the faith to Ireland. And what he preached grew, took hold in the hearts and minds of the Irish and ever since then they have been known for their tender and filial devotion to Mary the Mother of God.

"People were so thrilled with the recognition given to Mary and God's greatness in her that they started to greet her—over and over again—with the greeting of the Angel Gabriel that we find in the Gospel itself. '*Hail, full of Grace, the Lord is with thee...*' It was natural that Elizabeth's greeting would be added to this— '*Blessed art thou among women, and blessed is the fruit of thy womb*' ...All that became one prayer taken directly from the Gospel—and it became so popular and spread everywhere until by the early thirteenth century the Church placed it beside the Lord's prayer and the Apostles' Creed as one of the three basic prayers for all the faithful.

"As the great monastic orders like the Dominicans, Franciscans and Carthusians encouraged the people to greet Mary through the simple greetings of Gabriel and Elizabeth, devotion to Mary increased and people began to realize that the same Mary interceded for them. So they began to say, '*Holy Mary, Mother of God, pray for us sinners now and at the hour of our death..*' By the fifteenth century that petition was added to what was known as the biblical or scriptural '*Ave*' and the *Hail Mary* as we pray it today was completed.

"People liked the prayer. They felt close to Mary and they believed in her closeness to Jesus and her power to bring them to Him, so they prayed the *Hail Mary* over and over. Gradually that custom replaced the old custom of praying the one hundred and fifty *Our Fathers*, the custom that was carried over from the Old Testament. And so we move into the third stage.

"That's what I call the meditative stage—meditating upon the mysteries of the lives of Jesus and Mary. If you study the spiritual background of the middle ages, you can see how easy and natural it was for the faithful to move into a meditative mood when praying. The people of the middle ages lived in the age of deep faith. They led simple uncomplicated lives, and they thought and spoke much about Jesus—His joys and sufferings and the glory of His resurrection. As they thought about Him, they were reminded of Mary and her role in the great mystery of the Incarnation. So they began putting it all together—the mystery of the birth of

Christ—and his life and sufferings and finally His triumph. In this they were always helped and encouraged by the great preachers of those times who went from place to place focusing the minds and hearts of the medieval people upon the message of Gabriel to Mary and the mysteries of the lives of Jesus and Mary that flowed from that one great moment when Mary accepted God's invitation to be the mother of His Son. The fifteen Mysteries of the Rosary were formally established. Ten *Hail Marys* were fixed to be said for each of the mysteries, and that corresponded to the fundamental number of one hundred and fifty that found its roots in the one hundred and fifty psalms of the Old Testament. And so the mysteries of the lives of Jesus and Mary were divided into the Joyful, the Sorrowful and Glorious periods of His life, and each mystery was introduced by the *Our Father*, with the praying of the *Hail Marys* as the vocal background, and, bringing each mystery to its conclusion—in acknowledgment that each mystery is in the plan and will of God and to His glory, is the *Glory be to the Father*.

"It was a real blessing to me to discover through my own study and research how the Rosary has its roots way back in the Old Testament and evolved through the Word of God in the New Testament, and through the guidance of the Church and the acclamation of the faithful. It shows how one light leads to another if only we are open to accept it.

"Like all the works and events in the Church, the Rosary has the power and touch of the Holy Spirit upon it. Even Jesus had to be born and He had to grow in wisdom and age. It took centuries for the Rosary to come to us in its most complete form. It's the product of many ages and various cultures responding to the needs and desires of the people to offer God praise and adoration, to enter into the contemplation of His eternal plan—and to appreciate how He worked out salvation through Jesus and Mary. When the people could not read and had no books, no psalters, the Lord provided.

"It meets the needs of the modern family today—to get together to pray."

Not quite of this world

H. Austin Peterson first heard about Father Peyton from two friends from the Young and Rubicam days, Al Scalpone and Tom Lewis, two of the priest's earliest volunteers. Mr. Peterson's career as a radio and television writer and producer kept him hopping for forty-four years, and he did not meet Father Peyton until 1974. From that first meeting, he became another Hollywood notable who said "Yes" to Father Peyton's invitation to join up. He became a volunteer and, by the time of the production of the Christmas program, "The Most Joyful Mystery," he was spending full time working with Family Theater.

"I have been exposed to hundreds of star personalities, from Fred Astaire to Efrem Zimbalist, but I don't believe that any personality has so impressed me as Father Peyton," Mr. Peterson said. "The thing that impressed me most was his honest sincerity. You believe because he believes. He is absolutely dedicated to the family and its salvation."

In those years as a volunteer, "Pete" photographed Father Peyton at rallies in many parts of the world. He recalled one of those times in Mexico when eighty-five thousand people stood in the blazing sun for hours to hear Father Peyton's message.

Looking back upon his impressions of Father Peyton, Pete wrote:

> What impressed me most, I guess, was to see photos of Father Peyton conducting a rally with five hundred thousand in attendance at Golden Gate Park. San Francisco is my home town and I didn't think you could get a half million people out for anything less than the Giants winning the World Series and the 49ers taking the Super Bowl the same day!
>
> I am constantly amazed at his Rosary films. In the mountains back of San Juan I have seen hundreds of Puerto Ricans standing in the rain to watch the films projected on a sheet stretched between two trees. To think that these same films have been seen by almost 80 million people under similar situations boggles ·the mind—even to a TV man used to dealing in millions.
>
> Father Pat and his work have had a serious impact on me.

When I was in Rome in 1976 with Father and we stood in the beautiful St. Peter's Basilica I found myself declaring to Father I would like to convert to Catholicism. I was surprised as he was! You cannot be around this man and not be affected. We search all our lives for something in life that is really worthwhile and maybe the answer is the simplest of all—prayer.

There are times when I look at Father Peyton that he appears unreal—something not quite of this world. I can't think of another word except "saint". His boundless energy, his dedication to his belief that the family can be saved rubs off on you. He's quite a man.

Pages out of the Bible

John C. Fuller had been a film editor in Hollywood for forty years. His first work for Family Theater as a volunteer was in the early days of television production. Then his own work kept him busy, and it was not until thirteen years later that he was able to fulfill his dream of working again with Father Peyton. From that time on, he became the full-time volunteer chief film editor.

During his first stint with Family Theater, two of the telefilms he edited received the highest critical praise. He was nominated more than once for an Emmy award for the quality of his work.

The films that moved him to want to return to work with Family Theater were the award-winning *Hill Number One* and *That I May See* starring top Hollywood stars.

Hill Number One begins in a modern setting as an artillery crew hurls howitzer shells at an enemy hill, known only as "Hill Forty-Six." As they complain of the hardships and deprivation, their chaplain tells them the story of another hill—Golgotha.

The movie focuses back in time two thousand years to a denuded cross on the crown of that hill, with Mary the Mother of Sorrows weeping beneath it and with the taunts and shouts of Pilate's soldiers. The story follows Joseph of Arimathea as he begs for the body of Christ, and the disciples praying in the Upper Room, to the dawn of the first Easter with the tidings of the Resurrection breaking over Judea.

That I May See is based on the story of Bartimeus the blind beggar whose sight is restored by Jesus. He is at first grateful and then vain. He journeys from Jericho to Jerusalem and his faith wavers in mental turmoil when he witnesses the Crucifixion. He meets a fellow traveler, Simon the Cyrenean, who reproaches him for his ingratitude. He does not repent until he sees Mary, who has come to thank Simon for carrying the cross. On the lonely road back to Jericho, Christ appears to Bartimeus and his faith is completely restored.

"Johnny" wrote his own account of his impressions of those films and of his work over the years for Father Peyton:

I first met Father Peyton in 1951 while he was producing the first of the three films that I was to edit for him. It was a tremendous experience for me. I had been editing westerns and comedies but now the challenge of a religious film confronted me. The mechanics would be the same but this type of subject had to be handled carefully. In westerns you cut for action and in comedies you cut for laughs. But in these religious pictures the pace had to be slower. The scenes were sensitive. You had to have patience.

While I ran the film through the moviola I observed at close range the stark drama that was unfolding before my eyes. Every scene was like a page out of the Bible, come to life. The direction was so powerful and the actors were great. Many times during the editing, tears came to my eyes.

Two of the three films, *Hill Number One* and *That I May See*, were judged by the nation's TV stations to be the best films in the religious category in 1952. This critique was published in *Billboard Magazine*. It was at this time that I realized the impact that this man was making on the world with his belief in family prayer for a better world.

When I finished the three films I went back to the westerns and comedies, but my experience with Father Peyton never left me. I always thought of those scenes that affected me so much, and I kept hoping that someday I would again have the opportunity to work with him. That opportunity came thirteen years ago.

I was semi-retired and had plenty of free time. When I visited Father Peyton at the Family Theater he was getting ready to film interviews with fifteen prominent stars. One word led to another and I have been a volunteer worker editing film for Family

Theater ever since. I truly believe that the family that prays together stays together.

Over the years Father Peyton got help from many celebrities of all denominations. One day after we got through shooting an interview with Buddy Ebsen (who played Jed Clampett on the "Beverly Hillbillies" and now is TV's "Barnaby Jones") for the *Prince of Peace* series, Father asked all of us on the set if we would like to join him in a prayer. After we finished Buddy told Father: "When my minister sees this film on television he will want equal time."

The Second Glorious Mystery
The Ascension

The eleven disciples made their way to Galilee, to the mountain to which Jesus had summoned them. At the sight of him, those who had entertained doubts fell down in homage. Jesus came forward and addressed them in these words: "Full authority has been given to me both in heaven and on earth; go, therefore, and make disciples of all the nations. Baptize them in the name of the Father. and of the Son, and of the Holy Spirit. Teach them to carry out everything I have commanded you. And know that I am with you always, until the end of the world!"

(Matthew 28: 16-20)

As he blessed, he left them, and was taken up to heaven.
They fell down to do him reverence, then returned to
Jerusalem filled with joy.

(Luke 24: 51-52)

Father Peyton's meditation
on The Ascension

The Ascension like the Resurrection is another earth-shaking event. A sixth-century biblical picture interprets the scene of Christ disappearing from the sight of Mary and the apostles. Mary is standing beneath her ascending Son. His hands are raised in blessing. Her hands are raised in prayer and supplication. On either side of Mary are depicted the apostles, bewildered, shocked, in confusion. They are not able to cope with these unprecedented happenings. They feel safe, however, because Mary is with them. Her presence gives them the assurance of a mother. They are like children who in the face of a stranger or a strange event run behind their mother, clutch her skirts and with frightened eyes peer out from behind her to see how safe they are.

The apostles are taking their strength and courage from the person and the presence of Mary in their midst. She is mother—of this family—Christ's apostles and disciples. She is the same for us. She is our mother, too. We can lay claim to her love and care, her presence and her prayer by the same right as the apostles and early disciples, whose descendants we are. She is the safest and surest way for us to Christ.

The bishops

Jack Haley, who played the Tin Man who yearned for a heart in

273

The Wizard of Oz, one of the most famous of his many famous roles, proved that he lacked no heart in his response to Father Peyton. His was one of the frequent voices of Family Theater of the Air.

Asked for one of his most vivid recollections of an incident he witnessed in his years with Father Peyton, he told the story of "Father Peyton and the Bishops". Here, for the first time, is the story he wrote about two years before his death.

Father Peyton at Stonehill College

I accompanied Father Peyton on a flight from Los Angeles to New York City. We were on our way to Stonehill College, outside of Brockton, Mass., where Father Pat would receive an honorary degree. Upon arrival in New York, I registered him at the New York Athletic Club of which I am a member. We both had appointments to keep and would contact one another later in the day.

About five o'clock, my room telephone at the club rang, it was Father Pat. He informed me that he was in his room and about to read his breviary. I said, "Father, so soon as you are finished, meet me on the second floor in the tap room." "Oh dear Jack, is it all right for me to go there?" He asked nervously. "All right? You will probably meet a couple of other priests hanging at the bar," I answered. We both had dinner and nothing happened that the devil's advocate could dig up 50 years hence.

The next morning was Sunday and we both walked along 59th Street, through Columbus Circle on our way to St. Paul's Church on Tenth Avenue, which functions under the auspices of the Paulist Fathers. Father Peyton would say Mass on a side altar and I would perform as his altar boy. We had hardly arrived in the sacristy, when an out-of-town secular priest recognized Father Peyton, and asked if he would bless him. The priest knelt and Father gave him his blessing. As the priest arose, Father Pat quickly knelt and pulled me down with him, as he said, "Father, now you bless us." Father Pat, with his consummate humility, would not allow the out-of-town priest to exhalt him. He seemed to imply, my blessing is no more holy than yours, for don't forget, we both bless in the name of the Father, the Son and the Holy Spirit.

At the Stonehill commencement, I sat on the platform vestured in black gown and mortarboard hat, as I had been a recipient of an honorary degree several years before. Along with other lay

274

dignitaries, there were three bishops, one from Fall River, Mass., another from out of state and the third was a bishop from South America. Father Pat was introduced as the principal speaker. As he began his address to the graduates, their friends and relatives, I watched the bishops. The three of them leaned forward in their chairs to catch every word, expression and nuance that Father Pat would emit. It was much like in my profession, of a neophyte watching an established superstar.

They all had heard of Father Peyton and his love and devotion for the Blessed Mother. They had read of the many Rosary Crusades he had conducted all over the world, attracting millions upon millions of people. Now they were seeing him in the flesh. He began quietly. We were outdoors, still there was an obvious calmness. There was no scholarly eloquence in his voice, no rhetorical grandeur. But there was love. It shone all around him, a divine love, a special kind of love, that can come only from a man who has devoted his whole life, every step, every breath, every conscious moment to the Blessed Mother and her Divine Son.

The bishops seemed to lean forward a bit further. I watched the intensity on their faces. I speculated on what may have been percolating in their minds. Were they thinking of their bishoprics and the power they swayed over their dioceses and did they collate it, if only for a second, with the life of the vow of poverty priest, standing before them? Did they dwell at all on the early impulses that directed them toward their priestly callings? Did they think of the sentence they heard, so often during their seminarian days, until it became almost a litany, "The Following of Christ"? Did they recognize it in Father Peyton?

I began sharing my attention between Father Pat and the raptly absorbed bishops. "She's here, she's with us this very moment," pealed Father Pat. Suddenly, my thoughts shifted to the day Rosalind Russell and I agreed to act as co-chairpersons for his 25th anniversary dinner, and how he directed us to his chapel where he prayed the *Memorare* to our Blessed Mother and asked that the affair would be successful. I could hear Rosalind whispering to me, "Jack, this man's a saint." This triggered my contemplative mind and I thought, *Saints are not sanctified until after they have died. By the time the devil's advocate finished and the meticulous probing has ended, all those who knew the saint have also passed away. Then reliance is upon the writings of those who talked with him, supped, exchanged views and laughed with him.*

Wouldn't it be nice to have known St. Theresa, St. Patrick, et al? Or listen to the laughter of St. Francis and the brain of St. Augustine? What were these saints like while they were on this

275

earth? They must have functioned humanly, such as you and I do, but their lives were exemplary. They followed Christ, they had charity in their hearts, they breathed morality. And with their prayers, they caused mystical mysteries.

All of the above is Father Pat. Will he attain sainthood? I wondered. When priests become saints, is there celebration in heaven? I wondered further. I am sure I will not be permitted to attend Father Peyton's heavenly jubilation, but if he can just fix it, so I can peer in through the gate, I'll be happy. A salvo of applause stirred me out of my reverie. Father Pat had finished and as he walked back to his seat, the bishops were still agape, for how often does even a bishop share a platform with a saint.

Jack Haley's story shows the effect that Father Peyton has, even upon people who outrank him in position.

Jack Haley's son, Jack Haley Jr., a famed producer and another of Father Peyton's helpers, commented about the same time, "People who help Father Peyton have good things happen. I like to think that there is a little bit of Father Peyton in me and that he has helped me in the good fortune I have had in my chosen work."

The Third Glorious Mystery
The Descent of the Holy Spirit

When the day of Pentecost came it found them gathered in one place. Suddenly from up in the sky there came a noise like a strong, driving wind which was heard all through the house where they were seated. Tongues as of

fire appeared, which parted and came to rest on each of them. All were filled with the Holy Spirit. They began to express themselves in foreign tongues and make bold proclamation as the Spirit prompted them.

(Acts 2: 1-4)

Father Peyton's meditation
on The Descent of the Holy Spirit

Scripture tells us of the presence of Mary, in prayer with the apostles in the upper room, awaiting the fulfillment of the promise Christ made them before His Ascension. For more than a week they pray and they wait. At last the days of waiting are over. For this time of prayer and waiting, they are rewarded. Christ fulfills His promise. He sends the Holy Spirit, the Church is born.

Christ, through the Holy Spirit, is again present with His people. The power of the apostles, the courage of the martyrs, the ever increasing number of saints, and the multitudes down through the ages that transmit to their sons and daughters the Christian Faith, are all due to the Holy Spirit. Through His presence, we get life and love. Through His presence we are united with Christ into one body—His Mystical Body—the Church. Through His presence in the Church and in each one of us, its members, we are able to say "Our Father."

What an echo of the upper room is the Family Rosary home. Let every family who prays the Rosary daily expect like results—the Spirit of Christ comes when the family is united in prayer with Mary.

A film for a prayer

María Luisa Luca de Tena sat at her typewriter. The sheet of paper rolled into the machine was still blank. Her mind flashed over the years she had worked with Father Peyton, recalling many incidents of joy, sorrow, success, frustration, astonishment, enlightenment, inspiration, faith, prayer. There were so many! How could she choose one in response to an invitation to her to write a story of her most vivid recollection of Father Peyton.

She would never forget the impression of honest sincerity she had when she first interviewed Father Peyton for an article in the newspaper her father published.

It was shortly after the Málaga Crusade, and Father Peyton was trying to explain to the leaders the purpose and methods of the Crusade. But he knew very little Spanish. She had become his interpreter for some of his interviews with high-ranking bishops and businessmen. During one of these sessions, the man being interviewed was very negative. He was also blunt and so disagreeable for a person of his position she got the impression he revealed a lack of faith in the efficacy and method of the Family Rosary Crusade.

When she and Father Peyton came out of the interview, Father Peyton was as red as a tomato because of the humiliation he had suffered. Neither one of them said a single word until on the way home in the automobile.

Then María Luisa could not help but exclaim, "Father, it was painful. It was terrible." Father Peyton, who had already recovered his serenity, replied with a smile, "Oh, dear María, this is one of the small, the very small, prices that I have to pay for the great victory of Our Lady."

María Luisa believed that simple incident revealed the character and deep faith of Father Peyton as well as any. She started to write and soon filled the sheet of paper with the words of description that she was so apt with in the practice of her journalistic career.

Then her mind started wandering again over the years and her experiences and impressions of Father Peyton. There was one

278

more story she had to tell. The vividness of her recollection might have something to do with her own personal involvement with that incident, but it was revealing of Father Peyton's methods of persuasion.

She wrote, swiftly and with few pauses:

In search to strengthen the Family Theater Hour,—to continue Family Theater programming of inspirational films—Father had seen in Madrid a film by a Spanish producer. His name was Caesar Gonzáles. Father decided he must obtain this film for one of his programs. Finally, he was able to obtain an interview with this person, who was generally known to be a hard businessman and certainly not very Christian in his way of living and thinking.

I was the interpreter for this interview. Mr. Gonzáles received us in his office, which was impressively luxurious. After we had gone through several secretaries and sub-secretaries, we finally reached him. And Father Peyton began explaining his desire of acquiring that film, which was called. *El Golfillo.* Señor Gonzáles told him immediately that he would sell it for a hundred thousand dollars. Father Peyton tried to convince him that this film, once it was shown in Spain, was already finished. He couldn't give him such a sum of money at all. He could only give him a percentage after he had seen what way he could use it in the United States. Well, Señor Gonzáles didn't even want to listen to that, and they began to talk about figures and to bargain. But Señor Gonzáles did not surrender in the least. Finally, Father Peyton remained silent for a moment, and then he said, "Mr. Gonzáles, I'm not a businessman. My only business is prayer. So let us pray together before finishing our bargain." And at that, he immediately knelt down in the middle of that office. And I, although I was a little embarrassed, also knelt down. And Caesar Gonzáles, with great embarrassment on his part, could not do otherwise.

And there we were, the three of us, kneeling, and Father Peyton prayed away in most fervent prayer to Our Lady.

Suddenly the door opened and two men, businessmen, entered, and they were carrying briefcases and papers. And they looked at us with mouths wide open with astonishment, looking at this group of us, kneeling, Caesar Gonzáles and myself, we were blushing. And it occurred to me at that moment that those gentlemen thought, "Father Peyton is marrying them in secret. The fact is that we were so embarrassed and ashamed that our heads were literally down to the floor. And they did not know what was happening, and so they just left in astonishment.

Father Peyton, meantime, continued unperturbed and prayed

the litany to Mary. And when we got up, Caesar Gonzáles was so stunned that actually he gave him the film as a gift. And I believe that this film can be found today in the film library of Family Theater with the English title *The Urchin*.

Twice saved

Hugh T. Tunney, chairman of the Tunney Group of companies of Ireland, went to Mass on Sundays and felt that he fulfilled his religious obligation. He enjoyed the material benefits of his great wealth the rest of the time. It was not until after he met Father Peyton that he realized he had been quite lost, spiritually speaking.·

He had heard of Father Peyton but had not met him. When he heard that Father Peyton was coming to Dublin in August, 1977, he invited him to stay as his guest at Dublin's world-famous Gresham Hotel, which he owned. Father Peyton accepted gratefully and prayed with Mr. Tunney and gave him a set of Rosary beads.

Mr. Tunney believes that Rosary twice saved his life, the first time October 20, 1977, and again two years and one week later.

After meeting and talking with Father Peyton, Mr. Tunney practiced his Catholicism every day of the week, not just on Sundays. "Of all the people I have ever met, not one has had a more lasting effect or deeper impact upon me than Father Peyton," Mr. Tunney declared.

He wrote his own account of those incidents, as follows:

> I was driving home to Dublin in a Rolls Royce, and as I approached the village of Dunshauklin, County Meath, I was saying my Rosary, which is normal for me since I have a habit of saying the Rosary while I am driving alone in my car. As I came round a corner into Dunshauklin village, suddenly I saw a car parked on

my left hand side, petrol pumps and people on my right hand side, and a car coming toward me about to pass the parked car. As you will appreciate from the description I have related above, my way forward was totally blocked, and the result was a very serious accident, in which both cars were very badly damaged, and the occupants of the other car, a young husband and wife, were badly injured. The young husband recovered without any serious injury, but unfortunately his wife died in hospital about three hours after the crash.

I escaped badly shaken but without the slightest hurt. My Rosary beads were in pieces and when eventually I put them together again, I found three beads were missing. Those three beads were found by a friend of mine whom I asked to go to the place of the accident the following day.

I am convinced that the Rosary saved my life on that occasion, but you must form your own conclusions.

The second incident was on the morning of the murder of Lord Louis Mountbatten of Burma and members of his family. The date was the 27th August, 1979. On that occasion I was invited by Lord Louis to have dinner with him and his family on the evening of 26th August, at the Castle Classiebawn, in County Sligo in the west of Ireland, where Lord Louis Mountbatten and his family were my guests.

I found Lord Louis Mountbatten in great form and after talking with him until 12:45 a.m. we decided to retire. Breakfast was arranged for 9 a.m. and I asked to be called at 8 a.m. with an early morning cup of tea. I was duly called, dressed, and looking at my watch I found it was only 15 minutes after eight, so I decided that since I had plenty of time to spare I would say my Rosary novena then, rather than the evening which was my normal practice.

I came down to the dining room and Lord Mountbatten arrived in the room approximately one minute later. We were alone in the dining room awaiting the arrival of the remainder of the family. Lord Louis was full of life and full of fun. He was wearing a black naval jumper with the inscription the ''Fighting Fifth'' which he told me was presented to him by the widows and the survivors of the famous *Kelly* (the ship Lord Mountbatten loved).

As it was a particularly fine day, Lord Mountbatten with almost all his family decided to go fishing on *Shadow 5*, which was his boat built from timber from the estate and to Lord Mountbatten's own design. *Shadow 5* was used by Lord Mountbatten and his family during the month of August each year when he stayed at Classiebawn, and the rest of the year by myself.

After breakfast that morning Lord Mountbatten insisted that a number of photographs be taken of myself with members of his family and himself, which was something he never did before. The camera was lost at sea but was later recovered and all the photographs came out perfectly.

After the photographs were taken I went into the Morning Room to talk to Lord Brabourne, son-in-law of Lord Mountbatten, who was one of the survivors from the terrible explosion on the boat. At about 11:30 a.m. Lord Mountbatten got anxious to go to the boat with Lord Brabourne and the rest of the family. Lord Brabourne then asked me to come with them on *Shadow 5*, which I had done on previous occasions. However, due to the time and the fact that I was anxious to get back to business, I declined. Twenty minutes later Lord Mountbatten was dead, as was Lord Brabourne's son (a boy of fourteen years), the young boat boy, and the dowager Lady Brabourne.

I really believe that it was Our Lady who made me say no to the invitation to go on *Shadow 5* that morning, and thus my life was saved.

After meeting Father Pat and talking to him, which had a profound and lasting effect on me, I resumed the practice of the daily Rosary and the Sacraments and I can assure you that I feel much better, much happier, than at any other time in my life, and I shall always feel indebted to Father Pat and Our Blessed Lady for all the benefits, material and spiritual, that I have received, which I attribute without reservation to the practice of saying the Rosary daily.

The power of prayer

Harvey Bernhard's troubles began after he started helping Father Peyton in the late 1960s. He reached a low point in his film-making career and a ruptured disc in his spine left him temporarily paralyzed. It began to look as though Harvey Bernhard was not one of those people who had good things happen to them when they helped Father Peyton.

At this low point in his life, Father Pat and Father Heinzer took him to Family Theater and gave him a job.

He stayed at Family Theater for a year as director and produced *A Matter of Faith*, filmed interviews with world leaders, as well as a documentary on Father Peyton. Bernhard related, "Then my mind started to function confidently again. I got an idea for a picture and I raised the money and made the picture. From 1971 to the present, I have made eight motion pictures.

"The important thing was that here was a wonderful holy man who took me, a non-Catholic, to his heart and said to me, 'Harvey, you have a destiny to perform. God has something in mind especially for you.' He gave me this wonderful, I would say, intangible thing called faith."

The ill fortune that overtook Harvey Bernhard while he helped Father Peyton turned out to be the crisis in his life that led him to fame and riches. His production, *The Omen*, was an instant success, followed by two equally successful sequels.

Many have told how they were helped by Father Peyton's faith.

Danny Thomas revealed the serious nature underlying his public image as a comedian when he said that Father Peyton, whom he helped in the early days, was since then in his petition when he said his daily Rosary. He said, "I only know that, when I was in Father Peyton's presence, I always felt that I was standing beside a man who had been touched by the hand of God."

Actor Gene Kelly said of his encounters with Father Peyton, "I was struck by the amazing quality not only of the love he possessed for mankind but of the love he projected—a rare gift. I am proud to call him a friend."

A Korean veteran wrote to Father Peyton, long after the war, that while he was a prisoner of war, he made a Rosary out of seeds to pray every day for his release and return to his family.

The Cleve B. Bonners, who were inspired to a lifetime of nightly family Rosary after attending a triduum by Father Peyton in their home city of Pasadena, California, said they "felt great surprise, utter joy and happiness" when they walked into their daughter Mary's half-darkened bedroom unannounced one evening after dinner and heard her praying the Rosary along with a recitation over the radio.

Maureen Kearney grew up in awe of her world-renowned great-uncle. She recalled her childhood impression of him as a man whose infrequent and unannounced visits to the family home in

Scranton sent her grandmother, his sister Beatrice, and the rest of the household into a frenzy of activity. He was, she recalled, "so big, so quiet, so holy...always dressed in black, not at all like the other priests in the family who wore casual clothes and played with us when they came to visit."

Father DePrizio saw in Father Peyton a man of this world, of flesh and blood, radiating the power of a deep living faith so eminently in touch with God that he said, "Most of us miss it but are attracted by it. He reaches out beyond the barriers and walls that we erect. He speaks the message without the mask on. He was always ecumenical. His message of the Rosary is the message of God. He was always way ahead of his time in pioneering the mass media for religion."

Father DePrizio visited Father Peyton's boyhood home in Ireland in August of 1977. He visited the church where the young Patrick Peyton used to serve Mass and the cemetery where his parents are buried.

He said, "As I walked the same little alleys and lanes he walked as a boy, I had the same feeling I had when I visited the famous shrines of the saints. I thought, 'Who knows? Maybe someday people will be coming here for the same reason. Who knows?'"

Father Peyton's sister Sarah, crippled and in a wheelchair and faced with the growing illness of her husband, Seamus Owens, one day cried out, "Oh Mary, send me someone to help." At that moment, she heard coming from the other room the voice of her brother. Father Peyton, arriving on one of his infrequent visits home to Ireland, prayed with his troubled sister. She told him that afterward she had become able to cope with the problems.

On another occasion, Father Peyton said Mass in the hospital room where his sister Mary lay weakened with cancer. During the Mass, she later told her doctor, she felt "an uplift." A few days later she returned home.

Father Peyton said, "I give all of my Masses to Mary, and she has the ability to give them to my worst enemy if I have one, but she chooses to be generous with my family and friends."

Some people claimed that Father Peyton's prayers wrought "miracles" for them. He replied, "If extraordinary things happen, it isn't extraordinary for me, for what I am doing is enlisting the beautiful overwhelming influence of Mary with God, who makes them happen. I unite my prayers, feeble though they are, with the overwhelming power of the prayer of Our Blessed Mother. Anybody that will do that can get the same results.''

A great friend and helper of Father Peyton in Madrid, the Duchess de Bournonville y Oregon, sister of Queen Fabiola of Belgium, related that once she was so worried when her husband became ill that she called Father Peyton, who came and prayed. Father Peyton placed his hand upon the area causing pain, she wrote, and said to her, "Don't worry. This is over and Sunday he'll go fishing," as he had planned. The duchess added, "Everything turned out exactly as he had predicted."

Denny Leonard was a good bricklayer and he reached for the last brick to put in place before the noon whistle blew the end of the Saturday's work and the beginning of a weekend with his wife Ceil and their three children. He lost his balance and plunged sixty-five feet to the Schenectady, New York, street below. Arms, legs, skull and back were broken. Doctors did not think he would live through the day. They gave up hope. Father Peyton rushed to the hospital bedside when Ceil Leonard called him for help. For days she and Father Peyton appealed for help to Our Blessed Mother, reminding her that the Leonards were a Rosary family, Denny joining them when he came out of his coma. Denny recovered and resumed a normal life.

Kitty O'Grady met Father Peyton in 1943 when he spoke at a telephone operators' Communion breakfast in Cleveland. She was so impressed that she founded the Cleveland Friends of Father Peyton, which raised more than forty thousand dollars over the years for Father Peyton's work.

On February 7, 1961, her family learned that "Aunt Kitty" had terminal cancer.

Father Peyton telephoned her from San Francisco in early April to see how she was. She told him she had "an itch that is driving me crazy." She and Father Peyton said the "*Memorare*" together over long-distance telephone. He promised to visit her in July. The next day the itch went away and never returned.

On July 26, three months longer than doctors had given Aunt Kitty to live, Father Peyton visited her and said a Mass in her home. She died on August 18. Her nephew Patrick Corcoran said, "It was as though my Aunt Kitty was waiting for Father Peyton."

Her nephew Patrick became coordinator of fund-raising for the Cleveland Friends of Father Peyton and by 1980 the group had raised another sixty-nine thousand dollars toward a goal of one hundred thousand dollars for Father Peyton's "All for Her" fund.

When Patrick Corcoran told Father Peyton it was hard raising that much money, Father Peyton replied, "It was hard at Calvary too."

Anthony J. (Joe) Dolan was admitted to the Albany, New York, Medical Center Hospital in early 1979 for surgery on his neck for a blood blockage. He also suffered from very high blood pressure and renal disease. His doctor advised him that the surgery was necessary, even though the result of it could be critical, or even fatal. Father Peyton, responding to the plea of a relative, went to the hospital and prayed with Joe and his brother Martin, the three kneeling beside the bed. The next day, in further diagnosis, the physicians discovered that the blockage had disappeared and that surgery would not be required. Joe was home with his wife Mary and their eleven children by Thanksgiving. "To this day," Mary Dolan wrote on March 15, 1982, to Father Peyton, "I do not have to take Joe's blood pressure, which I had to do for years three times a day, lying and in a standing position. His blood pressure is normal and he is completely cured of his blood pressure condition." She wrote, "Praise God and Our Blessed Mother for her dear advocate Father Patrick Peyton. We will be indebted to Our Lady all the days of our life."

The Fourth Glorious Mystery
The Assumption

The assumption of the Blessed Virgin Mary Mother of God, body and soul, into heaven, is celebrated in the *Mass of the Assumption* on August 15.

Almighty God, You gave a humble virgin the privilege of being the Mother of Your Son, and crowned her with the glory of heaven. May the prayers of the Virgin Mary bring us to the salvation of Christ and raise us up to eternal life. We ask this through our Lord Jesus Christ, Your Son, who lives and reigns with You and the Holy Spirit, one God, for ever and ever. Amen.

(Collect, Mass of the Assumption)

The Assumption was defined and proclaimed as Church dogma by Pope Pius XII on November 1, 1950, in St. Peter's Square in Rome.

After having addressed humble and incessant prayer to God and invoked the Light of the Spirit of truth, for the glory of Almighty God, Who has lavishly bestowed such precious favors upon the Virgin Mary, for the honor of His Son, immortal King of ages and conqueror of sin and death, for the increase of the glory of the august Mother of that Son, for the joy and the happiness of the whole Church, by the authority of Our Lord Jesus Christ, and by our own authority, we pronounce, declare and define as a dogma revealed by God, that the immaculate ever-virgin Mary, Mother of God, having completed the course of this earthly life, was taken up body and soul to the glory of heaven.

(Pope Pius XII, November 1, 1950)

Father Peyton's meditation
on The Assumption

We believe that we are destined for eternal life. Body and soul we shall live forever in the eternal bliss of Heaven. This is our faith. This is our victory. This is the driving force that keeps us going. We believe that Mary, the Mother of our Savior, is already there body and soul. As we journey on in our pilgrimage, so often tired and weary, we are strengthened and encouraged by this fact that Mary, one of us, our sister—truly human like the rest of us—has already arrived. She is our Morning Star. She is our courage and our hope. We must never forget that where she is now, we shall be there some day.

She is the first of the redeemed and the first to enjoy to the fullest the gift of Her Son's Redemption. Body and soul, she is in heaven with Him. She has arrived ahead of us. As day by day we continue our pilgrimage on the same paths she trod, we get our strength, hope and courage from knowing that where we are headed for, Mary, our mother and our sister, is already there.

What a glorious heritage our forefathers have given us in the Rosary that ever comforts and encourages us to keep going on, no matter how difficult the way.

Runway for the future

"My work of the past forty years has been but a runway for the future," said Father Peyton. The record of the Family Rosary Crusade was history, as he had told Pope John Paul II. "I am working now for the benefit of our children's children in the year twenty hundred and one and the years that follow in the next century."

While working to insure a Crusade organization that could carry on without him, he continued to minister to individuals in need of his prayers and to extol the practice of daily family Rosary to his extended family of man through rallies and the media. As he prayed his own private Rosary each day, in chapels and churches, walking along streets, in moving vehicles, before the picture of the Madonna and Child in its place of honor wherever he stopped for a night, a new concept took root and grew within him. He realized that his private prayer of thanks and petitions for the salvation of the world's people was also family prayer, that anyone's private prayer prayed for the whole family was family prayer. While the whole family praying together could assail heaven with a louder voice, Our Blessed Mother would respond to the lone petitioner with her blessings for the whole family.

Father Peyton made several trips to Ireland and to the Philippines in 1980 and 1981. He spoke at five rallies in County Galway and County Mayo, including one at Ballina near his birthplace. He also spoke at several rallies in the troubled southern island of Mindanao in the Philippines, where two teams were at work with the Rosary films.

Ireland welcomed its native son, and church leaders repeatedly invited him to come back. He was the speaker for the first "Open Day" in three hundred years of the cloistered Carmelite nuns at Loughrea. At the request of the media for more interviews, he also made a separate trip to Ireland.

He was invited back for a second, and then a third, consecutive year as the principal speaker for the annual Family Day celebration at the pilgrim shrine at Knock. When he returned there for the second time in July of 1980, the lord mayor of Dublin, Deputy Fergus O'Brien, gave a reception in his mansion for the Family Rosary Crusade. Some days later, as Father Peyton passed through Sligo, he was greeted with the sight of a bishop leading his people through the streets with a loudspeaker, praying the Rosary. Father Pat got out of the car and greeted the bishop and his people. From that meeting there developed the friendship between Bishop Dominic Conway and Father Peyton that helped promote the mission of the Rosary priest.

Even while still at work on the making of the first television program on the Rosary mysteries, Father Pat was preparing to attend the triennial Synod of Bishops in October of 1980 in Rome. He saw this gathering as a providential opportunity to call the attention of the bishops of the world to the help the Rosary recited daily in the home could give to family spirituality.

The subject for the 1980 synod was to be the Christian family. If these delegates from around the world should make even a brief statement on the value of the Rosary in the home, and if the Pope should promulgate it to the faithful, it would clear up the misunderstanding about Mary that arose after Vatican Council II and bring a definite end to her eclipse. It would vindicate Father Pat's stubborn adherence, in the face of opposition, to devotion to Mary and the Rosary.

Father Pat contacted many of the delegates, asking them to support the cause of the family Rosary. Typical of the responses was one from Cardinal Sin of Manila, who pledged to espouse the Family Rosary in the Synod.

Father Pat went to Rome and mingled among the bishops in their assemblies, lobbying for the family Rosary.

Then, commending the outcome there to the will of God and the help of Mary, he flew from Rome to Mindanao for the crusades there.

Archbishop Antonio Mabutas had written to Father Peyton back in May asking him to come to his archdiocese of Davao in October. He hoped, he wrote, that the visit would be "the beginning of a more dynamic and widespread apostolate for the whole of Mindanao," describing the island as "now rent by strife because of the Muslim problem here and many other problems confronting my people."

That first rally on October 26 was the beginning of many more rallies for Mindanao.

The Crusade teams continued to work always ahead of Father Pat's arrival by three or four months. With thirty projectors and sets of films, the volunteers could show the films simultaneously in thirty locations in one night.

Father Peyton joined an assemblage of the bishops of the Visayan Islands in Cebu City one June day. Julio Cardinal Rosales, the archbishop of Cebu, gave him an opportunity to explain the Crusade to those bishops at a luncheon at his residence.

Cardinal Rosales wrote to Father Pat on July 17, saying, "The teams here have to move on from one diocese to another after spending three or four months. If only you can spare more projectors and films, tremendous results can be acquired with greater speed and more remote areas can be reached."

Father Peyton left the Philippines to work in the United States and Ireland in 1981. In June he went to Washington, D.C., to begin filming his third television special featuring Mother Teresa of India. He had given her a choice and Mother Teresa, Nobel Peace Prize recipient for her humanitarian work among the sick and poor of India, had chosen the Visitation Mystery for its special meaning to her.

"Oh Mother, you're the personification of this mystery," Father Pat said to her in a segment of the show.

He asked her to explain the meaning of her choice. Mother Teresa, in her gentle tone, replied, "The Visitation Mystery is very special to me because I think that's where Our Lady is the first missionary of charity because she was the first one to carry Jesus as the handmaid of the Lord. The moment Jesus came in her life, immediately she went in haste to give Him to others, and that going is what we as Missionaries of Charity should do. We too, like her, go in haste and visit the sick and the dying and the crippled and the lepers and unwanted and unloved. She has a very special, special place in our life and especially that she went in haste and she must have gone with joy, and that's why she's the cause of our joy. And I do the same thing by going in haste to meet our people, her people, her children, which I do because of joy."

The rest of the drama was filmed at Notre Dame University and in London with the London Players performing the Bible scenes. Featuring narrator Bob Newhart and Notre Dame's head football coach Gerry Faust and including recitation of a decade of the Rosary, "The Visitation Mystery" was telecast over some one hundred stations in the United States and Canada and the Philippines during the 1981 Thanksgiving and Christmas seasons.

Father Pat returned to the Philippines for an October 1 rally in Zamboanga. There thirty thousand people gathered in pouring rain. Army tanks and groups of armed soldiers every thirty yards or so stood guard. An armed helicopter hovering overhead made so much noise that people could not hear. Father Pat asked them to fly it away. Father Pat had earlier been told that on an average five are murdered every day in that neighborhood.

Zamboanga Archbishop F. Cruces wrote on January 18, 1982, to Father Peyton, "Our Christmas this year, has been very peaceful, no grenade explosions as in past years, many people in church, communions in hundreds. I attribute the improving situation of peace and order conditions to our Family Rosary Rally and to our continuing prayers for peace in our area."

Father Pat considered certain occurrences as signs of God's blessing upon the future of the Crusade. One such sign was the designation of its slogan as a proverb and documentation of the genesis of the expression for all time by a prestigious publication.

"The family that prays together stays together," the slogan that Father Peyton had disseminated for so long and so widely that its origin had become obscured, was designated as a proverb in the fall of 1981 by Oxford University Press for entry in a dictionary of proverbs.

By far the greatest in the reinforcements for Father Pat's message came out of the Synod of Bishops. It came more than a year after he had commended the outcome of his efforts at the synod to God and Mary. It was a strong statement on the Rosary and family prayer included in Pope John Paul II's Apostolic Exhortation, "The Role of the Christian Family in the Modern World," given in Rome on November 22, 1981.

Father Pat said, "It's a signal from God that Mary and the Rosary are of such strong value in helping the family spirituality that it had to be put on record for all time. It will be a powerful motivation for the bishops to take up the banner for Mary and the Rosary and carry on the Crusade."

The Fifth Glorious Mystery
The Coronation

A great sign appeared in the sky, a woman clothed with the sun, with the moon under her feet, and on her head a crown of twelve stars.

(Revelation 12: 1)

The litany of the Blessed Virgin Mary tells us that she is queen of angels, of patriarchs, prophets, and apostles, of martyrs, confessors, of virgins and of all saints, queen conceived without original sin, queen assumed into heaven, queen of the Most Holy Rosary and queen of peace. Mary is queen of heaven and earth.

The Queenship of the Blessed Virgin Mary, formerly May 31, is celebrated each year on August 22. The feast of the Queenship of Mary was instituted by Pope Pius XII on October 11, 1954, in his encyclical *Ad Caeli Reginam*. He also decreed that on that day "there be renewed the consecration of the human race to the Immaculate Heart of the Blessed Virgin Mary."

Father Peyton's meditation
on The Coronation

What is so good about the Rosary is that it goes all the way in telling the whole story of Jesus and Mary and ourselves. The Rosary takes us in hand at the beginning and leads us to the end. It tells us of the Resurrection of Christ, the Assumption of Mary, and now it gives us a glimpse of how God thanks her, glorifies her, honors her and rewards her for how nobly and valiantly she cooperated in His plan to redeem and save us. For a better way of saying it, we call all this the Crowning of Our Blessed Mother as Queen of Heaven and Earth.

But it isn't God alone who gives her that thanks, honor and glory that is signified by the word "Queen." Men and women through the centuries have outdone each other in expressing their recognition of Mary and their wish to crown her "Queen." Elizabeth is the first of this endless line of devotees. Her greeting to Mary, *"Blessed art thou among women and blessed is the fruit of thy womb"* forms part of that famous prayer, the *"Ave Maria"* or *"Hail Mary"*. With that prayer countless millions through the centuries ceaselessly extol her greatness, recognize her excellence and crown her Queen.

With the *"Hail Mary,"* we cry out to heaven and earth who she is, why she is, what she has done for us, and how much we owe to her. With the *"Hail Marys"* of our Rosary, we proclaim to the heavens and earth that the Son she bore is Our Redeemer, Our Savior and Our God.

This is the secret of the Rosary. This is its power. This explains why the Rosary has come down through so many centuries. It is the heritage our forefathers thought best to preserve and hand on to their sons and daughters.

The crowning years

Much had been accomplished, but there was still much to do to insure the permanence of a global Family Rosary Crusade. Father Pat had followed Father DePrizio's advice always to expand by crossing geographic and organizational boundaries. The Crusade had evolved into what one bishop called "a movement rather than just an organization." Its leadership had extended beyond the Congregation of Holy Cross to Dominican, Franciscan and diocesan priests, the Sisters of Mercy, and lay men and women.

Active Crusades were being carried on in Spain and the Philippines. Father Pat had every hope that the same would be true soon in Ireland. Father Armijos, who had become director of the Latin American Crusades, had completed seventeen campaigns since 1980 in Argentina, Mexico, Peru and Bolivia. And a beginning in Colombia was imminent. The Adveniat grant of the German bishops had helped generously in providing the sets of Rosary films and projectors and other equipment to show the films in Latin America. The generosity of other benefactors had provided more films and equipment.

The trilogy of television specials based on the Mysteries of the Rosary had been produced and aired, to great public acclaim, on free television time. Father Pat was constantly at work to complete programs based on all fifteen mysteries. Shooting of scenes from the Bible was to begin soon in London.

Father Pat intended while in London to complete arrangements for an ecumenical recitation of a decade of the Rosary for one of the television specials. He had contacted the leaders of England's Ecumenical Society of the Blessed Virgin Mary and learned that they would be receptive to his idea to demonstrate the belief that all Christians as well as Catholics can pray the Rosary. A decade of one of the Joyful Mysteries would be prayed by Anglicans, Methodists, Greek Orthodox and Catholics. Among the clergymen he planned to visit with a personal invitation and who had assured him of their acceptance were two widely read authors—the Methodist minister the Rev. J. Neville

Ward, author of many books including *Five for Sorrow, Ten for Joy*, a definitive book on the Rosary, and the Anglican priest the Rev. John de Satgé, author of *Down to Earth*, a book on the Blessed Mother.

Father Pat was also planning a revised set of instruction manuals, one each for bishops, priests, lay leaders and teachers, which, he said, "will provide complete instruction so they will have no need of rallies and no need of me."

The "All for Her" trust fund set up for the interest income to provide a measure of financial security for the future was still considerably short of its five-million-dollar goal.

Father Pat had a calm and peaceful confidence that, if it was God's will and Mary wanted him to complete those plans for his legacy to future generations, this fifth decade would be the crowning years of his work.

Father Peyton pushed himself beyond fatigue into one activity after another. The blue eyes shone out of the pallor of his gaunt face. His doctor ordered him to slow down, to rest, and finally ordered him into the hospital. Father Peyton spent his seventy-third birthday on January 9, 1982, confined to a hospital bed in New York City. He was still there toward the end of January when the anniversary gift of red roses arrived and was placed on the stand next to the reproduction of the Murillo painting of the Madonna and Child that represented his only constant companion. It was with him wherever he went. January 31 was the fortieth anniversary and the actual day of the beginning of the fifth decade of that work that had been inspired long ago on the last Sunday in January. In age, as in youth, Father Peyton knelt by a hospital bed before a picture of the Blessed Mother and prayed.

His doctor told him that a new medication for heart patients was helping him and released him from the hospital upon his promise to rest.

After a few short weeks in New York and Albany, the hollows and some deepened lines in his face disappeared and he again stood tall. Although he still tired after hours of intensive work, he felt ready for the trip to London, shortly after mid-March. He planned first to visit his family in Scranton. His sister Mary was back in the hospital, her cancer terminal.

"I don't feel sad because someone dies," Father Peyton said with a smile, shortly before he left Albany. "I know that my sister Mary will be in heaven."

297

Then, as his voice and the smile both broke, he added, "but I will feel sad because I am separated from my beautiful sister Mary, even for a brief time, even though I know I will soon join her."

He had just arrived in New York when he received a phone call urging him to hasten to see his sister Mary for a last time. He was able to get a flight that same evening for Scranton.

He went to her at once and talked to her and prayed. Although she could not answer him, he felt that she knew he was there.

The next day he said Mass in her room. A half hour later, Mary Peyton, who had worked and devoted her life to her family and had helped support her brothers Thomas and Patrick while they were becoming priests, left them. Mary Peyton passed from this world on Saturday, March 20, 1982, the first of the nine children of John and Mary Peyton to go since Nellie had left them as a young woman of thirty-five.

Father Peyton cried a lot. The priest who knew without doubt that his sister Mary was reunited in heaven with their parents and their sister, cried for his separation from her and for the separation of one from the other, by death or by distance, of that Peyton family who had so loved one another and had so loved him that they had willingly given him to the world.

Pictures of their lives together flashed upon the screen of  Father Peyton's memory. One in particular remained with him—the picture of his sister Mary as a beautiful young woman. He heard again in his mind the sweetness of her voice and her gentle words of love for and about him.

His sister Mary had once answered a comment about being a member of the famous Father Peyton's family with, "He doesn't belong to us. He belongs to the world."

After a few days in Scranton, Father Peyton returned to New York, where he boarded a plane on Saturday, March 27, for his scheduled flight to London. He had much to do and miles to go.

Glory be to the Father, and to the Son, and to the Holy Spirit.

As it was in the beginning, is now, and ever shall be, world without end. Amen.

AMEN

Epilogue

As I look over the past, I see that harnessing the air was the secret of Family Rosary Crusade's success. I'm also struck by a pattern that runs through its forty-year history. In each decade, a thousand obstacles preceded and accompanied each of its successes. There was frustration, hostility, futility, outright opposition:

"The Rosary is bad radio."

"It's like a broken record."

"You can't hold an American audience by praying the Rosary on television."

All these statements from leaders in the field of communication. Yet despite their dire predictions, Family Rosary leaped into the world of radio and television and succeeded where failure had been predicted. Clearly the work was in God's hands.

Now, with hindsight, it is more evident than ever that to keep abreast of changes in society, Family Rosary had to move from the pulpit in the parish church to the pulpit in the studio, that the message "The family that prays together stays together" could today ring from one end of the world to the other.

The decade of the Eighties finds society weak in belief and amoral in values. Perhaps this is good for the Church, for as history has proven over and over again, the greater the opposition, the more intense the faith.

Now, more than ever before, I hear the cry of the multitude for Mary and the Rosary. Thousands of letters from different parts of the world testify to her power. Tens of thousands of people come to hear of her through Family Rosary rallies. Even in the United States, where a certain sophistication has disdained the Rosary, hearts are opening again. Today the television industry provides valuable airtime for specials on the Rosary. The response to these programs tells us again and again that hearts have been touched.

The signs and symbols about us augur well for the future of the Family Rosary Crusade.

Since its inception, the Crusade owes its life to the generosity of its friends. The "All for Her" fund, as explained in this book, will help provide financial security for the years to come. The Crusade leadership, starting with the Holy Cross Fathers, has extended to the Sisters of Mercy and to Dominican, Franciscan, diocesan priests, and lay men and women. These are the leaders who direct the teams in the Americas, Asia, and Europe, with every hope that they will extend to the other continents.

Perhaps the greatest sign of God's blessing and the assurance of the Crusade's future is in the statement on the Family Rosary made by His Holiness Pope John Paul II in his Apostolic Exhortation, *The Role of the Christian Family in the Modern World*, given in Rome on 22 November, 1981:

> While respecting the freedom of the children of God, the Church has always proposed certain practices of piety to the faithful with particular solicitude and insistence. Among these should be mentioned the recitation of the Rosary: "We now desire, as a continuation of the thought of our predecessors, to recommend strongly the recitation of the family Rosary...There is no doubt that...the Rosary should be considered as one of the best and most efficacious prayers in common that the Christian family is invited to recite. We like to think, and sincerely hope, that when the family gathering becomes a time of prayer the Rosary is a frequent and favored manner of praying."* In this way authentic devotion to Mary which finds expression in sincere love and generous imitation of the Blessed Virgin's interior spiritual attitude, constitutes a special instrument for nourishing loving communion in the family and for developing conjugal and family spirituality. For she who is the Mother of Christ and of the Church is in a special way the Mother of Christian families, of domestic churches.

Rev. Patrick Peyton, C.S.C.

Patrick Peyton, C.S.C.

The Family Rosary, Inc.
Executive Park Drive
Albany, N.Y. 12203
May 31, 1983 – Feast of the Visitation

*Paul VI, *Apostolic Exhortation Marialis Cultis*, 52,54: AAS 66 (1974), 160-161.

301

About the author

Gabriel Gosselin, one of the earliest French settlers of Quebec, Canada, was so paralyzed in the neck and arms that he could not lift or turn his head without great pain. One day in 1684, as he prayed in the chapel of St. Anne, the paralysis suddenly went away. His cure is one of the first miracle cures recorded in the annals of the shrine of St. Anne de Beaupré near Quebec city.

Jeanne Gosselin Arnold, the author of this book about the twentieth century crusader for Mary the Mother of God, is a direct descendant of that seventeenth century beneficiary of the grace of the mother of Mary. Studies and records indicate that the Gosselins of America, a family that has produced many priests, are all descended from that same Gabriel.

During a thirty-year career as a reporter, columnist, feature writer and editor at the Albany, New York, *Times Union*, a Hearst Corporation newspaper, Mrs. Arnold covered a variety of beats, including police, minorities and religion, and wrote extensively on such subjects as the depraved, the deprived, the disabled, the elderly and the altruistic. She is the holder of a number of awards and citations including a New York State Bar Association top award for a series of articles entitled *Court of Secret Sorrows: Family Court*.

She is the mother of Eugene R. Arnold (USAF, Ret.) and Mrs. Linda Beattie, who is also a newspaper columnist and who did the original bead design art work and the composition for this book. Mrs. Arnold is also the grandmother of Carol Jeanne, Eugene, Jacqueline and Leilani Arnold and Dawn, Jeanne, Robert and Linda Beattie, and she is a great-grandmother. She lives at R.D. 1, Box 265, Westerlo, N.Y. 12193.

The structure of this book parallels that of the popularly prayed five-decade Rosary. Part 1 represents the pendant cross and beads on which are prayed the *Apostles' Creed*, the *Our Father* and three *Hail Marys*, serving as an introduction to the decades. Each of the other five parts has eleven chapters, representing the *Our Father* and ten *Hail Marys* of each decade. All of the introductory prayers and the *Our Father* that begins and the *Glory be to the Father* that ends each decade are written into the text. Although some but not all of the *Hail Marys* of the decades are contained in the text, all fifty are implied by the progressive addition in the headings of the beads that represent them. The reader who has finished reading this book has therefore, in effect, followed the five-decade Rosary and perused the meaning and Father Peyton's meditations on all fifteen Mysteries of the Rosary.